$PREAD

$PREA

THE BEST OF THE MAGAZINE THAT ILLUMINATED THE SEX INDUSTRY AND STARTED A MEDIA REVOLUTION

Edited by

RACHEL AIMEE, ELIYANNA KAISER, AND AUDACIA RAY

THE FEMINIST PRESS
AT THE CITY UNIVERSITY OF NEW YORK
NEW YORK CITY

Published in 2015 by the Feminist Press
at the City University of New York
The Graduate Center
365 Fifth Avenue, Suite 5406
New York, NY 10016

feministpress.org

First printing March 2015

Cover design by Herb Thornby, herbthornby.com
Text design by Drew Stevens

Library of Congress Cataloging-in-Publication Data
$pread : the best of the magazine that illuminated the sex industry and
started a media revolution / edited by Rachel Aimee, Eliyanna Kaiser, and
Audacia Ray.
     pages cm
  ISBN 978-1-55861-873-2 (ebook) – ISBN 978-1-55861-872-5 (pbk.)
1. Spread (New York, N.Y.) 2. Sex-oriented businesses. I. Aimee, Rachel
editor. II. Kaiser, Eliyanna editor. III. Ray, Audacia editor. IV. Title: Spread.
PN4900.S67S67 2013
051–dc23

                                                              2014037096

CONTENTS

11 Preface: The Sex Worker Rights Movement
    in the Early 2000s—A Primer
    Rachel Aimee, Eliyanna Kaiser, and Audacia Ray

17 A Short History of *$pread*
    Rachel Aimee, Eliyanna Kaiser, and Audacia Ray

PART I: WORKPLACE

37 Introduction
    Lulu

39 Indecent Proposal: Fucking the Movement
    Eve Ryder

42 Positions: Is Sex Work a Sacred Practice
    or Just a Job?
    Vero Rocks and Tasha Tasticake

46 American Brothel: A Photo-Essay
    Erin Siegal

59 Stripping While Brown
    Mona Salim

66 Positions: No Sex in the Champagne Room?
    Mary Taylor and Carol Leigh

69 Menstruation: Porn's Last Taboo
Trixie Fontaine

80 Diary of a Peep Show Girl
Sheila McClear, writing as Chelsea O'Neill

PART II: LABOR

89 Introduction
Radical Vixen

92 Positions: Can We Justify Working for Pimps?
Anonymous and Eve Ryder

95 The Sex Workplace: No Day Without an Immigrant
Rachel Aimee

104 Respite From the Streets: A Place to Retire for
Mexico City's Elderly Prostitutes
Marisa Brigati

113 Black Tale: Women of Color in the American
Porn Industry
Mireille Miller-Young

122 The City's Red Lights: Mumbai's Boomtown of
Migrant Laborers
Svati P. Shah

PART III: FAMILY AND RELATIONSHIPS

131 Introduction
Kevicha Echols

133 Wives
Jenni Russell

134 Keeping Her Off the Pole: My Daughter's
Right to Choose
Katherine Frank

142 Hot Topic: People Who Date Sex Workers
Peter, Natalie, Allen, Bob C., and Fred

146 I (Heart) Affection, and Other Forms of
Emotional Masochism
Hawk Kinkaid

153 The Coldest Profession
Eliyanna Kaiser

156 Hell's Kitchen: Growing Up Loving a Working Mother
Syd V.

PART IV: CLIENTS

167 Introduction
Sarah Elspeth Patterson

169 Cher John (Dear John)
Mirha-Soleil Ross

175 Indecent Proposal: Bento Bitch
Miguel

177 Empower: In Defense of Sex Tourism
Chanelle Gallant

187 Haikus for Mistress Octavia
Jimmy Bob

189 Honest John: An Interview with Caveh Zahedi
Kristie Alshaibi

196 Hot Topic: Would You Steal From a Client?
Moxy, Violine Verseau, and Jessica

199 Indecent Proposal: Tiny Town
Audacia Ray

203 Healthy Hooker: Condoms 101
Eliyanna Kaiser and Dorothy Schwartz

211 The Last Outcall
Fabulous

PART V: VIOLENCE

221 Introduction
Brendan Michael Conner

224 Paradise Lost, Paradox Found: Or, Don't Get Caught
Slipping in the Big Hypocro-Easy
Cha Cha

231 Tsunami Report: Sex Workers in South Thailand
Empower Foundation

235 Epidemic of Neglect: Trans Women Sex Workers
and HIV
Mack Friedman

244 The Unicorn and the Crow
Prin Roussin

250 Escort Rape Case Causes Uproar in Philadelphia
Catherine Plato

253 Bodies Across Borders: Experiences of Trafficking
and Migration
Melissa Ditmore and Juhu Thukral

PART VI: RESISTANCE

265 Introduction
Bhavana Karani

267 I Have Nothing to Say: A Story of Self-Defense
Lynne Tansey

273 The Cutting Edge: On Sex Workers, Serial Killers,
and Switchblades
Sarah Stillman

281 Fashion with a Function: The Aphrodite Project
Erin Siegal

283 2 Young 2 B 4Gotten: Youth in the Sex Trade
Brendan Michael Conner, writing as Will Rockwell

294 Alphabet Hookers: B is for Bobbi
Morgan Ellis

PART VII: MEDIA AND CULTURE

301 Introduction
Damien Luxe

304 Sex Work and the City: An Interview with Tracy Quan
Rachel Aimee

315 Up in Buck's Business: An Interview with Buck Angel
Audacia Ray

322 Intercourses: An Interview with Pro-Choice Activist
Joyce Arthur
Eliyanna Kaiser

329 In Her Own Words: An Interview with
Deborah Jeane Palfrey
Radical Vixen

340 The Real Media Whores: Uniting Against
Sensationalism in the Wake of Spitzergate
Caroline Andrews

348 Dirty Words: An Interview with Craig Seymour
Brendan Michael Conner, writing as Will Rockwell

356 The History of *$pread*: A Timeline

367 Acknowledgments

PREFACE:
THE SEX WORKER RIGHTS MOVEMENT IN THE EARLY 2000s—A PRIMER

Rachel Aimee, Eliyanna Kaiser, and Audacia Ray

Like any movement for social change, the sex worker rights movement has gone through many phases and been challenged both internally and externally by people, ideas, and events beyond its control. It has experienced wins and losses, and it has reimagined its goals and values with each successive generation of leaders and activists who have taken up its banner. To better understand the writings of the sex workers who wrote for *$pread* magazine, this preface will attempt to provide some context to the movement in its historical moment.

"Sex Work" and "Sex Workers"

Major news networks use it today, but the term "sex work" was first coined by Carol Leigh (aka Scarlot Harlot) at an activist conference in 1978. While its contemporary, popular usage might suggest a polite synonym for "prostitute," its intended meaning is much broader, encompassing anyone who exchanges money, goods, or services for their sexual or erotic labor. The purpose of inventing the term wasn't about being polite, although "sex work" does nicely sidestep the stigma embedded in some of the more charged monikers. But more significantly, the idea of connecting all professions that exchange sexual or erotic work under one umbrella served as a linguistic labor organizing tool, connecting porn performers, fetish workers, exotic dancers, prostitutes, phone sex workers, and others, with one label, recognizing their shared stigma and struggle, regardless of their differences. And, since the first job of any social change movement is a gathering of its ranks, or what some feminists have called "consciousness-raising," the invention of the term "sex work" most effectively jump-started today's sex worker rights movement.

Back when *$pread* began publishing in 2005, it was uncommon for sex workers to identify as sex workers, and while it has become much more common over the past decade, its usage among non-activist sex workers is still relatively rare, for various reasons. Some strippers, pro-dommes, and others whose jobs may not actually involve having sex for money, are offended by the suggestion of commonality with prostitutes. Other people reject the identity because they don't think of what they do as a job, or because they are uncomfortable with the stigma associated with the term. In the years since *$pread* ceased publication, the mainstream sex worker rights movement has begun to acknowledge that the term sex worker doesn't work for everyone.

Feminism and the Politics of "Choice"

Far more insidious than its infamous cousin, the virgin/whore complex, the choice/coercion dichotomy has complicated the relationship between sex worker activists and feminists for decades. In the early 2000s, mainstream feminists approached the issue of sex work with a near copy/paste of some of their foremothers' arguments from the 1970s and 80s. What was once considered the radical thinking of the feminist sex wars had gone mainstream: the idea that sexualized labor, particularly pornography and prostitution, is inherently degrading to and exploitative of women. Meanwhile, the opposing view advanced by "sex-positive" feminists essentially argued the opposite: sex work represents an empowering way for women to use their bodies, leveraging financial independence from sexual self-expression. (This narrative, of course, ignored the fact that not all sex workers are cisgender women.) While it would be too simple and reductionist to suggest that no nuance existed within either of these two philosophical factions, it would be close to the truth.

As sex trafficking became recognized as an important problem in the United States, many "anti-sex work feminists" began to use the words "trafficking" and "prostitution" as synonyms, both in their rhetoric, and in their policy-making and lobbying. Proposals to combat trafficking enjoyed easy support—both political and financial—and anti-prostitution efforts could easily pass for anti-trafficking ones. Throughout the early 2000s, a near-constant onslaught of laws and policies heavily curtailing the rights of sex workers were adopted as "anti-trafficking" measures.

And so, just as sex workers had begun to come out in droves, harnessing the relatively anonymous power of the Internet to self-identify and self-articulate, they found themselves in a predicament. To claim choice meant challenging institutional feminism. And to claim coercion meant being trapped in victim-status. No sex worker activist or group easily escaped reacting to this reality.

It's not surprising that many young sex worker activists allied with the sex positive feminists. They at least acknowledged that sex workers had enough autonomy to be capable of choice and self-determination. Sex workers have long been in the crossfire of warring feminists, and the rhetoric of empowerment was understandably more alluring than degradation. But the alliance forged between sex-positive feminists and the sex worker rights movement was sometimes problematic because it led to a culture in which it was necessary to constantly assert one's autonomy, even if that meant not speaking up about experiencing violence, coercion, or personal difficulty with sexual shame, thus favoring those who were most empowered (or able to pass as empowered) by their work: mostly white, middle-class, non-immigrant, cisgender women.

Rhetorically, this led to some of the main messages of

the sex worker rights movement further isolating less privileged sex workers. The constant assertions that sex work was "just like any other job," that it was experientially rewarding, richly enumerating, or spiritually significant, or that sex workers "weren't all homeless junkies working the streets" naturally alienated those who hated their work, struggled to make ends meet, used drugs, or were homeless. A dominating narrative of empowerment also contributes to a growing stigma against sex workers whose experience isn't strictly empowering.

None of this is to say that a more diverse group of sex workers were not speaking up or were not active at the time. They most certainly were. With some very notable exceptions, they largely worked within other movements, particularly anti-poverty, harm reduction, and criminal justice reform movements. While today's sex worker rights movement remains far from perfect in terms of representation and meaningful leadership, the last few years have seen a noticeable shift toward acknowledging how many communities of sex workers have been left out of the conversation.

The Work of the Sex Worker Rights Movement

The United States lags behind most other nations when it comes to sex workers' labor organizations and social movement building. In India, for example, the Durbar Mahila Samanwaya Committee is an active union representing 65,000 prostitutes; while in the United States, the Lusty Lady, a peep show, which was the only unionized sex workplace in the country, recently closed its doors. While prostitution is decriminalized in New Zealand and the Netherlands, and not fully criminalized in many other countries including Canada and the United Kingdom, it remains illegal in the United States (save a few counties in Nevada, where licensed brothel workers find many of their basic civil liberties curtailed). So while those new to sex worker activism might assume that this movement spends its time lobbying to decriminalize prostitution or unionizing strip clubs, the day-to-day work being done by most activists is usually much more defensive and reactive, modest in its goals, and incremental in its approach.

In terms of policy change, much of the work being done by sex workers and their allies focuses on reducing the harm sex workers experience because of existing laws and policies, both globally and locally. For example, in 2011, activists were successful in repealing a Louisiana law that required some sex workers to register as sex offenders. And in New York and other cities, sex workers continue the campaign to stop the police practice of confiscating condoms from sex workers (and those profiled as sex workers) as evidence of prostitution. Sex workers across the country also provide a wide range of peer-led services, including health care, distribution of condoms and clean needles, legal advocacy and court support, résumé-writing skills, parenting and relationship support, self-care and self-defense workshops, and more.

Sex workers are disproportionately victims of violence, both physical and institutional. Violence against sex workers, by police as well as clients and others, is common, and the criminal status of prostitution makes it virtually impossible for sex workers to report these crimes to the authorities. Since 2003, sex workers have been coming together on December 17 to mark the International Day to End Violence Against Sex Workers. Originally conceived by Annie Sprinkle, one of the pioneers of the modern day sex worker rights movement in the United States, as a day to remember the victims of the Green River Killer in Seattle, WA, December 17 has become a day when sex workers hold vigils in cities and towns across the globe to remember those who have been lost, and to draw attention to the violence that continues to be committed against sex workers everywhere. If there is a common note to American sex worker activism across the country, it is each community coming together on this date.

Another priority for activists is changing the way the media talks about sex work. This means challenging the harmful stereotypes in the mainstream media, and sex workers creating their own media. The ways in which sex workers do this has changed dramatically. In 2005, sex worker-made media consisted of a few books—mostly academic, some memoir, and mostly focusing on the idea of sex work as empowering. The past decade has seen a heavy shift toward online spaces: community blogs such as Tits and Sass, Sex Worker Problems, The WhoreCast podcast, and community forums and conversations on Twitter and Facebook have become the primary places where sex workers go to find community and create their own media. Back when *$pread* began publishing, however, none of that existed.

A SHORT HISTORY OF $PREAD

Rachel Aimee, Eliyanna Kaiser, and Audacia Ray

How It All Started

Social movements don't spring forth fully formed, and the sex workers' rights movement is no exception. The adage that prostitution is the "world's oldest profession" may or may not be accurate, but whenever people began trading sex for something they needed or wanted, others marked their actions as immoral, unhealthy, and against the grain. Injustice was born. Yet as people struggle against injustice, amazing things can happen, including stories and documentation of the people living the struggle to exist against the grain.

That is a grand way to imagine a struggle for justice, one that we—the editors and staff of $pread magazine—can lay claim to today, though we didn't set out with that gleam in our eyes. In the spring of 2004, Rebecca Lynn, Rachel Aimee, and Raven Strega, three young activists living in New York, met while organizing a benefit for PONY (Prostitutes of New York). (The magazine quickly grew beyond these three women, and the "we" of this history was always a shifting one.) We got talking about our frustration with the mainstream media's sensationalizing portrayal of sex workers as either glamorous, highly paid call girls or drug-addicted victims without agency. We had read some accounts of sex work written by actual sex workers, but most of these were academic essays written for a college-educated readership. We recognized the need for a space where sex workers could write about their experiences in an accessible format—something lightweight and fun to read, that could easily be distributed among sex workers from a wide range of backgrounds. And so, knowing very little about the changing realities of independent publishing in the early twenty-first century, we set out on this journey, picked up and dropped off many more volunteers along the way, and created a magazine.

From the start, we conceived of *$pread* as a community-building tool that would appeal to all kinds of sex workers, though our notion of "all" sex workers was very much limited by our personal experiences and frames of reference. (Not everyone who worked for *$pread* was a current or former sex worker. Our staff also included allies who cared about the rights of sex workers. In fact, we were very careful not to disclose which of us were and weren't sex workers. This allowed people who didn't feel safe about being "out" to still be part of *$pread*.) We imagined a magazine that strippers would flip through in dressing rooms. We imagined a magazine that a body worker would hand over to her coworker after she was done with it. We imagined a magazine that a porn performer would browse while in a clinic waiting to do his panel of STI tests. We imagined a magazine that a phone sex operator or webcam performer would read between clients. Since many of us had experience in the sex industry ourselves, we knew that sex workers who work indoors spend a lot of time flipping through magazines while waiting for clients. The magazines that sex workers we knew had in their workplaces were fashion magazines or weekly news tabloids. But what if they had access to a magazine especially for them?

We thought that the simple act of holding a magazine in their hands and knowing that *sex workers made this* would encourage sex workers to feel like part of a community. Though several among us were bloggers and otherwise involved with and excited about the Internet, we felt that a physical magazine just had more weight. Over the next five years, during which we published four issues every year, we would come to understand so much more about the literal weight of the magazine as we hauled the boxed-up print runs of each issue into our various offices and then to the post office in carefully zip code-ordered stacks.

We entered the arena of publishing at a moment of epic transition from hardcopy to digital. We had been inspired by lovingly handcrafted, desktop-published, and photocopied sex worker zines like *Danzine*, *Whorezine*, and *PONY XXXpress*. We were fans and hoped to be the peers of small independent magazines that had real print runs and distribution, like *Bitch*, *LiP*, and *Clamor*. If we had known from the beginning just how hard everything would be, we almost certainly would have been too intimidated to undertake such a lofty project. But we didn't. So we did.

Getting Off the Ground

In the process of producing the first issue of the magazine, we tried to cast our nets wide, gathering articles and artwork from people we knew and people we'd like to know. We made "Write for *$pread!*" flyers and handed them out at strip clubs, brothels, and outreach centers. We met weekly in an East Village coffee shop, the name of which became our default password on our email accounts. We camped out at the Brooklyn apartment of the brave new recruit who stepped in as art director (even though she had no experience) and spent a month solid hunched over her shoulders as she taught herself how to use the design software and laid out the first issue. We planned fundraisers to cover what we estimated to be the expenses of printing the first issue of the magazine, leaving no budget to spare. The final product, which almost didn't make it to New York after it raised the eyebrows of customs officials when our Canadian printer shipped it to us, had the word "prostitution" misspelled in several places and almost no margins. But we had made it, and we loved it, warts and all.

In 2004, when we sent that first call for submissions into the universe, *$pread* had a post-office box, a one-page, hand-coded website, and an email address as its "we're a real magazine!" markers. The call announced that the first issue would be published in March 2005—a totally arbitrary date that we somehow managed to stick to. When submissions began rolling in, we were amazed and intimidated. It was the beginning of the weighty feeling of responsibility that would dominate every staff meeting: all these people, all these sex workers—including sex worker activist celebrities we looked up to—were counting on us to make this happen. The submissions and the notes of encouragement that arrived in our PO box and email inboxes proved to us that we had real potential to shift the isolation that many sex workers were feeling.

With no startup capital and no operating budget to speak of, we set our sights on raising $2,000, which was the cheapest quote we'd gotten from a potential printer (based in Winnipeg, Canada). We raised the money the best way we knew how—by throwing parties, resplendent with burlesque and go-go dancers, leaning hard on the performers we knew both inside and outside of strip clubs, the denizens of which peppered the New York City social scenes we all gravitated toward. We printed flyers and posted them all over the streets of the East Village, as well as in sex work business places. During the hot August leading up to our first fundraiser, in a stifling apartment in Bushwick, we hand-silk-screened piles of two-dollar thrift store T-shirts with the first of many $pread logos: a smirking woman with a bob haircut, holding a lit matchstick, illustrating the magazine's tagline: "Illuminating the Sex Industry." The shirts were mostly hideous, but people bought them anyway. And the fundraisers brought something more important than money into the fold: volunteers eager to get involved with the magazine. The $pread family began to grow beyond the founders.

We launched the first issue on March 16, 2005, at a party that advertised the first out lesbian Playboy playmate as our headlining performer (although she didn't show up). The press, however, showed up in droves, eager to find out what a magazine by and for sex workers looked like, probably expecting porn. We didn't meet expectations for salacious content, though we joked to *Time Out New York*, "It's not intended to arouse, but people are aroused by all kinds of things, so maybe someone will be turned on by sex workers fighting for social justice." Most sex workers deal with quite enough erotic content on the job, so much to the disappointment of readers expecting breathy *Penthouse*-style letters, *$pread* articles covered the business of sex, which as it turns out is often not that sexy. The first issue featured articles on safer sex negotiation skills and analysis of the representation of black women in the US porn industry, and subsequent issues featured reviews of lube and lipstick, health and advice columns, and real stories of labor issues and violence in the workplace.

In our first year of publishing, we often described *$pread* as a "trade magazine" for the sex industry. Later we expanded this by saying that we covered arts, culture, news, and politics from the perspectives of sex workers, which seemed a better way to describe the magazine's content as we grew and evolved. By the end of our first year in business, we had published four issues that looked increasingly professional. Thanks to the generous donation of design software and advice from a graphic designer who was a supporter of the magazine, we developed a consistent look.

We also came up with recurring features for the magazine that had clever titles: "Indecent Proposal," a popular section illustrated by New York underground comics artist Fly, in which sex workers detailed their weirdest requests from clients; "On the Street," where *$pread* staff approached unsuspecting people in parks and other public places to ask their opinions about aspects of the sex industry ("What would you say to your daughter if you found out she was a stripper?"); "Positions," a point-counterpoint column in which two sex workers debated questions like,"Should sex workers be honest with their partners about their jobs?"; "The Cunning Linguist," a space where we defined specialty terms used by different kinds of workers; "Intercourses," which featured interviews with potential allies who hadn't necessarily given sex workers' rights a lot of thought (a politician, a reproductive rights activist, a labor organizer, a john, and even a priest); "No Justice, No Piece," our activism how-to column; and more.

Besides successfully launching and coming up with the bread and butter of how every issue would be put together, *$pread* had a lot to celebrate at the end of 2005: we won the *Utne Reader* Independent Press Award for Best New Title, beating out several better-funded publications. "They think we're a real magazine!" we crowed when we learned of the award. And we were. The sense of legitimacy that the award gave us was more important than the business advantages; we gained the confidence needed to motor on. But we also had a lot more to learn.

Defining "By and For"

In January of 2006, our ragtag group trekked up to a rented cabin in the snowy Catskills to have our first retreat. It was at these annual retreats that we addressed topics like "how to avoid burnout and hating each other" (an actual written agenda item) and talked through branding, strategic plans, and generally making the magazine's future less abstract.

At our first retreat, we bonded over steaming bowls of minestrone and played in the snow with the art director's pug. But there were also serious issues we needed to talk about. Unsurprisingly, we didn't always share the same opinions editorially. More critically still, we didn't yet know who we were as a magazine. "By and for sex workers" got us started, but it wasn't enough to endure, largely because the idea of "all" sex workers wasn't actually as inclusive in reality as it was in our intentions.

Despite our differences, we had important common ground: our core value was self-determination; we all believed the magazine was (and should be) a community-building tool; the pervasive public problem we sought to address was stigma; and we wanted *$pread* to be a forum for all sex workers, not just a privileged few. With these ideas in mind, we hammered out our mission statement:

We believe that all sex workers have a right to self-determination; to choose how we make a living and what we do with our bodies. We aim to build community and destigmatize sex work by providing a forum for the diverse voices of individuals working in the sex industry.

Determining this mission informed our editorial development. Many of us had spent years in a defensive position, talking about sex work with other "progressives," but tailoring our words to avoid the unpleasant. We weathered the fear that unguarded stories might be taken out of context and used against us. Had we become so used to self-editing that, even with other sex workers, we were afraid to be critical of our sex work experiences? We thought so, and we worried that it was slipping into our editorial habits.

The problem was exacerbated by the fact that our submissions pile trended toward people writing about their more positive experiences. Early on, the pages of *$pread* were, with a few notable exceptions, filled with happy hookers, cheerful strippers, and flog-happy dommes; if there was rage in an article it was usually directed at the outside world, not the industry itself.

The difficult but radical conclusion we came to changed the magazine: we would take no positions on political or ethical issues. Those whose experiences included critiques of their professions would be actively sought out to balance the self-selecting submissions pile. This was the implication of our newly minted mission statement: the magazine would belong to *all* sex workers by making space for the full range of experiences and opinions. We spent years both reaching for and failing at this goal, but the reaching made us a better publication.

The subtext of the bias in our pages was that *$pread* was primarily a space for the voices of sex workers with privilege, partly because we were not and never would be a publication that was able to pay our writers. This was also reflected in who was reading the magazine. Our first readers' survey showed that our readership wasn't as diverse as we had hoped. A majority of readers were white with college or master's degrees. We weren't reaching sex workers who were trans women, nor we were reaching cisgender or transgender men. As for industry diversity, we weren't reaching porn performers or street-based sex workers in the numbers we wanted to.

Looking back, we can see why we had these problems. Our staff and contributors largely consisted of white, cisgender women with relative class privilege. This mirrored the US sex workers' rights movement that was most visible to us, so when we "cast our nets wide" at the founding, we only reached as far as our privilege would take us. Our content slanted in this direction, and as a result, those with less privilege were excluded. (This is not to say that more diverse groups of sex workers weren't doing organizing and solidarity work. They were. We just didn't see it.)

At our first retreat, we came up with a plan to address these issues: we would start sending free copies of the magazine to outreach organizations across the country, and include fliers with ideas for contributing to $pread in forms other than 2,000-word articles. We hoped this would encourage submissions from sex workers who didn't necessarily have a lot of formal education, or even a mailbox.

Gathered in a friend's condo in Albany for our fourth staff retreat a few years later, we reflected once again on who the magazine was supposed to be by and for. This time, due in part to new recruits with new ideas, we decided to take the magazine in a different direction. At its inception, we had envisioned a magazine that would one day join the shelves of glossies at Barnes and Noble, but with a few years of experience under our belt, this dream was feeling like a practical impossibility. Since a core part of our mission was community building, we decided that broadening our outreach base was more important than pleasing the fickle distributors that would (at least in theory) carry us to major bookstores. So instead of gunning for new distribution contracts, we poured our resources into shipping 30 percent of each print run to mobile vans, shelters, and needle exchanges, reaching sex workers who couldn't otherwise afford $spread. Once again, we sought contributions with each outreach box we sent out, and further built our outreach distribution program through stronger relationships with organizations and agencies that centered the priorities of low-income sex workers, queer sex workers, people of color who had experiences in the sex trades, and people trading sex for shelter, food, drugs, or other things they need.

Change started to register in $spread's pages. The scales tipped from consumer shorts on false eyelashes to "how to" tips on safe injection of hormones and drugs; from interviews with the industry's star performers to reporting on sex worker organizing against "move along" powers of police enforcing Prostitution Free Zones in Washington, DC. It soon became clear that centering different voices in the magazine's pages fundamentally changed what was being said.

However, we eventually recognized that $spread needed a shift in editorial power. This was acknowledged—if only for a single issue—when a handful of people of color came together as a guest editorial collective to put together an issue (which also happened to be $spread's last) about race and racism in the sex trades.

From its conception, "The Race Issue" had a process that looked different than other issues. The original motivation for the issue came from sex workers and allies of color who were part of a broader sex worker community that wasn't being represented in the magazine. Although "The Race Issue" editorial collective acknowledged that $spread played an important role within the sex workers' rights movement, both as a reflection of what was happening and as an instigator calling for change, the collective also recognized that $spread was part of the problem. Many people of color felt alienated by $spread's content. They would search the magazine for photographs of sex workers of color, for significant and ongoing contributions from people of color, and for incisive racial analyses of the industry and the sex workers' rights movement. Although such items existed in fleeting, memorable moments, sex workers of color largely found them lacking in the magazine's five-year run.

In featuring mostly the voices of white sex workers, the magazine manifested the racism and perpetuated the exclusionary practices that exist everywhere, including in the broader sex workers' rights movement, where voices of marginalized groups are addressed as an afterthought. "The Race Issue" editorial collective considered how $pread defined the sex workers' rights movement by writing about it, and about how this could expand who is represented within the movement and who is supported by it. In making the decision to guest edit an issue focusing on racism in the sex trades, the collective hoped to create a more inclusive magazine that presented a multidimensional portrayal of the sex workers' rights movement and inspired critical thought on the intersection of race, racism, and community organizing with the sex trades. To do so, the collective selected articles that explored and connected individual experiences of racism to larger trends that exist across the various arenas of sexual exchange, such as discriminatory hiring practices, racial profiling, and race-based policing.

The collective saw "The Race Issue" not as the final word on racism, but as the beginning of a conversation. In the letter from the editors, they wrote "[I]ndeed, for as many voices that are represented in this issue, there are several that are not represented—including more representation from people of color with different lived experiences in the sex industry/trades, non-English speakers, greater indigenous community representation, men, differently abled individuals, and many more. Our aim in pointing out what is missing is not to delegitimize the voices present in the issue, but to recognize the challenges of creating a 'representative issue.'" The editors discussed at length what it meant to be representative. In deciding to focus the issue geographically in the United States, the collective chose to use the term "people of color" in the call for submissions because of its resonance in the United States. In doing so, the collective recognized that this already precluded including the experiences of sex workers dealing with racism in the sex trades in other places around the world and their accompanying movements.

There were hopes that this issue represented a shift in the direction of the magazine, and that it was the beginning of a new phase. Unfortunately, as "The Race Issue" was underway, $pread made a decision to fold due to capacity issues, so what was envisioned as a hopeful shift in new directions ended up being the final issue of the magazine.

As a volunteer-driven project, $pread's greatest strength was its flexibility, allowing for the magazine to take on new directions with the visions of all the people who created its many issues. In turn, the magazine transformed the people who worked on it, showing us what sex worker-made media could be.

Fitting In

Before many of the staff became involved with $pread, most had been involved in various social justice movements. And the way that $pread became integrated into these social movements was something we all watched closely from our different vantage points.

Since a number of us were LGBTQ identified, we made sure that $pread marched in each year's New York City Pride March. The LGBTQ community was one of our most consistent allies, partly because both of our communities face stigma because of gender-and-sexuality-based discrimination, and partly because a disproportionately large number of LGBTQ people have worked in the sex trades (which connects to the appalling lack of resources for LGBTQ youth, and the resulting epidemic of homelessness). When we threw ourselves a first birthday party at the opening of our self-curated sex worker visual arts show called "Sex Worker Visions," the LGBT Community Center volunteered space for the party and hosted the show for months afterward. We could see by the sea of sex workers mixing with non-sex worker LGBTQ folk at the event just how much love there was between our communities.

Our relationship with feminists was more complicated. Many of us had come out of the feminist movement, and there was probably no other social movement that had so much interest in sex work issues, but the 1970s anti-porn crusades of feminism had not gone out of vogue, and some of this interest was decidedly unfriendly. Many of us—including the feminists among us—held a deep distrust of feminism because so many self-described feminists expressed considerable hostility toward sex workers. There was probably no other social movement we interacted with that left us feeling so unsure of our footing.

Our tactic became to reach out, educate, wait, and see. We mailed boxes of our first copies to college women's studies programs, feminist bookstores and distributors, feminist organizations, and feminist websites. The reaction we received was mixed. One memorable reply arrived in a manila envelope that also contained the shreds of the latest issue of $pread:

Dear Prostitutes,

Were you smoking crack when you sent [a sample copy of $pread] to me? Or did your syphilis get in the way of doing any research into my company? I'd rather turn tricks myself than get within 100 feet of this crap you call a magazine. A true feminist works to secure the dignity and safety of all women, while you only care about yourself and your "liberation." Meanwhile, you're helping to destroy the country.

I hope you go down in flames.

(heart) One Angry Girl, Anti Porn Star Extraordinaire
Old Saybrook, CT

Hate mail notwithstanding, the majority of responses from feminists were supportive, especially from our publishing idols at Bitch. Still, there were times when our policy of not taking editorial positions on issues—including feminism— irked. In Issue 1.3, former call girl and author Tracy Quan said in an interview, "an attachment to feminism is, in American life, a sign of needing approval or affection from your mother. It may even be a sign that you spent your childhood in the suburbs." A few weeks after the issue's release, Lisa Jervis, cofounder of *Bitch*, submitted a letter to the editor expressing her disappointment that we didn't call Tracy on her "ridiculous comments about feminism" and challenging us with this:

> *You'd feel a responsibility to correct the record if someone said that it was always emotional damage that led folks to work in the sex industry, wouldn't you? You should feel the same obligation to counteract stereotypes about feminism.*

Tracy Quan, from our perspective, was the ultimate expert in what feminism meant (and didn't mean) to her, and our purpose was to give her, as a sex worker, a platform to speak her piece. As we noted in our response, "We are a publication that tries to foreground the diverse views of sex workers." And in fact, some sex workers do feel that emotional damage leads people to work in the sex industry, and their views were always welcome in the pages of *$pread*.

Still, we found ways to work with feminists whenever we could. *Bitch* welcomed us into its pages by publishing a major feature interview with the editors about sex work as a labor issue. And we partnered with them on a letter that was sent to all New York City Council Members to express our joint displeasure at a silly, publicity-seeking resolution to symbolically "ban" the words "bitch" and "ho."

Another group that embraced us from the beginning, but that not all of us saw eye to eye with, were the anarchists. Many sex worker activists are politically radical and many of the independent bookstores that sold *$pread* were anarchist bookstores, so anarchist activists made up a core part of our readership and frequently invited us to table and present at book fairs and conferences. The book fairs were always fun— at one particularly memorable event in Baltimore we decided to give away a free firecracker with each magazine purchase and quickly sold out.

Anarchists related to sex workers (and yes, there are also sex worker anarchists) in that they work "outside the system" and sometimes don't pay taxes, but they had a hard time with the fact that *$pread* explored sex work in all its facets, which included a discussion of sex as commodity in a way that didn't mesh easily with anti-capitalism. When we began subletting office space from the radical newspaper *Indymedia*, we stenciled a gold dollar sign on our newly painted pink door and spent weeks giggling at the uneasy looks caused by our implicated worship of the mighty dollar. At one anarchist bookfair, a fan of *$pread* approached us and said that she loved our "Consumer Report" feature, which she described as a "parody of consumer reports in mainstream women's magazines." We exchanged looks: "Consumer Report" was far from parody; it was real-life sex workers rating real-life products—because many sex workers need and buy a lot of products and care a lot about product quality.

We suppose that this is the inadvertent power of the written word: there was room for the content of *$pread* to have many different (sometimes even contradictory) meanings to many different audiences. In a broader context, something else happened which we didn't expect; *$pread* staff became de facto spokespeople for a growing sex workers' rights movement in the United States.

What $pread Meant to Sex Workers

Back in 2005, there were very few people speaking up as insider experts about sex work issues. So when news concerning sex work happened, or when researchers or public health officials wanted access to our community, our phones rang. By the end of our first year of publishing, we had become official media spokespeople whose jobs went well beyond responding to questions about the magazine. This role complicated our editorial mission: on the one hand, we didn't take positions; on the other hand, we didn't want to lose opportunities as they fell into our lap to correct erroneous assumptions about sex workers in the mainstream media (and to promote magazine sales while we were at it). Mostly, we passed generic media requests along to people in our circles who were most appropriate. But it wasn't easy, and if we felt that we had too much of the weight of responsibility for our community on our shoulders, these added tasks didn't lighten our load.

There was no moment when we felt more inundated than when New York Governor Eliot Spitzer was revealed to be the regular client of an expensive escort service in March of 2008. Some of our staff worked with press "on background," answering general questions about escorting for print reporters, while others appeared on live broadcasts of major outlets and radio shows. While it was good that we were ready for this onslaught, it was also a major distraction: we weren't a media operation, we were a magazine with a subscriber base that expected us to be focused on our next issue.

This adaptability did allow for *$pread* to become a known platform and voice for the sex workers' rights movement. In this role, our "no positions" position was often awkward to uphold. In 2006, when we attended the inaugural Desiree Alliance conference in Las Vegas, Nevada, the Sex Workers Outreach Project (SWOP) asked each attending organization to cosign a letter advocating for the decriminalization of prostitution. We were forced to stand up in front of this inaugural, historic meeting of our peers and explain that *$pread* couldn't endorse the letter. It wasn't a popular stance, but we knew that for any sex worker who didn't support decriminalization, adopting a political stance would effectively be hanging out a "Not Welcome" sign. We kept to our editorial policy with the zeal of a First Amendment enthusiast, and it served us well in making room for a range of ideas and opinions.

The ever-beckoning call to be everything our community needed us to be was a challenge. At one point, we applied for and received a grant from Citizens Committee for New York City to provide free tax preparation services for sex workers. It was a good program, but ultimately it was a time suck; we weren't a social services organization or a non-profit public purpose group. That doesn't mean that our forays into extracurricular activities weren't fruitful in other unexpected ways. In 2007, we collaborated with Transmission, a friendly Christian organization, to hold an Easter service focused on Mary Magdalene. We certainly aren't all Christian, but for those in our community who are, it was an incredible thing to attend a sex worker-positive Christian service.

At the same time, being the only magazine by and for sex workers meant that we received a lot of support and validation from our community:

"After reading the first issue I started to cry because I saw that there were others out there like me."—Remy, Minnesota (Issue 3.4)

"I love receiving [$pread] and feel like I'm hanging out with my best sex worker friends every issue."—Juline, Brooklyn (Issue 2.1)

"I just got my three back issues today and I am savoring them like a delicious treat. Even though I work in a big city, I often experience feelings of isolation as a sex worker. Reading $pread is like finding one person who speaks your language in a foreign country. Thank you so much for giving sex workers a voice."—Fae, San Francisco (Issue 2.2)

Letters like these reminded us of the important role that $pread played in the sex worker community, and kept us going whenever we began to burn out.

What $pread Leaves Behind

Probably the most important reason we succeeded was that we didn't know what we were getting into. And yet for five years we put out a quarterly magazine, celebrating each small success as the major victory that it was. At the end of this journey, we leave a legacy of making space for the voices of people who have been silenced, and we feel confident that our community will always have more to say.

This anthology represents a sample of *$pread*'s significant breadth over its five-year run. Choosing meant making difficult decisions about what to include and what to leave out. Ultimately, the selected pieces collectively demonstrate our mission: how sex workers with a range of viewpoints and lived experiences can come together through the pages of a magazine to listen to each other; and how by doing this, we broaden our sense of community. We were lucky to find and work with an incredible number of sex workers and allies from all over the world. To the volunteers, supporters, and readers who gave their time, sweat, and money to make the magazine a reality, we echo our words in *$pread*'s final issue:

> *Because of this outpouring of support, hundreds of sex workers who had never before been given permission to describe their lives or name their dreams for themselves finally had a platform to speak. Because they spoke, thousands more sex workers saw their lives reflected in the pages of $pread magazine, and many of them felt for the first time that they were not alone. Because so many sex workers shed the bondage of isolation, the world has shifted. We feel no hubris in saying this. We watched it shift.*

RACHEL AIMEE cofounded *$pread* magazine in 2004 and was an editor-in-chief for four and a half years. Now a parent and freelance copy editor, she also organizes for strippers' rights with We Are Dancers. She lives in Brooklyn with her family.

ELIYANNA KAISER is a former executive editor of *$pread* magazine. She is currently raising her two children in Manhattan. In her spare time, she writes fiction.

AUDACIA RAY is the founder and executive director of the Red Umbrella Project (RedUP), a peer-led organization in New York that amplifies the voices of people in the sex trades through media, storytelling, and advocacy programs. At RedUP, she publishes the literary journal *Prose & Lore: Memoir Stories About Sex Work* and she has taught media strategy workshops for sex workers in New York, San Francisco, Las Vegas, and London. She is the author of *Naked on the Internet: Hookups, Downloads, and Cashing in On Internet Sexploration* and has contributed to many anthologies. She joined the *$pread* staff in 2004 and was an executive editor from 2005 to 2008.

WORKPLACE

INTRODUCTION

Lulu

I guess the atmosphere that I've tried to create here is
that I'm a friend first and a boss second, and probably an
entertainer third.

—Michael Scott, *The Office*

Our workplaces say a lot about who we are. When
you spend every workday in a place, it molds against you
and becomes like a second home. In this chapter we are
reminded that, just like nine-to-fivers, sex workers experience
stupid bosses, arbitrary rules, and tricky relationships with
coworkers. Dungeons, brothels, strip clubs, and other sex
workplaces may be exoticized by the mainstream media, but
in these pages they are tangible, everyday settings.

The legal Nevada brothel industry is the subject of Erin
Siegal's stunning photo essay, "American Brothel." In providing a rare and intimate look at everyday life at Donna's
Ranch, these striking photos illuminate a segment of the sex
industry that intrigues us all.

Like the rest of the United States, the sex workplace is
shaped by race, as Mona Salim illustrates in "Stripping
While Brown." As one of only a few Indian women working
in the New York City strip club scene, she describes how race
informs her interactions with bosses, customers, and dancers
alike—with consequences that are sometimes hilarious, sometimes upsetting, but always revealing of the racial hierarchies
underlying our sexual desires.

Sex workers have a range of opinions about their jobs,
as illustrated in *$pread*'s regular point/counterpoint column,
"Positions." In "Is Sex Work a Sacred Practice or Just a Job?"

two pro-dommes explore whether sex work is spiritual in nature—or not. Meanwhile, in "No Sex in the Champagne Room?" a dancer and a prostitute debate the pros and cons of turning tricks in strip club VIP rooms.

For those sex workers working independently over the Internet, the solitary workplace is not without its challenges. In "Menstruation: Porn's Last Taboo," webcam pro Trixie Fontaine relates the social stigma around menstruation to her battle with camsites and credit card processors around showing menstruation porn.

On a more lighthearted note, in "Fucking the Movement," Eve Ryder describes her encounter with a client who asked her to dress as an anarchist protester. Meanwhile, Sheila McClear's "Diary of a Peep Show Girl" gives us a peek at daily life in the peep show worker's fishbowl "office."

All of these essays remind us that sex workers' lives aren't so alien. Vicariously bare and plainly told, the stories in this chapter reveal the sex workplace for what it is—no smoke-screens, no media glitz. Welcome!

LULU worked on *$pread* during her undergraduate studies on all things related to design and art. Since leaving *$pread*, she has attempted to learn to cook, started a photographic series of food portraits, and is trying to see the world. When she is not working or in school, she likes European art, looking at cat pictures, and anything tech related.

INDECENT PROPOSAL: FUCKING THE MOVEMENT

Eve Ryder

ISSUE 1.2 (2005)

He says he decided to call me because I look like a college student and my ad seems smart. I'm not much into role-playing and it says so in my ad, so I balk a little when he asks if I take clothing requests.

He begins to describe what he's looking for: Would I wear jeans? Of course. How about safety pins on the jeans? Okay. What about a *lot* of safety pins? Um, okay. Do I have any ripped T-shirts? Sure . . . Are any of them political? Wait, come again? What? When he asks me if I own one of "those black sweatshirts, with the attached hat thing," I start to laugh at him. You want me to wear a *hoodie*?

Then he begins to spill. He's an investment banker and ever since he watched the Seattle riots on TV in 1999, he's had a fantasy of fucking an anarchist protestor girl while she lectures him about being a big, bad capitalist pig. Oh, and would I mind not showering or putting on deodorant before our session? I tell him I was in Seattle for the WTO protests, although I'm not an anarchist, I'm a socialist. He stops me before I explain the difference; this he wants to hear in person.

The next day, I find myself in an office in the financial district, stripping out of some stinky protest ware I slept in the night before. My usual escort-perfected, hushed, fem-bot voice is replaced with tones of authority as I delineate the subtle political variances of the Left. "Socialism," I say, "teaches me

Illustration by Fly.

that what you do on Wall Street has no use value. You only exist to extract surplus value for the ruling class."

I ask him if he knows what commodity fetishism is. He thinks it sounds dirty but guesses that I'm the commodity and he has a fetish for me. I tell him he is a stupid capitalist and that his freaky little protestor thing is a pathetic manifestation of his patriarchal and class privilege. He moans harder.

The date culminates with a solid round of spankings. "Bad protestor," he teases, "you smashed the Starbucks." He wants me to stay longer, but he hasn't paid for more than an hour and I tell him that, "I just can't rationalize being alienated from my labor. Oh, and by the way," I add, "you got it wrong. I'm not the commodity, but my time is, and it's up."

EVE RYDER is a former streetwalker and call girl who lives in New York City.

FLY has been a Lower East Side squatter since the late 80s. She is a painter and commix artist, illustrator, punk musician, sometimes muralist, and teacher. She is the author of *CHRON!IC!RIOTS!PA!SM!*, a collection of her zines and comics, and *PEOPS*, a collection of 196 portraits and stories. Fly was a recipient of a 2013 Acker Award for Excellence Within the Avant-Garde. She is currently working on a multi-media project called *UnReal Estate; a Late Twentieth Century History of Squatting in the Lower East Side*.

POSITIONS: IS SEX WORK A SACRED PRACTICE OR JUST A JOB?

Vero Rocks and Tasha Tasticake

ISSUE 3.1 (2007)

These guys come in and they want something they can't ask for. They try, though, each of them awkwardly trying to name the ineffable: "GFE," "sensual," "good personality," "release," "relaxation." They say they want all kinds of things, but we know why they are really here: to connect with genitals. They want to jerk off. Or get jerked off. Or get hard and go jerk off at home. Or fuck to get off. Or get someone else off. It's all about the genitals.

The word "genitals" comes from some old Latin root (gen-) about beginnings, like generate, or genesis. Genitals represent the creation of me, and by extension, they represent everything I could possibly create. Religious impulse originates in the awe we experience when confronted by our own mortality. I could make a million references to ancient practices of sacred prostitution, but that was a million years ago and who knows whether all those ethnocentric anthropologists got anything right anyway. I want to stay in this moment.

Right here is a man whose senses have been sealed off by a lifestyle of eating in steak houses and drinking martinis. Sacred prostitutes are not part of his reality. He thinks she needs to be young, or tall, or clean-shaven, or whatever. That doesn't matter. He doesn't have to know that by visiting a sex worker, he's receiving a sacrament. He is connecting with the origin of his being and his own capacity to be creative.

The more clearly I hold this model for sex work in my mind, and believe that I am a priestess and my clients disciples, the more meaningful and interesting my work becomes. It can be hard to maintain this perspective when there is so much social pressure to see sex as antithetical to the sacred. I work toward a different vision of sex in society. I hold my consciousness as a single point of resistance in the sea of the collective. This is my spiritual practice.

—Tasha Tasticake

Is the pursuit of money sacred? Honey, I'll call anything sacred if you pay me enough, but after our time is up it's up to you to decide if I believe it.

Sex workers, like other workers, expect to be afforded the ability to be cognizant, self-determining, and real. We're not simply the fictitious airbrushed images of the 72 dpi screen, or the anal sluts of video release, or unfortunate creatures destined for every bad thing that happens. We exist as other people who wake up in the morning and ride the train—people you could know.

In my work, I use a Superior Female persona, among others. But I maintain that, since I choose both to work and to construct that identity, I am not somehow naturally predestined for either. My innate self doesn't have to hearken to a higher power to play games for an hour. I can get down and dirty and take the illusion off while on the subway home. I'm happy to keep that balance.

When some of us define their work as "sacred" off the clock, a few things happen:

1. Our regular humanity is compromised by the need for a spiritual dimension. If you have to apply a higher power to make doing sex work OK, that's a problem. It should be OK whether you're getting "blessed" or not.

2. Sex work becomes a calling, not a job. Suddenly, regular

Illustration by Katie Fricas.

girls and guys aren't qualified. I thought half the point was that regular people, not unearthly uber-creatures, but people with a bit of huevos and business sense could go make some scratch.

3. Workers lose their separate, personal identities. It's easy to laugh at someone who, both in and out of work, identifies as a goddess, sacred whore, or chakra-channeling medium, but it's also worrisome. It means that the identity that johns use to read that person manifests outside of work hours, so what the goddess is and what she's selling are sleeping double to a crowded, single bed.

You can argue that the way you deliver sex heals, enlightens, and brings positive change. But so do books, LSD, and a well-received membership to the Church of Scientology. Sure, some sex is sacred some of the time, but all sex can't be sacred all of the time. Claiming to sell a sacred exchange is necessarily selling its illusion.

—Vero Rocks

TASHA TASTICAKE argued that sex work is a sacred practice in the Positions column for Issue 3.1 of *$pread.*

VERO ROCKS is a New York City-based, professional dildo-wearing ass fucker.

KATIE FRICAS is a cartoonist and illustrator in New York. She drew for *$pread* from 2007 to 2010. Her comics have appeared in *WW3 Illustrated* and *Juicy Mother*. In 2014 her comic *Terry + Terry* was named best comic by people named Terry.

AMERICAN BROTHEL: A PHOTO-ESSAY

Text and photos by Erin Siegal

ISSUE 2.4 (2007)

Donna's Ranch is a brothel in Wells, Nevada, one of about twenty state-sanctioned cathouses across the state. The small whorehouse has become a staple of the rural town's diminishing economy. Although brothels are technically legal in Nevada (in counties with populations of under 400,000, which excludes Carson County, where Las Vegas is located), Wells is one of only eleven counties that have embraced the state's acceptance of the world's oldest profession.

With local industries shifting overseas and the slow demise of Nevada's mining economy, the town of Wells relies heavily on the taxable income it receives from Donna's Ranch. The brothel regularly donates money to local causes such as Little League, girls' soccer, military organizations, and community events. The brothel logo, however, is not displayed alongside those of other sponsors.

Depending on their location, brothels are required to pay anywhere from $200 to $100,000 in annual licensing fees. Each individual prostitute must also register with the government and pay a multitude of fees to the State. Nevada state law requires licensed prostitutes to take weekly STD tests, practice mandatory condom use, and get monthly blood tests for HIV/AIDS, all of which must be paid for by the workers. Prostitutes must also pay for tools of the trade, such as condoms, lube, and baby wipes. "Trick sheets," the plain, white flat sheets that cover the bed during dates, are provided by the brothel, though each prostitute must launder her own bedding. "The washing machine is the most important thing in this house," jokes owner Geoff Arnold. "If it goes down, we go down."

Local governments can establish trade regulations independent from the state, prohibit houses of prostitution in certain areas, and impose restrictions on prostitutes' lives. In many counties, severe rules have been instated to maintain a dramatic separation between the working prostitutes and the general population. Workers from the Wells brothels are banned from being in town after 5 p.m. without a sheriff or brothel manager as an escort. They cannot go to restaurants, bars, grocery stores, pharmacies, or even to the doctor without a chaperone.

After signing up to work for a certain period of time, ranging from a few days to a few weeks, women move into their bedrooms, where they will both work and live for the duration of their shifts. Girls are generally allowed to decorate their rooms as they see fit.

As a smaller brothel with between three and eleven working women, Donna's clientele is made up of roughly 90 percent truckers and 10 percent miners and cowboys from neighboring towns. To attract business, girls utilize CB radios to talk to truckers passing by on the interstates. Donna's also offers free showers, coffee, and tea to truckers, an enticing offer given that most truck stops charge fees for washroom use.

Each girl expresses herself via her clothing, and workers' outfits range from lingerie to tropical sarongs and mini-dresses. One by one, each woman steps forward, introduces herself simply by stating her name, and tries to maintain eye contact with the john. Any other kind of appeal from the prostitutes—a wink, lick of the lips, or even one additional word outside of the standard greeting—is regarded as "dirty hustling." "Dirty hustling" is deeply frowned on by working girls, and can be cause for infighting. After the john chooses the woman he wants, they retreat to her room to negotiate services and a price agreeable to both parties.

Some brothel workers report feeling little control over their working conditions, and dissatisfaction with the permanent record created for licensed prostitutes by the state of Nevada. The requirement for only prostitutes—and not clients—to undergo background and health tests is also fundamentally discriminatory, making the safety of the johns a higher priority than that of the working girls. While prostitutes set their own prices for services, they are generally required to split their income fifty-fifty with the house. Because of their official status as independent contractors and not employees, brothel prostitutes are unable to receive unemployment, retirement, or health benefits. However, the strict rules imposed by both the brothels and the state inform the argument that working conditions should preclude the women from being legally classified as independent contractors.

ERIN SIEGAL is a senior fellow at the Schuster Institute for Investigative Journalism and the author of the books *Finding Fernanda* and *The US Embassy Cables: Adoption Fraud in Guatemala, 1987–2010*. She was *$pread*'s first art director from 2004 to 2007. She currently lives in Tijuana, Mexico.

STRIPPING WHILE BROWN

Mona Salim

ISSUE 5.4 (2011)

When I was first hired to dance, the DJ asked me where I was from. "India," I said. He told me that he would have guessed "South American or Middle Eastern," and that the club had never had an Indian girl before. "You're going to do well. You're exotic and that's going to be an asset for the club."

It's been almost two years since that day, and every day, I am confronted with just how prominent our racial and ethnic identities are on the job. People talk about stripping as a form of sex work. I want to talk about it here as a form of race work.

A gentlemen's club is not just gendered, it's deeply racialized. And classed. Race is an essential dimension of how the strip club is experienced by dancers and customers.

As a woman of color, I've been made hyper-aware (by customers, management, and coworkers) of the fact that my racial identity isn't secondary to my identity as a woman. I'm not even sure I can separate those dimensions of who I am. In the literature I've read on stripping, it seems that all too often race gets "added on" to a larger discussion of gender and sexuality. I have trouble trying to compartmentalize pieces of my identity; now I'm Muslim, now a woman, now middle-class. The reality is, all of those pieces are imbricated, inextricable, and inflect themselves in my work and my life. Bringing race to the center of my analysis is a way to displace the dominance of gender and sex in popular discussions of sex work. It's an exploration of what exactly transnational feminists mean when we talk about intersectionality.

Strippers don't just sell beautiful smiles, perky breasts, thick hair, and great conversations. We sell racial fetishes. We fulfill fantasies of the exotic. We comply with certain notions of racial purity.

The work that sex workers do ultimately gets relegated to the realm of the "body," of sexuality and physical beauty. But all of our bodies already exist within the world of politics, politics that have rendered our bodies thin, curvy, dark, fair, desirable, or flawed. It's important to know that our sex and race are written onto our bodies by deep contours of history and politics. We can't talk about our bodies without talking about how they've been ordered, arranged, and labeled by structures larger and older than any of us.

The strip club is actually a perfect site for challenging this mind-body duality. A strip club is a place that is explicitly commodified and exotic. At the same time, it's deeply intimate. To demonstrate what I mean, I share with you here some commonplace experiences from work:

I exit the stage into the dressing room. Three other girls are back there, smoking and fixing their makeup. I sort my stage tips and bundle them into a rubber band and then put on my dress. "Girl, do all Indians have a body like that under all their clothes?" one of them jokes. I laugh. "No," another girl chimes in, "I lived in Jackson Heights and all the Indian girls were skinny and had no ass. You sure you don't have any black blood in your family?"

An Indian man comes into the club. The other girls warn me that he's no good and he never spends any money. When he asks me for a lap dance, I'm surprised. He ends up visiting me every two or three weeks and spending about a hundred dollars on each visit.

He tips me extra on Christmas, Valentine's Day, and my birthday. He tells me he started going to strip clubs because he and his wife haven't had sex since the birth of their youngest son, now fourteen years old. He says that even when they were sexually active, he and his wife never kissed or had oral sex. He tells me that he loves me, and that his wife wasted his life. He offers me money in exchange for sex on multiple occasions, but praises my "Indian values" when I turn him down. He tells me that I'm the first dancer he's liked. He claims that the other "blacks and Russians" who work there are uneducated, don't understand him, and are just interested in money.

An older white man who's visiting from Texas is having drinks with me at the bar. He wants me to get drunk, so I order a "gin and tonic" (Sprite). He is annoying, but he keeps tipping me so I put up with it. He keeps talking about the girls on stage as drug-addicted, stuck in abusive relationships, excessively promiscuous. I ask him why he feels comfortable telling me this, and he responds that I, as an Asian woman, come from a background that prioritizes family values and education.

Ricardo, a married graphic designer, asks me why Indian women are always all covered up. He says we always look attractive, but never dress in revealing clothes. "I'm lucky to have found an Indian stripper, or else I'd never get to see the body of an Indian woman."

These stories are just a few instances in which I was perceived in accordance with, or in contrast to, some preconceived notions of what an Indian/Muslim/South Asian woman is expected to be.

In this context I become hyperaware of how race is written onto my body. For instance, my very presence in the club separates me from those "skinny" Indian girls the girls I work with see on city streets and brings me into dialogue with others in the club. For Ricardo, my nudity separates me from the conservatively dressed Indian women he encounters. For several of my customers, my race indicates that I am free of

HIV or any other STI. I've been assumed to be a virgin by several customers.

The racial terrain I observe in the strip club is unique and nuanced in ways that conversations about race in the "real world" are not. Outside the club, I don't sip champagne and chat with a married conservative man about how the Republican Party should revitalize itself. In the club, I gain access to otherwise inaccessible people. Unlikely alliances and impossible connections are enabled.

A South Asian man in the club is sitting alone. I approach him and introduce myself. "Mo," he says as he shakes my hand. "Mo . . . hammed?" I guess. He gets visibly uncomfortable and nods. "I'm here for a blonde." He's not the first to assume an ethnically neutral alias. One of my regular customers, Arjun, introduces himself to all the other girls in the club as "John." Because he knows I'm South Asian, he has shared his real name with me.

"Mystique and Amanda to the stage!" the DJ announces. "Scratch that, Mystique and Gabrielle." I'm standing next to him and ask him why he changed his mind. "We can't have two black girls on stage at once," he tells me. "Management tells us that there should be variety on display." I comment that no one ever complains when there are two blonde girls on stage, and he agrees.

Champagne is on stage. As usual, I am in awe of her. Amazingly limber, she does all sorts of pole tricks and is accessorized beautifully. It's so much fun to watch. When she gets off the stage, the manager tells her not to dance like that anymore. "No booty-dancing. It's not classy."

In these cases, we see race being performed by dancers, management, and customers. We see the strip club as a place where racial pretenses are presented and race is constructed. The music, dancing styles, and attire are all deliberately chosen to create an image of a particular type of club, a specific sort of femininity, ethnicity, or class. Playing reggaeton and rap might pigeonhole the club as a "black" club, or a less classy establishment, as might a girl "booty-dancing" on stage.

Requesting music that constructs my own identity as authentically Indian or Asian has been financially lucrative. (Truth Hurts' "Addictive" features a Lata Mangeshkar sample that is just ethnic enough for several of my customers.)

Deliberately signaling my identity in this way is, for me, a conflicted act. When customers praise me in comparison to "ghetto" girls, or make offensive statements about other dancers' English competency, it becomes profitable for me to use my cultural capital in the club. In fulfilling a customer's fantasy by playing the part of a virginal Indian girl, a Muslim woman rebelling against a sexually repressed childhood, or the "intellectual" with an exhibitionist streak, I at once reinforce stereotypes about myself and the other strippers that I've been differentiated from. It is both a disturbing and rewarding performance.

The daily scene in the dressing room is also explicitly racialized: girls flatiron their curls, put on wigs, use body makeup to cover tattoos and stretch marks. Management enforces these internalized desires, encouraging women to wear wigs and body makeup. A sign in my club's dressing room reads: "TASTEFUL JEWELRY ONLY. NO 'BLING.' NO GHETTO GOLD. NO BAMBOO-STYLE EARRINGS."

I'm getting really sick of Ujin. Conversations with him fluctuate between him convincing me to meet him at a restaurant because "we're from the same culture" and "we should always trust our own people," and him disparaging me doing this kind of work. He encourages me to get married, quit, and find a job where I don't have to degrade myself. He gets very frustrated when I continue to turn him down for dates. "Where else are you going to find a desi man who's willing to date a stripper?" he asks.

"Are you really Indian?" he asks. "Yes." "Say something in Hindi. And tell me what part of Bombay you're from."

"Asl mein, waha ki paydaish hain, lekin yaha baday huwe."
*He seems satisfied and puts his arm around me. "Some
girls tried to tell me they were Indian, but they were actually like Guyanese or from Trinidad. But, listen, I really
like you, but I can't buy a dance from you. Let me just give
you the money instead. I don't want to do this with someone like you . . . You could be my sister or something."*

*Gia is from Tibet but tells all the customers that she's
Hawaiian. She doesn't want South Asian men giving her
any trouble. I always tell her that it might make her more
money to be upfront about her background, as it has for
me, because there are so few South Asian strippers. She
feels uncomfortable with the idea for reasons of safety. She
thinks guys "from our culture" would treat a South Asian
woman very badly for being in this line of work.*

These anecdotes suggest that the dynamics in the strip
club often rest on notions of racial purity, conformity, and
authenticity that may or may not actually exist. Scholars who
have studied stripping have documented the ways we allow
the customer to perceive our identity and personality. What
should be emphasized is that these perceptions are anchored
to race, culture, or ethnicity.

My experiences show that notions of racial purity abound
at the club. There have been several occasions where my
competency in Hindi, Urdu, Arabic, or "standard" English
have been the foundation for a long-term connection with
a regular customer. Linguistic skills were proof that I was
a particular type of immigrant woman, separate from the
women who often lacked legal documentation or had limited
English proficiency. Several times, customers told me that
even the way I introduced myself "gave away" my race and
class identity within seconds.

My status as a graduate student also often came into question by customers. One man, himself a university professor,
said that several girls pretended to be students, but "it's clear
that they're not, and it's clear that you're some sort of gradu-

ate student." In fact, the "Indian emphasis" on higher learning has come up several times by customers with whom I discuss my schooling.

Several customers ask for information about my family. Do my parents try to arrange my marriage? Aren't they really strict? Are they accepting of my decision to be in graduate school? Again, these questions reflect assumptions about what my people are expected to be like.

Yes, it seems undeniable that race shapes the daily realities of strippers at work. Our bodies are powerful symbols. They are not separate from our minds, from politics, from our social subjectivities. In spaces of commercial intimacy, it is never just a body that is bought or sold.

MONA SALIM is a writer, educator, stripper, and graduate student in New York City. She hails from Mumbai, India, and blogs about the surreal, aggravating, hilarious mash-up of race/class/gender/sexuality that unfolds in the low-lit mirrored walls of New York City's gentlemen's clubs at Civilundressed.blogspot.com. She dreams of a world in which sex work is decriminalized and social scientists can find jobs after earning a doctorate.

POSITIONS:
NO SEX IN THE CHAMPAGNE ROOM?

Mary Taylor and Carol Leigh

ISSUE 2.1 (2006)

An average dancer in the 1980s earned anywhere from $500 to $2,000 a week—an honest day's pay for an honest day's work. By the mid-1990s, the industry took a turn. Dancers no longer got paid by the show—instead they got sixty dollars per shift. Recently it has declined to getting paid nothing at all. When lap dancing and contact with customers kicked in, many dancers were forced to quit their jobs; some threw in the towel, others resorted to lap dancing or turned to drugs or alcohol to cope. Nothing could change the path that dancing was headed toward.

When word got out that you could earn at least twenty dollars for every three-minute (dirty) dance, prostitutes came in off the cold streets and moved their business into strip clubs. Dancers that would normally never do dirty dances felt they had no choice but to follow suit. If they didn't, the other girls would. Club owners realized how much money was being made in the VIP rooms and began charging the dancers fees to go to work. Hence, they became pimps. And clients got spoiled, receiving big services for twenty dollars.

VIP rooms and champagne rooms—I don't think so. Used condoms and cum-stained furniture are common and women are seen blatantly giving clients hand jobs, or allowing clients to finger them. Dancing? I don't think so! How can a legitimate dancer make money these days? The club owners won't pay her for her talents and the clients won't pay her unless she performs sexual acts. The lines have been crossed so badly that the strip clubs have become bawdy houses. I feel uncomfortable referring to these women as "dancers." They are not dancers! They are prostitutes!

I don't have a problem with women that choose to be prostitutes, have their own business, work from their home, or do outcalls. What I have a problem with are the prostitutes that use strip clubs to provide their services to the strippers' clients. They know NOTHING about the art of slowly and seductively removing their clothing while teasing and entertaining clients.

In closing, all I have to say is get out of the strip clubs and go back to the streets or use your own venues.

—Mary Taylor

I never worked at the strip clubs. I've been a prostitutes' rights advocate, so I am primarily concerned with prostitutes' perspectives. Conflicts between workers about prostitution in the strip clubs are old news, but have been newly exacerbated due to the changing sex industry.

This issue is particularly confusing because of evolving definitions of prostitution. Is lap dancing prostitution? Many lap dancers insist it is not. Cities have different answers, and it depends on case law. My Australian prostitute activist friends explain that where "shop-based" prostitution is legal, dancing and prostitution can exist at the same club. In countries where overt "shop-based" prostitution is prohibited, like the United States and Canada, the enmity between dancers and prostitutes is exacerbated.

It's a no-win situation. The booming exotic dance industry is the flip side to the prohibition of prostitution. The tease is legal, but actual sex is not. Criminalization of prostitution and stigmatization of "The Slut" pits women against each other, separating the "good girls" from the "bad girls," and the "bad girls" from the "very bad girls."

In this environment, with market demands lowering prices

so that one can no longer make the big bucks for a beaver show, certainly dancers have a valid interest in keeping prostitution out of the clubs. But when people insist there should be no prostitution at all in strip clubs, we say, "But there is." This reminds me of the old days when the neighborhood groups seemed to have good reasons for getting prostitutes off their streets. But where should prostitutes go with their limited options? NIMBY and NIMSC. Not In My Back Yard. Not In My Strip Club.

Some may propose a return to the old days; the price women have paid for decreases in sexual protectionism has resulted in greater expectations and perhaps more potential for exploitation. The challenge for sex workers is the very long haul of owning our erotic labor as individuals and communities and learning to work together through these divisions.

—Carol Leigh

MARY TAYLOR, a former stripper of twenty-one years, was the founder of the Exotic Dancers' Association of Canada and the author of *Bedroom Games*. Ms. Taylor is an expert in the exotic entertainment industry, founder of the "Peel and Play" workshops, and president of Live Girl Productions, Inc.

CAROL LEIGH is a sex worker activist, performer, and filmmaker. Leigh coined the term "sex work" in 1978. She has been a spokesperson for COYOTE, a member of SWOP and Desiree, and was a founder of BAY-SWAN. Leigh coordinated a street outreach project, volunteered at a needle exchange, and represented the SF Commission on the Status of Women on the Board of Supervisor's Task Force on Prostitution. In 1999, she founded the San Francisco Sex Workers Film and Arts Festival. She is the author of *Unrepentant Whore: Collected Works of Scarlot Harlot*.

MENSTRUATION: PORN'S LAST TABOO

Trixie Fontaine

ISSUE 1.3 (2005)

"Will you pee for me?"

It was one of the first requests I got as a webwhore during a private webcam show, and I was happy to oblige my customer for $2.99 a minute. I grabbed a Tupperware bowl, aimed the cam at my pussy, and pissed until my bladder went dry. Cha-ching! I envisioned logging into the camsite every morning to empty my bladder and line my pockets. Who knew webwhoring could be so simple and the customers so easy to please?

A week later I found out it wasn't so simple; yellow shows were (and still are) against most camsites' rules and many camgirls' accounts had been closed for disobeying by spraying. I was flabbergasted—doesn't a piss ban on a porn site violate common sense? You can see men eating urine snow cones by going to your neighborhood video store and renting *Jackass the Movie*, so what's wrong with videos of a sterile body fluid being streamed over the Internet to a porn consumer? I grudgingly stopped doing pee shows to avoid being kicked off the camsite, but the rationale of the no-piss rule eluded me.

Even more befuddling than the camsite's no-piss rule was the no-menstruation rule. What could possibly be wrong with me masturbating my own pussy at the wettest time of the month? Doing period shows seemed a lot more natural, less offensive, and safer than women doing the ever-popular (and camsite-acceptable) extreme penetration shows, fucking themselves with baseball bats, footballs, and beer cans.

Over a year later I opened my own Internet porn site selling monthly memberships to people who wanted to see my spycams, photos, and videos. Owning my own site meant I was out from under the thumb of the big corporate camsites and could set my own rules. I did pee shows and integrated my period into shows like "Bloody Body Painting" and photo sets like "Blood in the Studio."

I enjoyed showing off my period not because I got any customer requests to see it, but because menstruation is so conspicuously absent from porn. I was determined that my porn site be honest about me, my sexuality, and my body—how could my site be genuine and real if I ignored and hid the fluid coursing through my cunt once a month? I didn't want my site to portray only the typical skewed porno version of women's bodies and sexuality; I can think of no greater misrepresentation of premenopausal women's bodies than having 100 percent of porn pretend that 15-25 percent of our vaginas' monthly experience just doesn't exist.

While none of my members requested to see me on the rag, they didn't complain when I shared my period with them. Some of them chose not to look at it because they couldn't handle blood, some of them said it didn't exactly turn them on but it was "interesting," and some of them just thought it was no big deal. I was happy my fans were tolerant and supportive, but I was still mystified by men's disproportionate interest in pee versus menstruation. It surprised me that guys were so much more interested in a fluid that comes out of our pee holes than one that comes exclusively out of women's pussies.

As it turns out, pee is more easily eroticized by men than menstrual fluid because pissing is something they can relate to and urine more closely resembles semen. The only association most men have with blood is pain. Even scat is far more popular and sought after among porn consumers than menstruation. In the world of Internet porn, chances are you'll run across more enema enthusiasts than menstruation enthusiasts. You will find more guys on the web talking about how they want to give a chick's dirty asshole a tongue bath than you will guys who want to eat bloody pussy. Of course, none of this makes rational sense since menstruation is literally the "sexiest" of these three bodily functions (peeing, pooping, and menstruating), since it's part of the reproductive process and menstrual fluid exits the body through the vagina.

After a while, I found a menstruation fetish site run by Tuna, a man who commissioned period porn from amateurs like me. I was really excited to discover an eager (if small) market for the bloody photos and videos I wanted to make. The webmaster sent me a link to his page for models, describing the types of poses he wanted with sample pictures to illustrate what he was looking for. My excitement waned and transformed into disgust when I saw the emphasis was less on menstruating women and more on waste products: bloody maxi pads, anonymous twats with tampon strings, garbage cans with bloody tampons and panty liners, and a rear end view of a woman with her panties pulled down to reveal a dripping tampon that had overflowed onto a pad.

My naïve fantasy of presenting menstruation as a natural, healthy, and inoffensive occurrence worthy of integrating into sex and porn was overshadowed by images of things that belong in a landfill. I wanted to make period porn so people could start thinking of period sex as good, clean fun, not reinforce old perceptions of menstruation as something dirty and stinky. I wanted to display my period as a fresh, free-flowing, messy puddle of fun, not just something to be stifled and absorbed by a piece of garbage.

In spite of my distaste, I tackled my commissioned photo set with as much enthusiasm and creativity as I could, reminding myself that the webmaster was polite, generous with advertising, and couldn't be resented for fetishizing the one component of menstruation that's visible in our society: "feminine hygiene" products. A boy's first exposure to menstruation isn't wet, red pussy; it's advertisements for tampons, it's the package of Kotex his mom keeps under the sink, its his sister's used maxi beckoning mysteriously from the bathroom wastebasket. As with most die-hard true "fetish-ists," a single thing or one small piece of the whole captures the attention of someone in immaturity and sticks with him as he grows and focuses on the thing, amplifies the thing, and sexualizes the thing. It could be white panties or high heels or armpits or rubber swim caps . . . or pads and tam-pons. Because a lot of women don't want to have sex while they're on the rag, observing her bulging panties or dangling strings, or inspecting used pads and tampons (and tampon applicators) are the closest their male partners ever get to experiencing the intimate details of menstruation.

Even if I didn't like the focus on "sanitary" napkins and tampons, I grew to enjoy catering to menstruation fetishists anyway. It didn't adhere to my ideal vision of period porn, but it did appeal to my nonconformist desire to make provocative porn, even if the main reaction I provoked was disgust. I've always enjoyed grossing people out and if that meant I could make money in an underserved niche by dripping blood into my mouth from my oversaturated tampons, it was fine with me. I liked confronting people with my body fluids and knew that even if my members didn't exactly like it, they would remember me for it. There was plenty of other noncontrover-sial content on my website to entertain them, so I felt that including the unique red content could only help establish my brand and set me apart from other solo girl paysites. Unfortunately, it could also ruin my business.

Rather than get our own merchant accounts and infra-structure for processing payments online, most independent porn webmasters in the United States process credit card pay-ments through a third party, CCBill. CCBill is now the most popular and trusted third-party processor as others turned out to be unreliable and/or folded under new Visa regula-tions and restrictions deeming porn merchants "high-risk" accounts and requiring substantial registration fees. Not long after I started making period porn, CCBill suspended service on Tuna's account for violating their acceptable use policy.

CCBill also stopped processing payments for the woman-owned-and-operated site OnMyPeriod.com. When site owner

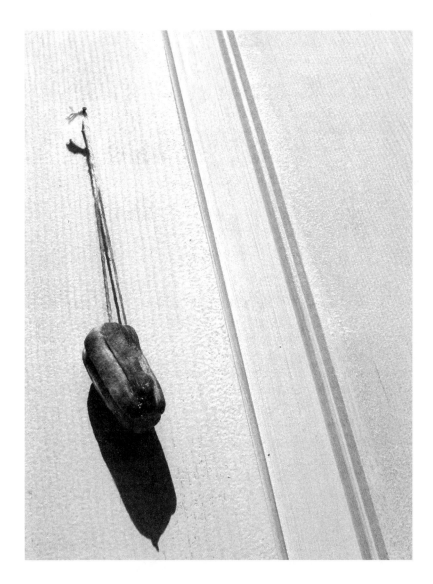

Photo by author.

May Ling Su couldn't find anything addressing menstruation in CCBill's posted acceptable use policy (besides restrictions on "extreme violence, incest, snuff, scat, mutilation, or rape"), she called to ask them where menstruation is mentioned in their AUP. May Ling Su says:

> *Talking on the phone with the people at CCBill, they explained to me that it falls under the bodily fluids and excretions clause. I asked them if they still provide services to sites containing male ejaculation.*
>
> *"Yes," he answered, "but that's different."*
>
> *"How is it different?" I asked. "Sounds to me like sexual discrimination."*
>
> *"I don't want to have a semantics argument with you," one of them started.*
>
> *"No, you don't," I answered. "You won't win."*

Even if they would entertain our arguments and we could prove that their policy equating menstruation with feces is primitive and discriminatory (their "Bodily Excretions" clause in its entirety forbids "any and all depictions and/or actual occurrences and/or references involving the content of, advertising, or marketing of scat/fecal matter, and/or a woman's period or menstruation,") and even if they agreed that menstruation is a more normal function to integrate into sex play than, say, a gang of twenty guys ejaculating on a teenager's face or a woman being double- or triple-penetrated anally (bukkake, dp, and tp are all "acceptable" in the porn world), CCBill is only bowing to the higher power of Visa, who couldn't care less if they lose revenue from porn transactions; in spite of unsubstantiated reports about pornography being a multi-billion dollar industry, Visa could certainly live without Internet porn's drop-in-the-bucket sales and the high charge-back rates endemic in our industry.

With no reliable alternatives for processing payments, May Ling Su made her site free, Tuna turned to a European processor, and I held my breath hoping no one would rat me out to CCBill by telling them I had menstruation content tucked in between my softcore photosets and striptease videos. Eventually I moved all of my red content to its own site, BloodyTrixie.com, to avoid having my white-bread-and-butter site's income compromised with CCBill (although I am still technically breaking their rules simply by providing a link to my red site).

I don't think any of us really blame CCBill for covering their asses with Visa, and I doubt that they relish shutting people down. It may sound counterproductive, but I actually appreciate CCBill's conservativism; we all want to have a reliable payment processor that follows the rules, prevents fraudulent transactions, and pays us on time, and we know the rules didn't start with CCBill or even with Visa. In fact, no one really knows what the rules are because obscenity laws are extremely vague and entirely subjective, varying from one community's set of standards to another's. As attorney Anthony Comparetto says, "the problem with obscenity is that it is the only crime in which you don't know when you have committed it. Think about that. You are driving down the road doing thirty-five miles an hour, and a police officer pulls you over to give you a speeding ticket. You tell him you were not speeding, and that there are no speed limit signs. He agrees that there are no speed limit signs, as it is up to the officer to determine if you are speeding . . . in his opinion. And you get the ticket."

The general public might assume laws against obscenity are just holdovers from bygone days, left on the books but never enforced, like laws against playing dominoes on Sunday or getting fish drunk. On the contrary, check out some of the steps made during George W. Bush's administration to combat obscenity:

1. Under the guise of protecting children, in 2003 Congress enacted the PROTECT Act with an amendment authored by Republican congressman, Tom Feeney, restricting judges from imposing sentences lighter than suggested minimums even in cases involving obscenity that does not involve children.

2. Record-keeping regulations (18 U.S.C. § 2257) requiring porn producers to keep model IDs on file proving they were eighteen or over at the time of the shoot were revised to include a level of detailed documentation and disclosure that jeopardizes the privacy and safety of porn actors and models and is nearly impossible to maintain without error.

3. Continuing the Ashcroft-declared war on pornography, in May the Department of Justice announced the establishment of an Obscenity Prosecution Task Force (in addition to the already-existing Child Exploitation and Obscenity Section).

With these kinds of steps being taken, we can expect the Department of Justice (DOJ) to file even more obscenity-related charges in communities specifically chosen for their conservative standards, increasing the likelihood of conviction. So what are community standards regarding sex acts involving menstruation? Judging from comments in online communities, both men and women are shocked by the censor-free area of BloodyTrixie.com, calling it "gross," "disgusting," and "disturbing." Even jaded adult webmasters accustomed to the most degrading hardcore porn imaginable respond to tame videos of intercourse with a menstruating woman by remarking, "Damn, that is some sick shit. People who enjoy that fetish are really messed up," and "I've seen a lot in this biz but that's some really nasty shit. Why not just wait till it runs its course or get a blow job? Takes unsafe sex to another level and generally it's not pleasant pussy."

On the other hand, plenty of people pipe up during forum discussions about period porn to say that they enjoy red sex and point out that the disgusted parties must not have a lot of experience with women if they're "afraid to get a little blood on their swords." On the legal front, the beginning of 2005 saw the US Supreme Court killing the PROTECT Act, and a District Court judge dismiss the charges as unconstitutional in this presidential administration's first high-profile obscenity case, filed against Extreme Associates. Of course, the DOJ appealed the judge's ruling, which stated that people's constitutional right to possess obscene materials is infringed on by the government's ban on the sale and distribution of obscenity (making it impossible to possess obscenity unless you create it yourself).

The core values forming the foundation of the US government's war on obscenity are the same as its core values opposing sex workers' rights across the board: they concede that sex itself is OK, but insist that it's not okay to actually sell sex. The government's anti-porn warriors continually defend the persecution of pornographers by claiming to support First Amendment rights and privacy rights, essentially saying that we have the right to create and view obscenity . . . we just don't have the right to distribute it or make any money off of it. We women (just barely) have the right to do what we want with our bodies, as long as we don't make money on it. In fact, the sentences for obscenity increase based on how much money you've profited through your "crime;" instead of being congratulated and sheltered from prosecution for your capitalistic ways as a good war profiteer, timber tycoon, or pharmaceutical company would be, the severity of your punishment increases proportionate to the amount of revenue you generate through sex.

We're encouraged to pay plastic surgeons to "beautify" our labia and stuff our cheeks, tits, and asses with implants, but we're breaking the law if we charge men money to fuck our cosmetically modified cunts. We're encouraged to pay tens of thousands of dollars to fertility therapists and remain on bed rest for months so we can distend our wombs with litters of artificially conceived babies, but if we sell pictures of ourselves with our girlfriend's hand in our twats we could be fined and go to prison for distributing the obscenity of fisting. We're encouraged to buy feminine hygiene products from "respectable" corporations like Procter & Gamble, Johnson & Johnson, and Kimberly-Clarke, generating over fourteen billion pads, tampons, and applicators for North American landfills per year, but God forbid we charge anyone money to watch videos of us actually using one of these products.

We're encouraged to buy hundreds (if not thousands) of dollars worth of pills individually to cope with menstrual cramps under a system that makes health care unaffordable for the average indie webwhore, but if we earn money by selling explicit videos demonstrating cramp reduction by masturbating ourselves to a juicy red orgasm we could find ourselves behind bars.

Menstruation may be the last taboo, but being a whore is the first . . . and we still haven't conquered that one. Before we can expect people to accept eroticized menstruation (or golden showers, or fisting, or a host of other "extreme" consensual sex-play elements) we must demand the basic right to sell sex in general. The current administration and its anti-obscenity posses are on the lookout for people like me, the kinds of people who turn public sentiment against the sex industry by our kinky ventures out of the mainstream, creating easy targets for precedent-setting court cases they can use later to further limit sex workers offering more vanilla fare. Is it worth it to make a big, red target of myself, and the industry in general, just to assert that I should be able to do whatever I want with my menstruating pussy AND make money while I do it?

Maybe I'm doing more harm than good, anyway; while failing to ever depict women menstruating in porn is a gross misrepresentation of our bodies, porn that caters to many red fetishists (e.g. "tampon munching teens") is also misrepresentative of the average menstruating woman's experiences—do I really want to pave the way for more male pornographers to jump on the red wagon and populate the web with their own ignorant, exploitative versions of menstruation?

Who am I kidding? The Internet is going to be littered with degrading, twisted, and moronic porn whether I'm present on it or not. The religious right is going to condemn us and sic their Rethuglicans on us whether I stay put or pussy out. The conservative element in government doesn't distinguish between sex workers except from a strategic standpoint in their efforts to eradicate all of us. Sex work has to be validated and legalized across the board; our rights won't be won by segregating our ranks between least offensive and most offensive, so I'm just going to keep on offending in whatever ways sound like fun.

TRIXIE FONTAINE lives in Washington State creating homemade auto-biographical porn with her partner, making Trixie a photographer, camgirl, model, webmaster, blogger, and overworked webwhore. She's addicted to computer solitaire. In theory, she could write lots of stories and fight the good fight(s) with the hours she wastes moving virtual cards around on monitors, but she's mentally exhausted simply writing this seventy-five-word biography. Now? She's deciding whether to play Solitaire Blitz or Dream Vacation Solitaire.

DIARY OF A PEEP SHOW GIRL

Sheila McClear, writing as Chelsea O'Neill

ISSUE 3.2 (2007)

The reason I started working at the peep show is because I couldn't go back to the strip club. The reason I couldn't go back to the strip club was because I had started dating one of its patrons. My ex-boyfriend, a forty-two-year-old Wall Street banker who had just broken up with me, was a regular there. Clearly, one of us had to go. Since he had more money, it ended up being me.

This place was not to be confused with an upscale strip club. No, this was the sort of establishment where dancers were actually not allowed to wear stiletto heels because of their ability to be taken off and used as weapons.

I tried to find work at other clubs, but it was hard. Unlike Frank's, Manhattan's other strip clubs had something called standards. Things like tans, manicures, and a wig that looked real were required. It is possible that many of these requirements might have been waived had I been in the possession of large breasts. Truly, while it would have been an achievable goal with a little work, I didn't have the drive to become a successful Manhattan stripper.

Luckily I found the peep show. Peep show girls are the slackers of the stripping world, the weird, countryish cousins to the exotic dancer. There are three live-girl peep shows left in Manhattan, all owned by the same company. I work at two of them. They probably employ, as independent contractors, about one hundred to 150 girls, who often depend on the peep show for the majority of their income.

One should never underestimate the pull of a live, nude girl on Eighth Avenue's foot traffic, a motley crew of Wall Streeters on their way home, street preachers, wannabe hustlers, small-time pimps, neon-overdosed tourists and college kids, runaways, the Port Authority crowd, and traveling Southern salesmen. They're lonely or half-drunk, they're high on acid or religion, and they're all coming into my store. The world of vice is truly democratic.

JULY 11

My first customer, somehow, ended up being my boss from the strip club I had just quit. Frank is a real character, bearing a disconcerting resemblance to George Costanza, wheeling around town in the same used-car-salesman outfit. It somehow made perfect sense when I saw him huffing his way up the stairs. "Frank?" I said. "What are you doing here?"

"Oh, hey, Chelsea," he said. "Nothin' much, nothin' much, just buyin' a dildo. What are you doing? You know, you're lucky. This place is real clean."

"Would you like a live fantasy show?" I asked. I gave my first show to Frank. It was incredibly awkward. It was the only money I made that night.

After the show was over, as he exited his side of the booth, sweating profusely, he paused. "You know, Chelsea," he said. "If you're going to be doing these kind of shows, you might want to think about getting rid of the rest of your hair . . ." I motioned to security and two guys loomed in. "Hey man, no talking to the ladies," they said. Frank put his hands up in the air, as if he was under arrest. "Alright, alright!" he says. "I just paid for a show! I'm leaving!" I watch with satisfaction as he is escorted down the stairs and onto the street.

JULY 18

I worked the graveyard shift tonight. "He seemed a little weird," Star says, watching a customer leave after a show.

"You never know when one of these niggas gonna turn out crazy and be waitin' for you after your shift with a baseball bat. That's why when I come to work, I come protected."

"Oh, fuck Mace," she continues. "I make my own Mace. I got my own special potion. You wanna fuck with me? Nigga gonna be blind when I'm done with him." Rumor has it that her "Mace" contains bleach, cayenne pepper, and Drano. She's right to be paranoid: yesterday I worked with a girl who had been followed home by a disgruntled customer several years ago. He sliced her across the face, leaving a long, jagged scar.

AUGUST 1

A very straight, business-looking guy kept hanging around tonight. He loitered near me for a while. "I love your outfit," he finally whispered. "Do you think if I took a show with you I could try it on?"

He was quite a large man, and my clothes were small. I wondered how this was going to work out. On my side of the booth I heard a muffled, sad voice. "What about the shoes? Can I try on the shoes, too?"

When he finally put ten dollars in the machine and shoved thirty through my money slot, I got to see him in his (my?) full glory. He hadn't been able to zip the skirt, and the bikini top and tank top strained across his skin, but he had done it.

"You look so pretty," I said. "If you were a woman, what color hair would you have?"

"I've always wanted to be a redhead," he said shyly, patting his head.

AUGUST 16

Today I called the manager, Chinese Danny, to cancel my shift for tonight.

"Why," he demands. "Why you no come in?"

"I can't work tonight because I started my period," I say. "WHAT?" he yells.

"I'm bleeding," I reply. "I'm bleeding from my pussy." "OK fine," he says quickly, hanging up.

AUGUST 20

Carla comes into work tonight, fresh from working a shift at the peep show down the street: "Man, those girls over there, they act like they never saw a dolla in they lives . . . Me and this other girl, we was supposed to do a pee show? Guess what? Bitch didn't pee! I mean, the guy paid for a pee show, he deserves to see one of us pee . . ."

OCTOBER 5

There was another bouquet of a dozen roses in the trash when I came into work tonight. Three young guys with crew cuts came in, drunk. They all took shows. I asked one what they were up to that night.

"Oh man, we're partying," one said. "We're all getting shipped off to Iraq next week."

I didn't ask any more questions after that.

NOVEMBER 2

This morning, the day shift girls found a homeless man in our dressing room, taking a shower. Understandably, they were startled and scared.

When a naked, unknown man came out of the shower as Carla was changing, she screamed at the top of her lungs.

"Come on, baby!" he said. "It's just me!"

"Who the fuck are you?" she asked. "You could be a rapist or a mugger!"

"I wouldn't want to rape you, anyway," he replied.

NOVEMBER 6

Two different customers asked me today what my "future plan" is. They seemed as concerned about my career path as I was; perhaps more so.

DECEMBER 8

Today they decorated the porn store for Christmas. Lights and tinsel are everywhere—all over the racks of she-male and her-maphrodite porn, on the staircase leading to the third floor, which is the gay cruising area—a glory-hole setup called the

"Male Box,"—and a big paper Santa is on our dressing room door. Someone has taped two round ornaments to his hand, so now it looks like Santa is holding his balls. The guys also taped candy-cane ornaments to the top of each of our booths. I'm not sure whether to be touched or deeply disturbed.

DECEMBER 11
Tonight I heard the following exchange outside my booth while giving a show:

"Are you serious, they have animal porn here?"

"They got animal porn, yo!"

DECEMBER 22
I do some Christmas shopping at the porn store before going back to Michigan for the holidays. I get 20 percent off all videos, merchandise, and sex toys. I was momentarily excited by this opportunity; however, after six months at the peep show, I've found I don't really want to have sex anymore.

JANUARY 5
The store is totally empty tonight and I'm working alone at 3 a.m. "Your Cheatin' Heart" is playing on the radio, and I can hear a dog barking, faintly. The barking noise is coming from one of the video booths, which means a customer is watching animal porn again. I put my head in my hands. No one is redeemable, I think. Everybody is beyond hope.

When I finally do quit the peep show, though, it'll be strange: here, in some ways, here was my perfect job, a place where I could walk into work two hours late carrying an open can of beer. Sometimes I think I'll miss it. Or not.

JANUARY 6
It's the weekend, and every hustler in New York is out and at the top of their game tonight. On the train, no sooner have the doors closed when a man shouts "SHOWTIME! FOLKS, HE'S ONLY EIGHT YEARS OLD!" The man hits "Play" on a beat-up boom box, and a small black boy steps into the mid-

dle of the train car, jerking and shuffling his way through a hip-hop song.

At work, a random man leads a toothless, drunk white guy into the peep show, points at us, whispers, and then collects money from the guy. This is a fairly common hustle in Times Square—men not associated with our store find a white tourist, or just somebody who's completely drunk—and promise them that they will find them some girls. Often this hustle is on the small scale, five or ten dollars just to lead them to the peep show, where they can then buy a show with one of us. Sometimes, however, like tonight—they trick the man into believing that we are prostitutes, and he is our pimp.

The hustler leaves, money in hand, and now the white guy is lurching over me, explaining that he has already paid the guy a hundred dollars for a "BJ" with me, and that he isn't going to leave until he gets one. I call security. They take care of him, and then Ron goes to the back to grab a mop, on his way to clean cum out of one of the video booths.

"You know," he says, wringing out a filthy mop, "there's gotta be a better way to make a living."

SHEILA McCLEAR (aka Chelsea O'Neill) is the author of *The Last of the Live Nude Girls*. She is a reporter at the *New York Daily News.*

LABOR

INTRODUCTION

Radical Vixen

Our lives shall not be sweated
from birth until life closes,
hearts starve as well as bodies,
give us bread, but give us roses.
—James Oppenheim, "Bread & Roses"

"What do you do for work?" Sex workers are often asked this question by our clients—after a phone sex session or a lap dance in a strip club—as if our jobs don't count as work. "Sex work is real work" has long been a slogan of the sex workers' rights movement. We may not have stereotypical work experiences—punching into a time clock, sitting for hours in a cubicle, putting in notice for vacation days—but we still want to be able to work safely and be treated fairly and with respect. Unfortunately, as long as sex work is not considered real work, the idea of labor rights for sex workers is seen as laughable.

Sex workers the world over have organized for labor rights. In 1942, brothel workers and madams in Honolulu went on strike for the rights to raise their prices and to travel freely throughout the city. After twenty-two days, they won the right to travel freely. In 1997, strippers at the Lusty Lady peep show in San Francisco unionized and eventually turned the club into a worker-owned co-op. The Durbar Mahila Samanwaya Committee in West Bengal, India is a sex workers collective with over 65,000 members, working to fight stigma and social exclusion of sex workers. But sex workers face unique challenges in organizing for our labor rights.

While all sex workers are denied rights and respect on some level, white, cisgender sex workers who work indoors typically have more opportunities to work in decent conditions and face less abuse from police and clients than those who are more marginalized. In "Black Tale," Mireille Miller-Young compares the working conditions of African American women in the American porn industry with those of their white counterparts. As Rachel Aimee illustrates in "The Sex Workplace: No Day Without an Immigrant," undocumented immigrants in the United States are doubly vulnerable to exploitation by pimps and unscrupulous managers because of their lack of legal recourse, compounded by the fear of deportation. Similarly, in "The City's Red Lights," Svati P. Shah reports on the vulnerability of female migrant workers in Mumbai, who sometimes resort to prostitution if they can't get construction work at the day-wage labor markets. And in "Positions: Can We Justify Working for Pimps?" two street-based sex workers, Anonymous and Eve Ryder, debate the pros and cons of working independently versus having a boss.

People who work in legal industries can count on social security and maybe even a pension upon retirement, but many prostitutes can't afford to retire from the industry—ever. In "Respite from the Streets," Marisa Brigati interviews Carmen Muñoz, founder of the Casa Xochiquetzal, a home in Mexico City for women over the age of sixty who are street workers. Against all odds, Muñoz, herself a sex worker, raised the funds, remodeled the building, and jumped through the bureaucratic hoops necessary to open this unique space for the city's elderly prostitutes.

Muñoz's achievements should serve as inspiration to anyone who thinks that the challenges facing sex workers are too big to overcome. As she puts it, "We need to get over this submissive attitude where we don't say anything, where we bow our heads before those who exploit us. They are not strong. We are the ones who make them strong. We need to stop helping them and start fighting for our own rights and the rights of our friends."

RADICAL VIXEN is a hippie, activist, and blogger. In addition to her own blog she wrote for $pread and Sugasm. An avid knitter, she dreams of one day raising llamas to spin their fleece into yarn. When not traveling, she and her husband live in the Southwest surfing the web off solar power. She blogs about peace, porn, and politics at RadicalVixen.com

POSITIONS: CAN WE JUSTIFY WORKING FOR PIMPS?

Anonymous and Eve Ryder

ISSUE 1.3 (2005)

There are females in the sex industry who work for pimps. I call it the underground sex industry. I feel that if a female is going to work, she should work for herself. It is also sad that a lot of women think that pimps don't exist. That is bullshit. Please, women of this industry, don't work for anyone but yourselves.

Pimps make all these promises that sound good and sweet, but they are lies. A pimp's job is to brainwash whores and to rob females of all their earnings. It's not a game when a whore does not come home to her pimp—mac, don, or whatever they want to call themselves—with a certain amount of money a night. If a whore has a bad date or gets robbed or raped, the pimp does not care. He will make her go out to make more money.

Keep in mind that a pimp is not your friend. A pimp does not care if you catch a disease or already have one. A pimp does not care if a whore uses a condom or not. Just because a female is a prostitute does not mean that she should die or risk death to make these pimps money. Our health is more sacred than all the money in the world. So please, all underground industry workers who are under pimp rule, don't let these men control your mind, body, soul, and peace of mind. No one should let a person have complete control of their being, including anything that you work for.

It's a shame how many whores want to get away or leave a pimp, but are frightened to do so because of the threats they get from these beasts. Just keep in mind, love yourself, work for yourself. There is a way out of this underground life. I'm living proof.

—Anonymous

No one would argue that anyone should work for a bad boss in any industry. And if working for a pimp means accepting beatings, rape, imprisonment, drug use, and then paying the perpetrator of these crimes for the privilege, that's obviously unacceptable. But "pimping" just means soliciting clients for prostitutes for a fee or managing a prostitution business. And although a fair number of whores choose to operate independently or cooperatively, many more work by choice or default for an escort agency, a traditional street pimp, a brothel madam, or another whore.

For many, working independently isn't desirable because of the extra time required, business skills needed, safety concerns, and isolation.

Working as an indy escort, I don't know how many times I have called my voicemail to feign calling my "pimp" to make a new client think I have protection that I most assuredly lack. I also wistfully remember the steady, reliable money I once made working for a "gang" who gave me access to the high-rolling casino crowd. When I first moved to New York, I got wet in the scene by working for another Indy escort. I took the calls she didn't have time for and paid her a referral fee. My bosses found it in their interest to procure my good temper and sincere smiling face, protect my health and safety, and ensure my job satisfaction.

So why did I go independent? I wanted to make more money. One day I realized that I felt confident about my ability to run my own business. I had mastered online advertising. I knew how to properly screen a client and sniff out LE.

Safety was something I worried about, but I had developed a list of regulars that wanted to see me and could rely less on new clients.

It is troubling to me that taking money from a whore is so vilified because it threatens our ability to have normal lives and relationships. The adult children, senior dependents, and partners of prostitutes face social and legal consequences for just being in our lives. A whore can't bring home her earnings like any other worker and feel proud of contributing to her family. Whores should be able to choose how we want to work without judgment.

Ideally, I want prostitution to be treated like any other business. "Whores" become workers. "Pimps" become bosses. And anyone who takes our money while beating us or raping us goes to jail. Not because of their relationship to the fact that we make our living having sex for money, but because they are hurting us and that's wrong.

—*Eve Ryder*

ANONYMOUS is a self-employed sex worker in New York City.

EVE RYDER is a former streetwalker and call girl who lives in New York City.

THE SEX WORKPLACE: NO DAY WITHOUT AN IMMIGRANT

Rachel Aimee

ISSUE 3.3 (2007)

In a surprising move that would further widen the gap between documented and undocumented immigrants in New York State, Brooklyn assemblyman Félix Ortiz recently proposed a bill that would require exotic dancers to obtain permits in order to work. Surprising, because the assemblyman is otherwise well known for his advocacy on behalf of immigrants. Apparently intended to fight human trafficking, sex workers believe that if this bill becomes law it will do little more than push undocumented immigrant strippers underground or into other kinds of sex work. "I'm going to get out of New York before that happens, obviously," says Vanessa, an exotic dancer from Spain who came to the United States five years ago on a now-expired training visa. Others think the change would create underground clubs and second-tier employment. Katana, originally from Montserrat, says she would "find a way to keep working under the table." Not one of the dancers I have talked to believes the change would encourage strippers to leave the industry. Vanessa says she expects dancers would go along with licensing simply because they are not in a position to do much about it. "The dancers that got families over here, they're not going to be moving, they're going to accept it, that's all. Just as they accepted the house fee[1], they're going to accept this bill now."

1. Exotic dancers in most strip clubs across the United States are required to pay "house fees" to work. Although it's illegal to charge house fees, few dancers take legal action against club owners.

Vanessa has a point: It's difficult for sex workers, especially those who are undocumented immigrants, to organize against legislation, even when it affects them negatively. An undocumented stripper won't want to risk speaking to the media, lawmakers, or even sympathetic advocates, for fear of drawing attention to herself and her family. When I set out to write this article, I hoped to cover the lives of different kinds of sex workers across the United States, but I ended up focusing on exotic dancers in New York City because, for the most part, the only sex workers who were willing to talk to me about their personal immigration stories were those who already knew and trusted me.

When the long-anticipated immigration bill was defeated in the US Senate on June 7, immigrants across the country let out a collective sigh of disappointment and frustration. That sigh resonated particularly loudly in the sex worker community. The sex industry plays a vital and undeniable role in the lives of undocumented immigrants. If sex industry employers were a more socially conscious bunch, the door of every brothel, strip club, dungeon, and escort agency in the country would have been firmly closed on May 1 for A Day Without An Immigrant. Despite the fact that immigration is such a hot-button issue, sex work is rarely on the table for the legislative discussions, or indeed the activist ones.

Ruby Corado is a political activist and advocate for the Latino LGBT and sex worker community in Washington, DC. She works with Latin@s In Accion, a community organization that helps sex workers to gain skills so that they can obtain work outside of the sex industry. With laws getting tighter, she expects to see more undocumented immigrants entering the sex industry. "Right now, sex work is the big industry that a lot of Latinos are going into." Considering the low-paying job options available to the undocumented, it's easy to understand why.

Immigrants come to the United States seeking a better standard of living for themselves and their families; adult entertainment is one of the few industries that offers the opportunity to make a decent living to people without any education or working documents. Even American citizens with college degrees often choose sex work because it is more lucrative than other jobs, so for undocumented immigrants whose other options are largely underpaid and often involve hard physical work and long hours, the potential to earn more in the sex industry, working far fewer hours, is significant. This is particularly true for women, since most traditional women's jobs available to immigrants pay even less than those available to men, whereas in the sex industry, women usually make more than their male counterparts. "If you can make $6,000 a month doing sex work or $500 cleaning houses, which one are you going to choose?" asks Ruby.

Twenty-six-year-old Katana came to the United States from Montserrat with her two-year-old son in 2002. At first she was working twelve-hour-days, including weekends, as a cashier to cover her basic living costs in New York City—while also sending money back home to support her family. In 2004, Katana began working as an exotic dancer. Since then she has been able to cut down dramatically on her hours. "Dancing brings in faster money, a little bit easier money, and you don't have to work those long hours," she says. "There's a lot of people that are illegal and they're trying to survive and support their family and they can't go in a regular place like a cashier job without having [legal working documents], so this kind of business helps people to survive."

While many immigrants find sex work preferable, being a sex worker and an undocumented immigrant in a culture in which both are looked down on can put one in an extremely vulnerable position. Anyone who does illegal sex work in the United States risks being arrested and serving jail time. Undocumented sex workers also face deportation and are at a greater risk for exploitation. Antoine, a twenty-nine-year-old undocumented escort from France, is well educated and gave up a good job to travel and explore a new continent, choosing to do sex work to support his adventures across the United States and Canada. Unlike most workers, if deported he could probably return to a decent standard of living in his home country, but it's still something he worries about.

"It is funny how paranoid I can get sometimes about immigration stuff, doing an illegal job in a country where you can't even work [legally]," he says. "When I see a new client, it is all about, 'Am I going to be caught by the police? Is this a trap?' To make my ad more attractive, I emphasize the fact that I am French—some clients get really excited about it—[but] I know that whoever [sees that] could find out that I am some kind of illegal worker."

Ruby Corado sees many less privileged Latina sex workers being exploited by men looking to take advantage of their ability to make what is often perceived by non-sex workers as "easy money." "There is a certain type of man who particularly targets illegal immigrants because [he] knows they are vulnerable so [he] can threaten them, [and say he will] call the police. Even if you have a green card it can be taken away [if you are convicted of a crime] and these men know that."

When sex workers are being exploited they face the additional burden of having nowhere to go for help, sometimes even within their own communities. Immigrants who come from cultures with a more conservative view of sex work, such as many Latino cultures, may be labeled as sinful and dirty and lose status within their own communities: "The stigma is so much that they can't leave to do some other job. They cannot be accepted anywhere else, so they get stuck," says Ruby.

While sex worker and immigrant activists have long been working with local police departments across the country to improve legal protection for those who are being exploited, lack of consciousness, anti-immigrant sentiments, bad laws, and police corruption mean that sex workers and undocumented immigrants still have a lot to fear from dealing with the police. Most sex workers don't report crimes at all.

Exploitation, when reported, can sometimes be used to get legal status, often on the grounds of political asylum or even, in some extreme cases, as a victim of human trafficking. Ruby Corado gives the example of a woman from Mexico who had been working as a prostitute by choice for many years but now wanted to leave the industry. A group of men she was working for tried to prevent her from quitting. "She was able to prove that she wanted to leave but they were trying to stop her."

The fact that the line between voluntary and forced sex work is not always clear-cut presents real problems for workers using these arguments to get green cards. Nonetheless, Ruby advises anyone who thinks they might be able to prove that they were forced to do sex work to speak to a lawyer and see if they have a human trafficking case. She also advises those who have been victims of persecution in their countries of origin to seek legal counsel to find out if they have a political asylum case; however, most undocumented workers do not fall into either the trafficking category or the political asylum category and must find another way to apply for a green card.

Harsh anti-prostitution policies can make the naturalization process even tougher for sex workers than it is for others. An applicant will be asked whether she has worked as a prostitute in the last five years and if she says yes, she's automatically rejected on the basis that she lacks "good moral character." Of course, most sex workers know better than to reveal something like that on legal paperwork, but a sex worker's reluctance or inability to reveal anything about her occupation can be a significant handicap when it comes to applying. While many undocumented workers in other industries can ask their employers for help to prove that they've been in the country for a certain length of time, sex workers may not have that option. Similarly, while regularly filing taxes is one of the best ways to prove you've been living in the country and obeying the law on a green card application, sex workers are especially wary of reporting their income to the IRS because of the nature of their jobs, so many opt not to file taxes. However, failure to file taxes is a felony-level crime that can not only result in deportation but also make it more difficult to get documented status.

Vanessa takes precautions to conceal her profession. "I always try to avoid even giving [my social security number] to strip clubs, because one day I might fix my situation and [the government] would know that I'd been stripping over here and that just doesn't look good. I don't see why I should be in the category of the stripper, which is then thought to be a prostitute, and I'd rather really that they wouldn't know about what I do."

However, for those who are "stuck" working here, supporting families back home but unable to travel back and forth to visit for fear of not being able to get back into the country, getting legal documentation can be a priority, no matter what it takes. With the immigration bill dead in the water and no comparative new legislation in sight, undocumented immigrants don't have many easy options. It is virtually impossible to obtain a green card through employment unless you can provide a compelling reason why a US citizen couldn't do your job. For many, finding a US citizen to marry can seem like the easiest path.

Two years ago, Katana married a friend who offered to help her get a green card in exchange for $6,000. "I had to find somebody to help me out, even if it means paying him a little something. At first he was saying he would do it for free, but I offered to give him something on my part." When she gets her green card, Katana intends to go to nursing school and save enough money to buy a piece of land back in Montserrat. "I want to stay [in the United States] but I also want to come and go. I want to have a house there, you know, so that when I go there I've always got a place to stay instead of staying with people." She also intends to have her son—who is now seven years old—join her in the United States when he is older.

Ruby cautions, however, that marrying for a green card doesn't always bring a happy ending. "Some might find a client who is willing to help them, but it's not like *Pretty*

Woman!" Of course, many "real" marriages end badly, but an undocumented sex worker who is dependent on a spouse is more likely to end up in situations where she is being exploited or extorted by a man who understands the power he holds over her.

Thirty-eight-year-old Patricia moved to the United States sixteen years ago from Hungary and has been working as an exotic dancer for thirteen years. For a long time she tried to find someone to marry for a green card but eventually decided it was the wrong path for her. "I was attracting the wrong kind of men because I was always thinking about [getting a] green card, never about love. I was attracting men with anger problems and no money, men who wanted to use me." Like many strippers and other kinds of sex workers, Patricia feels that working in the sex industry makes it more difficult to find decent romantic partners. "You have to lie about your job. If you tell the truth they don't trust you. You have to be very lucky."

Patricia was hoping the immigration bill would give her the opportunity to apply for legal residency, but since it was defeated she has decided to leave the country and return to Hungary. "I want to move on, get a regular job. I'm sick of this job, year after year, the same thing—no money, no future, you cannot visit your family, they cannot visit you. In the end you either have to pay somebody a lot of money for a green card or you have to wait for your luck to come, but it may never come."

While it seems irrefutable that undocumented immigrants are here to stay, policymakers have refused this reality. On August 10, the US Department of Homeland Security announced they would begin enforcing a rule that employers are required to fire any employee without a valid social security number or risk a fine of up to $10,000 per worker. At print time, the move had been temporarily blocked by a federal judge as a result of a lawsuit filed by the ACLU and other labor rights organizations. If the court ultimately allows the rule to be enforced, virtually every other immigrant organization—along with many national labor and business groups—predicts chaos.

Ruby Corado believes that the impact will totally disrupt normal labor patterns. "We talk about having twelve to twenty million people illegally, so now ten million of those people are going to be out of a job. There will be no one in the McDonald's—get your own burgers, honey! No one in Safeways, in the grocery stores. They don't think about that, but it's going to happen. Employers are not going to want a fine so they are going to let them go." She believes that many of the immigrants who lose their jobs will go into the sex industry, further crowding the supply side of an industry that is already becoming saturated. "Five or ten years ago you could make a lot of money in sex work, maybe $1,000 a week. Now you're lucky if you can make $1,000 in a whole month."

While falling prices in the sex industry can be attributed to several factors, from the loss of disposable income of clients affected by the dot com crash to the rise of Internet porn, the sheer number of people going into the industry in recent years has undoubtedly played a role. Just as in the "straight" world there are those who complain that immigrants are "taking our jobs," anyone who has worked in the sex industry knows there is plenty of immigrant-bashing going on in our own community. The derogatory remark that a strip club is "full of Russians" is understood to mean that it's full of girls who are willing to do more for less, lowering standards for "the rest of us." The current anti-immigrant climate only serves to perpetuate this kind of prejudice.

The reality is that anti-immigrant, anti-sex work legislation pushes people into more precarious, underground situations, rather than magically making them disappear. As long as there is poverty somewhere, people will come to the United States seeking work. As long as sex work pays more than other jobs, many of those people will work in the sex industry. Immigrants and advocates are hoping that after the 2008 elections a new administration will bring a change in direction and a more realistic approach to immigration. It is hard to imagine any politician ever explicitly standing up for sex workers, but a bill that prioritizes immigrant rights would, in many ways, be a bill for sex worker rights in disguise.

RACHEL AIMEE cofounded *$pread* magazine in 2004 and was an editor-in-chief for four and a half years. Now a parent and freelance copy editor, she also organizes for strippers' rights with We Are Dancers. She lives in Brooklyn with her family.

RESPITE FROM THE STREETS: A PLACE TO RETIRE FOR MEXICO CITY'S ELDERLY PROSTITUTES

Marisa Brigati
Translated by Elizabeth "Mark" Ramage

ISSUE 4.1 (2008)

Elizabeth and I have just arrived at Casa Xochiquetzal after walking through the busy streets of the Merced neighborhood in Mexico City, past stalls selling shoes, food, children's toys, electronics, lingerie, and sex worker clothes. Merced is a central district for street prostitution in Mexico City. In 2002, it was estimated that a few thousand sex workers were operating out of the neighborhood. Casa Xochiquetzal is a home established for women over the age of sixty who are street sex workers.

We sit in a tidy kitchen and a slight, white-haired woman in a knee-length skirt approaches us. She places Nescafé, sugar, and milk in front of us and politely welcomes us to the home. It's hard to imagine her selling sex in exchange for a plate of food or to avoid a night sleeping in a cardboard box.

Casa Xochiquetzal affords these elderly women something life has usually not provided: choice. The women are not permitted to bring clients to the home, but what they choose to do outside of it is not restricted. Some women take this opportunity to learn new skills or pursue education. They are hoping to make the house self-sustainable by selling crafts and wares.

The house is bright and cheerful, but plumbing and electricity are inadequate. More work is needed for these women to have safe living conditions. Our support and solidarity is crucial.

Carmen Muñoz, a sex worker and the founder of Casa Xochiquetzal, speaks with us about her experiences and explains why she was inspired to open this unique place.

MARISA: What inspired you to open Casa Xochiquetzal, and how did you do it?

CARMEN: Anyone who says they are a sex worker always has doors closed on them. [Before Casa Xochiquetzal opened] there were various shelters, but they treated sex workers badly, they humiliated them, so the women opted to return to the streets.

I met a photographer, Maya Godeth, who wanted to write a book about sex work, and I discussed the idea for the sex workers' home with her. I began writing to politicians but got no response. Then, in 2004, Maya introduced me to Jesusa Rodríguez [a prominent Mexican actress, playwright, and social activist], who promised to help us. I finally got a meeting with [politician] Andrés Manuel López Obrador and when we presented our idea and told him what the problems were, he couldn't believe that there were women older than sixty in sex work. He said he would help us, and in November of that year we were granted this house, which used to be a museum.

It was totally in ruins. There were cats, dead dogs, garbage. So we all came, the sex workers from La Merced, to clean, sweep, and mop. However, we couldn't get legal ownership of the building because we weren't an official organization, so we had to look for an institution that would do that for us. It was really hard until [feminist and anthropologist] Marta Lamas convinced [nonprofit philanthropic organization] Semillas to take responsibility of the project.

It wasn't until May of 2005, when [singer] Eugenia Leon gave a concert in the city theater to benefit the house, that we were able to start remodeling the doors and windows. The Women's Symphony of Mexico City gave another concert to benefit the house and with this money we finished the doors and windows.

We finally moved into the house in February, 2006. We were able to house fifteen women, who all slept in one giant room. And in April of 2006, the SEDUVI [Ministry of Urban Development and Housing] donated 2,000,000 pesos (about 188,000 dollars), and we were able to pay construction workers to remodel everything. In November, 2006, the house was inaugurated by Alejandro Encinas [the Mayor of Mexico City].

Now there are thirty-five women living here. But it has been a lot of work for the Instituto Por Las Mujeres, whose name it is under, and for the DIF [Department of Family Integration], who give a weekly donation of fifteen meals. It's not enough, but it helps.

MARISA: Are there more women who would like to live in the house? Is lack of space an issue?

CARMEN: There's room for more women, but we haven't been able to take in more because we lack a lot of things. For example, we sometimes run out of gas and have gone up to fifteen or twenty days without gas. The food, the medicine—we lack a lot. I would take everyone in right this second, but the point isn't just to take them in. The point is to give them a life with dignity.

I worry about this a lot because it's so cold on the street and the women have to deal with so many obstacles. There are times when they walk all day to find a client and in the evening their mouths are dry and they look exhausted. It's desperate not to have the resources to wash your mouth, no roof to sleep under. It's something that we should all care about—not just as women or as sex workers but as human beings.

A lot of people say "but we have good principles." We, too, have good principles, but we also have a lot of hunger. And that hunger was what made it necessary for us to do sex work.

MARISA: How are sex workers perceived by the rest of society?

CARMEN: To most people we are lazy, good for nothing, vicious thieves; we are the worst. For them we are like

Photo of Carmen Muñoz, courtesy of Marisa Brigati.

ugly dolls and should be hidden in the corner [this is a reference to a children's song]. But there are more of us every day, and it's because the core of the problem is never addressed. Why aren't the madrotas [female pimps] punished? Why aren't the padrotes [pimps], who extort the sex workers, punished? The fathers who sell their daughters aren't punished, the clients aren't punished, none of them are punished. Instead, we are punished.

The government should work on getting rid of child prostitution. In some towns, fathers sell their own daughters. They have seven, eight, ten children, so they send one daughter to a pimp to get a little money every month so they can give the others something to eat. This is what the government should be addressing.

The government should realize that a lot of us don't have an education because our parents couldn't pay for it, precisely because they had so many children. This is what we want people to realize and address, and to never again say that we are working because we like it, because that is false. They should do a little street work and see how things work and then they would stop saying stupid things like that.

MARISA: Are there organizations that work for sex workers' rights in Mexico?

CARMEN: There are various organizations that say, "We are working for the rights of sex workers," but please, they are the madrotas and they themselves charge a quota for what they are doing for the ladies. There is nobody that helps anybody here. Everyone who can screw you, will.

MARISA: Are sex workers involved in these organizations?

CARMEN: No. They say that they have been sex workers, but I believe they are sex workers as much as I believe that I'm a nun. A true sex worker would not take advantage of another sex worker, because it hurts in our own flesh, because we know what it's like to suffer for being in sex work. But those women, no, they are just taking advantage of the pain and need of others for their own financial benefit.

MARISA: How many sex workers are there in Mexico City, and what ages are they?

CARMEN: Look honey, I can tell you the age when they retire, but the age when they start, I would get myself in trouble. Some of them retire at seventy-five, eighty, ninety years old. Some don't even get to retire. They stay in the streets.

MARISA: How many of them live on the streets?

CARMEN: Here in La Merced there are about sixty, more or less, according to the last poll that was done, but I don't know. Every day another elderly person arrives. I heard that in Guadalajara there are many young sex workers as well as a lot of old women, women already really old who stay in sex work and who sleep in parks.

We all have the same needs but our heads are clouded. If we were smarter we would organize, like in other parts of the world. We should be fighting for our rights ourselves. Not the pimps, not the institutions, but us, the sex workers. We should be sharing knowledge and letting everyone know that they can be independent, that they shouldn't be exploited. We need to get over this submissive attitude, where we don't say anything, where we bow our heads before those who exploit us. They are not strong. We are the ones who make them strong. We need to stop helping them and start fighting for our own rights and the rights of our friends.

MARISA: They have problems of hunger and poverty. Do they have problems with violence as well?

CARMEN: Of course! There is hunger, a lot of pain, a lot of violence. Women have always been very oppressed. It starts with our fathers. We are told, "You have to obey your brother." So when some guy comes along and says, "You have to do this," we do it, because that is what they taught us.

In my case, I had to support the father of my children. Right after I had a baby, one or two hours after I gave birth, he would come and rape me like I was a beast. Or he would give me his feet and I would have to lick them, otherwise he would hit me. Horrible things, but you have to put up with them because that is what you have been taught, and when you open your eyes it's too late: you are stuck in a terrible situation, you have already been humiliated, beaten, mistreated.

They say that the law protects the women, but I have called like fifty times because my next-door neighbor is beaten almost every day, and nothing has been done about it. The other day the abuser told me, "Stop being nosy," and I asked him, "Why?" and he said, "You know why. They already told me that you are making calls." I didn't tell anybody. Who told him I was calling? The authorities, right?

Where are the people helping women? They take the sex workers away in paddy wagons, and when the women get to the police station they are raped, in the very same police cars. Meanwhile the hotels are crowded with prostitutes who are minors.

The problem that concerns me the most is that there are so many children in the streets, in the parks, waiting for their mothers to prostitute themselves to give them something to eat, to be able to pay for a hotel room, while there are so many people to whom the government gives four or five apartments. Why not to sex workers? The newspapers say, "The government is helping the sex workers, so they can give their children a dignified life." Where is that help? If you ask for money they say, "No, right now there isn't any," when you can see them handing over money to others, but for you there isn't any.

So you just have to tolerate it, keep paying for your little hotel, keep tending to your kids in the street, and one day your sons are street kids and your daughters are prostitutes just like you, because they don't see anything else. Just vice, vagrancy, prostitution.

One day I was invited to the Assembly of Representatives for a meeting to talk about a new law. They were saying, "Look, the ceiling is made of marble, it cost so much money, the desks are all made of whatever." They talk about how they spent so many millions of pesos on food in a few days and I say "Ay, my God, for me one million pesos would be marvelous! I would eat for who knows how many years, maybe until I die."

And everyone was like, "Ooh, look at the lamps, they are very expensive!" This is what was supposed to be important to us? We went to learn about the law but they said, "It is very important that you are familiar with the history." Why do I want to know the history? I am alive and I am hungry, I am cold, I have needs. So what do I care what happened before?

Maybe it's better if I just don't go to these meetings, because one day I might run out of patience.

MARISA: How can we, sex workers from the United States, help you?

CARMEN: You are sex workers from the United States?

MARISA: Yes, I am.

CARMEN: Ay, don't tell me that! Here I am talking so much! I believe that you, too, have experienced everything I am talking about in some form, right? This marginalization and all that. So we should be working together, communicating to see what we can do for each other, and traveling to see how we work in different places. You have the opportunity to travel, to see that we are independent, that we don't have to depend on a government or on pimps but on ourselves, and that we can teach ourselves to work for our rights. We should be working together because we are all really fucked! But we have to keep going forward, to take off these yokes. I think you already took yours off, right? That's awesome, I congratulate you!

ELIZABETH: But isn't there a more specific way to help? Are volunteers needed?

MARISA: Money, always.

CARMEN: Money, yes always, all the money you want. I'll send you a trailer! We also make jewelry. There is a girl from Denver who helps with the house, and sometimes she brings me money. One time she brought me one hundred dollars, and sometimes she sends money and I buy materials to make jewelry, and then she takes our merchandise to sell so we can make a few cents. In this way we help ourselves. There are also people who come and teach us things that we don't know, like the girl who taught us how to make jewelry.

I won't deny it, we have a lot of needs, but I don't think it's just us. At least we have this roof. There are many who don't even have that, so their needs are greater. So I ask that, when you see an old sex worker, help her if you can. The same with the young girls who prostitute. They need us. Together we will work toward our ideals.

MARISA BRIGATI is a sex worker and anarchist. Born and bred in New York City, she has traveled extensively and is particularly interested in the intersection of radical politics, the working class, and women.

BLACK TALE: WOMEN OF COLOR IN THE AMERICAN PORN INDUSTRY

Mireille Miller-Young

ISSUE 1.1 (2005)

"You are not supposed to talk about liking sex because you are already assumed to be a whore," Jeannie Pepper told me following her 2002 recognition ceremony for twenty years in adult entertainment, the longest career for a black actress. I had just begun to do fieldwork for my doctoral research project on women of color in hardcore when I met Jeannie Pepper, one of the first black porn stars of the 1980s. She, along with women of color like Vanessa del Rio, Angel Kelly, Linda Wong, Sahara Knite, Desiree West, and Kitten Natividad, broke down the doors of the adult industry, allowing the young minority women of today to be able to compete as porn stars. I wanted to excavate this history of women of color's participation in porn, from its beginnings in the age of early photography and film to the global multibillion dollar industry it is today, in order to understand the experiences of hardcore's most invisible workers. What Jeannie Pepper illuminated was key: the stigma of women of color as *always* whores in our society has a profound impact on how they negotiate sexuality and sex work.

For many women of color, we have been raised in families and communities that do not speak openly about sexuality. Whether because of religion or social or cultural traditions and taboos, as women of color we grow up being told that sex is wrong, keep your legs closed, and don't ask questions! Even among women, we have created enduring silences about sex as a mode of protection. Because women of color in America have been so exposed to harsh stigmas about our womanhood and disproportionate sexual violence against us, we have actively produced a culture of silence about sexuality in our own communities, as if such denials would force the dominant society to see our value and humanity. Instead of learning about sex from our mothers, aunts, and grandmothers, many of us find out from friends, lovers, or strangers. As we try to define our own sexual identities, we must always confront the images society and the media industries have manufactured about us—those rampant stereotypes of black ghetto hoes, spicy Latina mamacitas, Asian angels, hustling hookers, and crackhead pregnant inner city minority teens on welfare. Movies, magazines, music videos, and the evening news relentlessly repeat these images again and again, confirming them as truth even in our own minds. Women of color in America battle against these myths everyday. Our survival depends on a kind of guerrilla warfare challenging this ideological terrorism against our souls.

The sex industries are completely complicit. Beliefs about the sexuality of women of color as deviant and dangerous drive the disproportionately higher rates of incarceration for minority women street prostitutes. Because of poverty, discrimination, and social marginalization, black and Latina prostitutes are more likely to work on the street rather than from escort agencies, brothels, or from their homes. Exposed to the dangers of the street—including psychopathic johns, leeching pimps, and corrupt and abusive vice cops—women of color prostitutes are the victims of disproportionate levels of violence. Black women make up nearly 40 percent of arrests for prostitution. They are five times more likely than white women to live in poverty, and three times more likely to be unemployed.

For many women, the hardcore film industry offers the safest and highest status sex work. Aside from the higher pay rates, there are several advantages that sex workers find in the porn business. For instance, women can generally determine whom they want to perform with and what type of sex acts they are willing to do in an environment that is, for the most part, safe, clean, and *legal*. Although stigmatized, women in this legal terrain of sex work can attain a form of fame, visibility, and legitimacy that is generally impossible for workers in other parts of the sexual economy. Sex workers can gain notoriety in this entertainment-based industry that then helps them gain future exotic dance gigs, charge extremely high rates for private escorting, start their own members-only websites, and access modeling and promotional work for companies.

But women of color are consistently discriminated against in the pornography industry. On average they are paid half to three-quarters of what white actresses are offered. They are not offered nearly as many roles as white performers, and tend to be cornered into the so-called "ethnic market." As a result, African American, Latina, and Asian women working in the underfinanced ethnic market have fewer opportunities to "crossover" into the mainstream, white-dominated sphere of hardcore, and therefore gain less notoriety, and less pay. Few companies dealing in interracial and all-ethnic porn offer big contracts to women of color, and if they do, they are much less than the $100,000 per year that large corporations like Vivid reserve for white actresses. Historically, Vivid has only offered a handful of women of color contracts in that range. Porn companies rationalize these inequalities by arguing that women of color are not as desired by the mainstream audience (i.e. white men) as they are by urban men of color, and therefore make up a smaller market share of hardcore products. These companies spend less on ethnic video production and marketing budgets and offer smaller salaries for "ethnic talent."

In addition to discrimination in pay rates, contracts, and opportunities, women of color in hardcore also complain about experiencing prejudice at the workplace, including hostile, indifferent, or unprofessional treatment by production companies, agents, directors, the crew, and white performers. They have reported being sent home because white actors and actresses were uncomfortable having sex with them (viewing it as a risk to their careers), being unfairly criticized or ignored, and receiving less support on set. Unlike mainly white or even some interracial sets, all-ethnic sets often expect performers to do their own makeup, hair, and costumes. They rarely provide decent food for all-day shoots, and while white sets have catering, you're lucky to find more than sweets (to keep them working) and liquor (to calm them down) on ethnic-market sets.

But one of the starkest contrasts in the labor experiences of women of color sex workers in porn is the issue of roles. Since the development of an all-ethnic fetishized market in hardcore video in the 1980s, one of the most common roles for black and Latina actresses has been the maid. Although there is not very much logic to be found in the plotlines of porn features anyway, it seems that production companies cannot imagine letting women of color play the roles of wife, mother, sister, or daughter alongside whites. Instead, they continually figure women of color in supporting roles such as the servant, a character that lives in sexual servitude for whites. Drawing on a long history of stereotypical roles (remember the mammy in films like *Gone With the Wind*?), situating women of color as maids reveals that even though the primary role of pornography is to spark the (lustful) imagination of spectators, imagination is, in fact, one of the least significant components of the adult industry.

Pornography works hard to create a fantasy for predominantly male spectators, but because white men dominate the manufacturing of the fantasy, these images tend to reflect their desires and fears of the sexuality of people of color. Hence, women of color are figured as lusty Latinas, submissive Asian girls, and black ghetto hoes. In the political economy of the industry their discriminatory treatment is made invisible, while in the economy of desire, stereotypes of their race and sexuality are made distinctively visible.

These problems are linked to the devaluation of women of color in our society, and the rampant exploitation of our bodies. Measured against Anglo-American standards of beauty

Photo of Jeannie Pepper, courtesy of Mireille Miller-Young.

and codes of femininity, we are rendered grotesque, animalistic, dominant, and excessive. The ideal of beauty seems to be women who look like Jenna Jameson, Jenny McCarthy, and Pamela Anderson, and the widespread fame and acceptance of these women by the mainstream media underscores the ascendant value of white womanhood. Women of color are pressured to conform to these ideals, and as the miraculous transformations of J. Lo and Beyoncé to a nearly white, mulatta image attest, women of color tend to only be accepted to the extent that their exoticism is situated in a comfortable range of the blonde, white female aesthetic. Darker skinned and more "ethnic-looking" women are often pushed to the lowest status in the sex work economies; from street work to escorting to dancing, they are made doubly invisible.

In order to keep up with these expectations and compete in the game, we try to force our bodies to conform to these dominant standards. Cosmetic engineering through surgery is popular among women of color in porn, as they attempt to nip, tuck, and suck the voluptuous brownness out of their bodies while inflating their breasts to a marketable DD and beyond. Long, straight hair weaves and color contact lenses complete the look. They are told that an increasingly skinny and plastic image is what sells, that the porn consumers want a chocolate Barbie Doll.

What are we trying to prove? Can we love ourselves and demand that we are valued on our own terms in the sex industries? Jeannie Pepper lasted twenty years without altering her body with surgery. Even Ron Jeremy celebrated her natural body, saying at her recognition ceremony that Jeannie had the best breasts in the business and lamenting that they don't make them like that anymore. At the same time, however, while Jeannie maintained her own image, she was never completely embraced by the American adult industry. During her long career, Jeannie spent seven years living in Germany with her then husband, photographer John Dragon, because she found that she was more accepted as a black woman in the sexual marketplace of Europe than she was in the United States. While Jeannie found space to thrive in exile, the acceptable image for women of color in the US porn market narrowed.

As a result of the mainstreaming of hip-hop culture, the ethnic market has become more popular. The representations of darker and thicker women's bodies, especially their butts, have increasingly been deciphered as low class, as "ghetto." This aesthetic is somewhat celebrated in the new hip-hop pornography, but it remains a way to stigmatize women of color as *always* whores (and not in the feminist sense of the word). Instead of embracing a range of bodies, sexualities, and looks as part of the diversity of women of color, the industry has labeled some women "ghetto" and others "crossover," sustaining a hierarchy among women. These divisions have a lot to do with dominant fantasies of women of color as sources of desire and disgust, but they key into real cultural race and body politics between sex workers with different skin tones, body types, and class backgrounds.

Entrenched racism continually marginalizes women of color in this industry, while sexism facilitates the control of the production, distribution, and retail sectors of adult entertainment to remain in the hands of men. Because the industry is always searching for the next fresh face, tits, and ass of the eighteen-year-old girl next door, women workers are pitted against one another to compete for the scraps of opportunities left. And because white women easily benefit from the subordination of women of color in the porn market, they tend to embrace their race and class privilege in order to compete and ignore the struggles of minorities. Nina Hartley is one of the few white women who has publicly condemned racism and sexism in the industry, and has advocated for cooperation on the part of all women, who are the backbone of the porn business. Women of color actresses like Jeannie Pepper, India, Dee, Honney Bunny, and Sinnamon Love have also urged for unity, across race and class lines, for all women in the industry. What would such a coalition look like?

The recent HIV/AIDS crisis that hit the adult entertainment industry in the spring of 2004 sparked an important conversation among sex workers. Performers called industry-wide meetings to discuss the implications of the disease spreading to at least three sex workers who worked without condoms. Unlike the brave efforts of many street sex workers and escort services to normalize the use of condoms, the porn industry has largely resisted institutionalizing condoms, arguing that their fans believe that condoms make the scenes less erotic. Companies tend to allow workers to decide whether or not they want to use condoms, but performers who are condom-only often complain that they are offered less work than those who are willing to work without protection. This urgent issue drew a firestorm of complaints from performers who gathered together as the crisis hit. They began to talk about their frustration with companies not looking out for their best interests—in attempting to sell fantasies, these production companies neglected the harsh realities of sex workers' lives in the age of HIV/AIDS. As performers came together to work out their concerns about the porn business (a meeting largely sparked by black male actors in the industry), they were formulating a nascent sex labor politics in opposition to the status quo. Feeling their lives were at stake, they articulated concerns as sex workers, rather than as porn stars. Significantly, this mobilization was the blueprint for what is needed now in the industry, among not only women of color but all workers in the porn business.

The only way to improve the conditions for all women and men in porn is to demand improvement of and equality in industry standards. Because of the decentralized nature of the hardcore industry and the lack of a common workplace, it is difficult for porn workers to imagine forming a labor union like the Exotic Dancers Alliance (EDA) in San Francisco. Yet, professional performers need to follow the example of COYOTE (Call Off Your Tired Ethics) and PONY (Prostitutes of New York) to form networks with one another and mentor young workers coming into the industry. Such efforts have tended to be undermined by the nature of the industry in drawing mainly casual workers who do not remain long and lack an investment in forcing change, and young women who are ignorant of the acceptable rates for their work.

Perhaps these challenges could be overcome by forcing companies and agents to distribute information designed by a sex worker labor collective that informs new workers about industry standards and their rights. Another tactic might be to initiate an online database that all workers would be expected to consult, which would hold guidelines for workers and be used to coordinate meetings with others. Some forms of these efforts have already begun with Protecting Adult Welfare (PAW), directed by Bill Margold, and Adult Industry Medical Health Care (AIM), founded by former porn star Sharon Mitchell. Mitchell and Nina Hartley have joined forces to create *Porn 101*, an instruction video for sex workers in hardcore that explains how they can navigate the exploitative terrain of the industry.

More initiatives like this need to occur, and they need to be sure to have a sustained analysis of how both racism and sexism inform the labor experiences of porn workers. And any network that does form needs to connect porn sex workers to the broader community of sex workers in other arenas of the sexual economy, in the United States and beyond. As the adult industry is increasingly part of the globalization of capitalism and a mainstay of many national economies, all sex workers need to exchange information and strategies for resistance. Just as the re-election of the right-wing administration in the White House teaches us, we need to gain our resolve, collectivize, and mobilize to make a change. It will not be easy, but the survival of all of us and our rights to use our bodies as we choose with dignity is at stake.

MIREILLE MILLER-YOUNG is associate professor of feminist studies at University of California, Santa Barbara. Her research explores race, gender, and sexuality in visual culture and the sex industries. Her book, *A Taste for Brown Sugar: Black Women, Sex Work, and Pornography* examines the history of African American women's representations, performances, and labors in pornographic media. She is a coeditor of *The Feminist Porn Book: The Politics of Producing Pleasure*, with Constance Penley, Celine Parreñas Shimizu, and Tristan Taormino.

THE CITY'S RED LIGHTS: MUMBAI'S BOOMTOWN OF MIGRANT LABORERS

Svati P. Shah

ISSUE 4.3 (2008)

I walked over to sit with Subha, my main contact at a public labor market, known as a *naka*, in Mumbai, India. Subha was one of the women who moved freely between the clusters of men and women in the space. She was known by everyone, and had been extremely generous to me with her conversation and time. She would say with pride, "No one will even look at you wrongly, because they know I'm here right behind you. They're all afraid of me." When I would ask why they were afraid, she would smile and say simply, "They just are." After I had been going to the *naka* for a few weeks, various men began to ask me, "So, has Subha told you yet that she's a prostitute?"

I had been talking that day with Subha about other areas in the city where women use public spaces, a city street, or the red-light area, to find clients. Almost all of those women said they go looking for construction work from their local manual laborers' *naka* in the morning, but they also said, "If we don't find work there, we come here," adding, "*Pet ki liye karna pad ta hai.*" (It has to be done for the stomach.) I asked Subha what she thought about this "*pet ki liye*" (for the stomach) argument for doing sex work. She replied to me by saying, "*Hahn, izzat le kar ghar ka undar bayt satke hai, laykin . . .*" (Yes, for honor a person could sit in their house) but . . ." she trailed off, and would not speak about it further.

This article is part of a larger research project that examines the relationship between migration and sex work in India, focusing on the city of Mumbai. In poor migrant communities throughout the city, I talked with women who earned their livelihoods as day-wage laborers in the construction industry, as sex workers, or both. Most of the women were heads of their own households, and were either sole earners for their families or contributed along with their children. No matter how long they had lived in Mumbai, class and caste markers meant that these women and their families had been relegated to a semipermanent migrant status in the city, a status which, in this case, includes living in the vast slums of Sanjay Gandhi National Park at Mumbai's northern edge. This status of "permanent migrancy" has serious consequences for securing housing, food, access to safe drinking water, and education.

As a researcher I was looking for the untold story, the story that no one else was talking about. I found this in the numbers that India's National AIDS Control Organization (NACO) reported on the levels of brothel- and non-brothel-based sex work. According to NCO, an estimated 30 percent of prostitution in India is brothel-based. The rest, 70 percent, was non-brothel-based. This was the first reason I chose to focus on migrant women who do sex work, rather than focusing on full-time sex workers who are migrants. Seventy percent is a big untold story.

While Mumbai is iconic for prostitution in many ways—its red-light district is considered to be the largest concentrated red-light area in India, if not Asia—it has no large-scale sex workers' rights organization. There are, however, several prominent anti-prostitution and anti-trafficking organizations in Mumbai. The reasons for this are still speculative, ranging from the amount of money said to pass through the various rungs of the red-light district's hierarchy, to the high turnover of women entering and leaving Mumbai's red-light district. In formulating the research for my project, the absence of a sex worker-led organization in Mumbai was a sign of more untold stories.

Eventually, the research project that emerged was as much

about the growth of Mumbai as it was about the migrants, and sex workers, who built it. Understanding *nakas* was the key to all of this. *Nakas* formed at street corners and railway stations, and served as key meetings points for migrants, and a source of manual labor for the entire city. Both men and women provided this labor and, inevitably, competed with each other for day-wage jobs. Unlike the construction boom of the mid-1990s, when *naka* labor was used for large-scale construction work, today migrated communities typically use the *nakas* to look for short-term "contracts" for manual labor. Trade unionists and migrant workers' advocates in Mumbai estimate that some 300,000 people look for paid work from one of the dozens of *nakas* throughout the city each morning, in order to solicit work for that day's income.

According to construction and NGO workers, and union organizers, the day-wage construction and repair work in Mumbai available from the *nakas* is usually paid in the range of Rs100 (100 rupees, or around two dollars) per day for women, and Rs125–Rs150 for men. Workers at the Mumbai *naka* described here reported needing at least Rs2,000 per month, or roughly Rs66 per day. To earn this basic minimum salary, women working as sole earners in their households would need to secure twenty working days in a month; most women reported having eight to ten days of paid construction work per month. Although the provisional reason for the discrepancy between men and women's pay rates, given by almost everyone involved in the *naka*, is that "skilled" labor earns higher wages than "unskilled" labor, it is clear that a woman would never be considered a skilled worker, no matter how long she had been working in the industry. Instead, women were almost always identified with begari (helpers) work, a job that includes doing much of the heavy lifting on a construction site.

Some one hundred to 200 people passed through one *naka* in a northern city suburb each morning. Located on a street corner in front of a pharmacy, the *naka* was practically part of the street itself. The *naka* was the community's daily gathering space, with knots of people listening to someone reading out a newspaper story, drinking tea, and chatting. The *naka* was also one of the few spaces where members of the poor, Dalit (lower caste) migrant community could gather in large numbers in a public space without fear of having to answer to the police or a passing stranger. To sit around with one's friends was not seen as wasting time, since it could lead to paid work.

Most *nakas* are empty and disbanded by eleven in the morning, turning back into street corners, train stations, and roadways, until they become vibrant public labor markets again the next day. By eleven, most workers have either found jobs or gone home. At the suburban *naka* I mention here, the gendered geography of the space becomes even clearer after the crowd thins, with dozens of men and women sitting in groups next to one another, but generally not mixing too much. While it is not uncommon for women to sit and talk in the men's space, and vice versa, it is noticeable when this happens because only a few women do this with any ease or entitlement. For the most part, the women sit apart, interacting with each other and the one or two men who enter their section. All of the interactions, regardless of gender, convey the familiar and close-knit feel of this community. The viability of a kind of "double language" to discuss any form of paid sex or sex trade at the *naka* emerged through conversations like the one I initially described with Subha. I had many conversations in which the solicitation of paid sex was simultaneously affirmed and negated, the negations mediated by the need to protect against the police and against the loss of social standing in a relatively interdependent community.

For some, Subha's identification as a sex worker was a foregone conclusion, one that she both maintained and denied by her refusal to discuss it further. To be sure, all the women at the construction workers' *naka* were not necessarily read as sex workers. However, for women at the *naka*, having proximity to large groups of men, being unchaperoned by a family member in a public area, and visibly using public space to seek out paid work are all necessary to be hired for a day job by a contractor. These are also signs of transgression of gendered norms of propriety for these communities, and fulfill the current legal definition of solicitation for sex under the Immoral Trafficking Prevention Act's (ITPA's) current anti-solicitation clause. (ITPA is the main law that governs sex work in India. The exchange of sex and money is not specifically illegal under the law, but everything around this exchange, e.g. "living off of the earning of a sex worker," is. The law is currently under scrutiny in a highly controversial debate about how it should be amended.)

The language was more direct when accusations of prostitution were levied at members of caste or tribal communities who were deemed "other" by the dominant Mahar Navbuddho community at this particular *naka*. When I asked another woman worker whether she thought there was any kind of prostitution happening from the *naka*, she replied easily, "It's those tribals, look at them! They are always doing such things. And they only ask for fifty rupees for a whole day's work! Who else will work for so little?" She carried on in her screed against communities undercutting each other's wages at the *naka*, leaving the question of prostitution far behind.

South of this suburban *naka*, several areas of Mumbai are used as spaces where women solicit clients for sex. One set of side streets next to a major commuter railway station has been targeted by local NGOs for HIV/AIDS outreach. Arriving in the area at around noon, I realized that I had begun to think of it as "the other *naka*." The striking difference between the construction workers' *naka* and this one was that, while at the construction workers' *naka* the women all sat almost huddled together, both to avoid harassment and to make themselves more visible to contractors, women on this side street never congregated, even for a few minutes, without facing harassment from the local police. The only place we could sit and talk was at the local tea shop, where the worst harassment was the stares of the other clientele. I stood next to Uma to invite her to sit for a bit. A man approached her and whispered something in her direction. I heard her say "*panas*" ("fifty") before he walked away.

Once at the tea shop, Uma said, laughing ironically, "All

we have is *majboori*, (a compulsion, of necessity) and we say fifty rupees, and maybe they'll wear a condom, maybe they won't."

I said, "You all usually say 'If we don't get work on the *naka*, then we come here for this work.' Why is that? Do you like [construction] work better than this?"

"Hahn," (Yes), she replied, as though it were obvious. "That's *mehenat* (physical labor)." She raised her arms at right angles on either side of her body, imitating the motion that women do as they lift pans of wet cement and rocks onto their heads at construction sites. "This?" she said, motioning at the street behind her. "What's this? Sometimes you get a good man, sometimes a bad man, sometimes there's no work here at all, sometimes they refuse to wear a condom . . ."

She began speaking again about the police, about the one who was transferred to their area some three months before, whose harassment of street-based sex workers at his previous posting was legendary. "Once he chased us down the road with his scooter, nearly ran me over. Another time, we ran so hard, I thought that *budhi aurat* (old woman) was going to die for sure she was breathing so hard." She went on to describe a woman whom he had beaten with his nightstick so badly that she couldn't get out of bed for two days. "*Usko puchhna chahiye, humne kra galti kiya hai? Pet ki liye karte hai.*"

("Someone should ask him, what wrong have we done? We're doing it for the stomach.") When I asked the chief inspector at the local police station about the beatings and the chasings, he said "Who can tell who is a good woman and who is a bad one? This is a family area. There's a movie theater on that street that families like to come to. We have to keep the street safe for them."

Uma's expressed preference for doing construction work instead of earning money through sex is in keeping with the objective expectations raised by advocates for the abolition of prostitution. Rather than relating a story which complies with the idea of prostitution as inherently violent and a loss of bodily integrity, as per the iconic story of prostitution-as-trafficking, Uma located the main source of violence as police harassment, and the greatest hazard to her own safety in clients who refuse to wear condoms, making *mehenat* (physical labor) better than paid sex, which is implicitly deemed as something other than hard labor.

Female migrant workers in Mumbai's day-wage labor markets, like nearly all informal sector workers, move between different kinds of paid work. In addition to selling sex, women sometimes trade sexual services for paid work. Although the legal and public debate on migrants and prostitution has thus far been kept separate, the growing governmental trend toward conflating migration, prostitution, and human trafficking in the bodies of poor female migrants may throw *nakas* and migrant workers into the debate. As untold stories go, this one, too, must unfold into public view, as the sex workers' rights movement in India continues to make its mark domestically and internationally.

SVATI P. SHAH is an assistant professor in the department of women's, gender, and sexuality studies at the University of Massachusetts at Amherst. She is the author of *Street Corner Secrets: Sex, Work and Migration in the City of Mumbai*. She has worked with queer, sex worker, feminist, and secularist grassroots organizations in the United States and in India.

FAMILY AND RELATIONSHIPS

INTRODUCTION

Kevicha Echols

She works hard for the money so you better treat her right.

—Donna Summer

Waitresses, nurses, mechanics, models, athletes, and entertainers all have jobs that involve both physical labor and close relationships. After a hard day of work they expect to come home to people who love and support them. Sex workers want this too, but their reality is more complex. The exchange of sexual services for material or monetary compensation supposedly absent of any romantic feelings, emotion, or attachment is unimaginable for many outside of the sex industry. Yet some women and men support their families, friends, spouses, and partners on the economic opportunities that sex work provides—and they maintain these personal relationships as well.

For the single sex worker, finding love in the wake of paid encounters with clients can be a difficult and emotional process. In his personal essay "I (Heart) Affection and Other Forms of Emotional Masochism," Hawk Kinkaid takes us through the very heart of this matter, reflecting on the desire to have a "love connection" while learning to manage the boundaries between erotic labor, casual sex encounters, and personal sexual relationships. On the flip side, working in the sex industry opens the possibility of confrontation with the partners of clients, as Jenni Russell expresses in her poem "Wives." On a lighter note, Eliyanna Kaiser takes us to the animal kingdom where we learn about penguins and their trade in sex favors for shiny rocks. Families, too, struggle with the stigmas and challenges of sex work and its impact on both parents and their children. One of the questions that critics of the sex industry often ask of parents, as a kind of litmus test of moral outrage, is "Would you want your daughter doing this?" Mother and former stripper Katharine Frank examines this topic in her essay, "Keeping Her Off the Pole: My Daughter's Right to Choose." Syd V. provides insight on how a child of a sex worker came to understand a parent's job, learned to be supportive, and became involved in sex worker issues in her essay, "Hell's Kitchen: Growing Up Loving a Working Mother."

The decision to disclose work in the sex industry to loved ones can be a struggle. Fear of stigma or rejection may influence some sex workers' decisions to reveal or not to reveal their jobs. Similarly, the concern of how friends and family members might react or what they would think if they knew that their brother, sister, mother, father, son, daughter, aunt, uncle, or third cousin twice removed dated or married a sex worker crosses the minds of some who find themselves in these partnerships. Contrary to the belief of many, some sex workers who do make their work known have supportive families and friends, and so do their partners.

Communication is key in any positive and productive relationship, and honesty is a large component of this. Family, partners, and friends are our safe haven, and sometimes it takes just one person to help us feel accepted and respected.

KEVICHA ECHOLS, PhD, served as the outreach director for *$pread* from 2006 to 2008. Kevicha's work at *$pread* inspired her research investigating discourses in publications created by and for the sex work community since the 1980s. She lives in Brooklyn, NY, and is a professor at a local college.

WIVES

Jenni Russell

ISSUE 2.3 (2006)

Her eyes rove to the redhead
removing her thong on stage and back
to examine me, a nude specimen, winding my bikini top
   around a wrist,
grasping the wad of bills stuffed in my garter.
She crosses her arms over her sweater.
I fan my face with my hand.

No, I don't remember "Roger."
It was two weeks ago. Twenty to fifty a night.
A thousand wallets since have bought me a drink.
I may have known he was married, yes,
but most pocket the ring. I'm sorry,
I don't recognize him in that photo either,
with your son at soccer camp. What happens?

Twenty dollars.
Follow me, I can show you.

JENNI RUSSELL is a retired exotic dancer whose poetry was frequently published in *$pread*.

KEEPING HER OFF THE POLE: MY DAUGHTER'S RIGHT TO CHOOSE

Katherine Frank

ISSUE 1.4 (2006)

Comedian Chris Rock has become the father of a baby girl named Lola, and in addition to his jokes about racism, politics, and relationships, he has now added material on fathering. One of his main tasks as a father, he claims in one of his monologues, is to "keep her off the pole." And just to be safe, "My daughter is staying away from all poles. That includes monkey bars," he says. Rock believes that having a daughter who is a stripper is the ultimate failure for a father.

As the mother of a baby girl, and as a former stripper, I found that Rock's comments gave me reason to pause. Certainly, the news headlines and television stories often make me stop to think about how one should go about educating kids about sexuality. After all, despite all of the hype about abstinence, kids are experimenting sexually at young ages. Oprah interviews young teens about "salad tossing" (oral-anal sex) and "rainbow parties" (oral sex fests where the girls wear different colors of lipstick). A network news story breaks about a ring of middle school group sex parties outside a Southern metropolis. A wide range of near-erotica can be viewed on late-night television, and kids are definitely tuning in. Even parents are becoming familiar with the popular terms "fuck buddies" and "friends with benefits," used by youth to denote casual sexual encounters. *Girls Gone Wild* has become a profitable series of videos ("Girls Gone Wild on Campus," "Girls Gone Wild Doggy Style," "Girls Gone Wild

American Uncovered," etc.), in addition to being used as a description of a regular Saturday night, and young girls flash their breasts or butts in exchange for baseball hats, T-shirts, cheap glass beads, or simply a few whistles.

NBC conducted a poll on teen sexual attitudes and behaviors and found that 27 percent had "been with somebody in an intimate or sexual way" (despite the certain denials of their parents), 12 percent had engaged in oral sex, 13 percent had had sexual intercourse, and that half of those who had engaged in oral sex or intercourse had done so by age fourteen. Religion seems to quell early sexual behavior a bit, but not completely: teens from Protestant and Catholic families were equally likely to be sexually active (26 percent), while teens from nonreligious families were slightly more active (39 percent). In many of the news stories, unfortunately, it seems that girls are striking unequal bargains: they tend to claim that their exploits are primarily about pleasing the boys and they still tell stories about being judged negatively by those very young men that they are so interested in serving. ("Do you think any of these boys will ask you to prom?" Oprah asks some party girls. The answer: it doesn't bode well for a corsage and dinner.)

My primary concern is actually not about preventing my daughter (or anyone else's) from becoming sexually active early. Such prevention efforts may not be effective or worthwhile. Some kids do begin these explorations at young ages, no matter how their parents try to prevent them, and for many of us who blossomed relatively early, such experience is not necessarily negative. I was personally quite interested in sexual things at an early age and believe that my experimentations during my teen years were important in determining the woman that I would become. On the other hand, I know that I did sometimes engage in sexual activity of different kinds for reasons other than for desire or self-exploration. Sometimes I ended up in a situation because I wanted to be popular, wanted a particular guy to like me, or didn't want to seem too uptight since my friends were all "hooking up" at the same time. Sometimes I thought, "Why not?" and couldn't come up with a good answer. Sometimes I drank too much and made decisions that I later regretted. A lot of us did. And, it seems, a lot of young girls (and boys) still do. Luckily, I had been provided with enough information about sexuality that my regrets were primarily emotional—I did not end up with sexually transmitted diseases, unwanted pregnancies, or with bodily scars from physical violence. These risks are real and youth should be educated about them in multiple forums. Recitations of the "horrors" of sexual activity are not, however, very effective as preventive measures for some of us.

Clearly, Rock believes that when young girls turn to stripping, or some other form of sex work, it is an example of the widespread tendency to devalue their sexuality, to see themselves simply as objects for men, and to engage in sexual activity and exhibitionism for no good reason. Yet I'm not sure I'd necessarily agree. When I began stripping in my late twenties and met women working in all different areas of the sex industry, I learned things about my sexuality that I believe would have helped me in my earlier years to avoid negative sexual situations. First of all, through stripping I actually learned how incredibly valuable my sexuality was. Not just valuable in terms of female virtue ("be careful not to lose your reputation"), an idea I found fairly nebulous and unconvincing all along (perhaps because I had already lost mine). Instead, I found that my sexuality was tangibly valuable. Economically valuable. What I had once given away for free, I learned, men were willing to pay for, and quite highly. This simple realization changed the way I thought about a lot of things, including my decisions to engage in sexual activity or to show off my body for others outside of the club. I see cheerleaders now and wonder if they realize how much money they could be making for those peeps up their skirts. I view young girls dressed like Paris Hilton with an almost conservative eye: Why are they going out dressed like that? Why show all that skin for nothing more than a bit of attention? Can't they see that they could be paying off their school loans with such attire and behavior?

In this capitalist context, where sexuality is sold and used to sell in multifarious ways, I don't think a father's greatest failure would be for his daughter to become a stripper. In fact, her choice of job could be seen as an intelligent entrepreneurial decision. At least she's not shrugging her shoulders when asked later why she was disrobing onstage in front of men (the way so many spring breakers and Mardi Gras enthusiasts tend to sheepishly do). In his comedy routine, Rock also disputes the idea that girls are stripping to pay for their education: "I haven't heard of a college that takes dollar bills. I haven't seen any clear glass heels in biology. I haven't ever gotten a smart lap dance." Sure, the comment is meant to be funny, as if strippers would always look like strippers in their five-inch heels and glitter, or show up to pay their tuition with folded money pulled straight from their garters. Yet, what Rock is really saying is that the woman who profits from selling sexual entertainment is not going to be able to accomplish anything else. Fortunately, he is wrong.

Many of my stereotypes were also overturned when I became a stripper and recognized how hypocritical people's judgments of sex workers tended to be. At one time, for example, I believed that prostitutes must be miserable women, that strippers were most certainly exploited, and that porn stars probably had experienced all sorts of psychological trauma. My experiences and friendships in the sex industry made me rethink a lot of these assumptions. I came to understand the sex industry not as a panacea for sexual ills or a capitalist utopia, but as an industry with many of the same benefits and drawbacks as other industries. I began to question why it was that women who sold sex or sexual fantasies were criminalized and stigmatized, while women who gave it away for free were either accepted and valorized (as long as they didn't give away too much, to too many people) or pathologized (if they did give away too much, to too many people, or the wrong people, or enjoyed it too greatly). Perhaps, I came to believe, we are barking up the wrong tree when we assume that sex or sexual expression has some predetermined meaning or that it necessarily has to be coupled with romantic love (something the college students who are embarking on their one-night stands and friends-with-benefits relationships already know). Perhaps, I also came to believe, the distaste that people express when confronted with explicit sex-for-money (or sexuality-for-money) exchanges is also hypocritical, rooted more in ideology and fear than in any truth about sexuality.

One night, after a few margaritas and a lot of discussion about raising a beloved daughter in a sexist and sexual world, I wondered aloud to my friends about whether I might suggest that my own daughter sell her virginity on the Internet, as some enterprising youngsters have already been doing. It would give her a reason to save it, I surmised, and perhaps it will be legal to do so in the future. After all, why lose your virginity to some high school guy in the backseat of a car (or wherever it happens nowadays), while you are drunk or stoned (or whatever kids do to lose their inhibitions nowadays), when you could get paid good money for it? She might earn enough from that one encounter for a down payment on a house, or to buy a new car, or to put away for college tuition. She might like the guy or she might not. Who cares? It would be quick and painless, because she would have the knowledge to make it so. And liking someone can be a transient state anyway—how many people actually end up with the first person they sleep with in the long term, or even the short term? Probably fewer than one would expect (or than the abstinence folks are hoping).

After their initial horrified reactions, my friends began to see my point, even dressed as it was in hypothetical attire. One woman remembered feeling as if her virginity was a kind of blight to be gotten rid of as quickly as possible. She had made a bet with her friends to see who could lose it first, and though all of them successfully accomplished their missions right around the same time (not exactly Mission Impossible, after all), the experiences had been uniformly unimpressive. Several women told of wanting their first time "to be perfect," but "settling" for far less. One woman couldn't remember the first time she had sex, as she had downed a pint of whiskey to avoid worrying about the supposedly immanent (but never actually forthcoming) pain.

Some first-time stories are romantic and some are upsetting and abusive, but most are unexpectedly banal. Certainly, if a young girl was planning on socking away some cash for the "gift" of her virginity, she might at least use that sense of value if she decides to be generous and bestow such a gift on a boyfriend. She might negotiate. She might insist that he take her on dates, or buy her Valentine's Day presents, talk to her in the halls the next day instead of whispering behind her back with his buddies, or even use a condom—tall orders for some young men nowadays. And, it seems, high expectations for some young women. Perhaps she might even insist on having an orgasm, or at least require him to make some attempt at providing her with sexual pleasure as well. Perhaps she would decide that it was a gift of love, and would request that he accept it in those terms (rather than simply hoping that he might feel the same way someday).

And what about all of those experiences short of losing one's virginity? How might she feel about those? The quick gropes that were allowed to appease a drunk fraternity boy, the backseat blow jobs (with no reciprocation of any kind), the frantic dry humping (which does, in fact, often resemble an unpracticed lap dance)? What are those moments worth?

These comments are not offered to feed or stir up any kind of crazy passion for virgins or to suggest anyone engage in illegal activity. Nor are they meant to suggest that all young women would be served by working in the sex industry. This is a thought experiment: The issue at hand is not whether or not you actually sell your sexuality in some form or another, or give it away for free. The issue is whether or not young girls feel like they own their sexualities. How does one maintain one's own understanding of sexual value in a world where sex is both incessantly commodified, on the one hand, and invested with multiple layers of often contradictory meaning, on the other (love, fear, pleasure, sin, freedom, commitment, adventure)? Unfortunately, laws against prostitution mean that, legally, women do not "own" their sexualities outright. We cannot do with our bodies as we see fit in the sexual realm (although we are certainly allowed—even coerced—to sell our bodies for other forms of demeaning labor). Not yet, anyway. However, we can own our sexuality in the sense that we can consciously decide what counts as a good reason for having sex (love, money, pleasure, fame, popularity?) or expressing ourselves sexually in other ways, and we can still demand respect and care for our bodies from those people we interact with sexually. We might not always get that respect, but we should at least be confident enough in our own sexual value to ask for it. This is something that feminists have fought for over the years: a reward that we hope our children will also be able to reap.

So how will I respond if my daughter becomes a stripper someday? Probably with the same ambivalence that I'd respond to any job choice—they all require some amount of compromise (and as of yet I can't even imagine her leaving the house on her own, so this is really becoming a thought experiment). Certainly, I could imagine that stripping would teach her the value of her body, as it did for me; that it is acceptable (and wise) to set your own limits about what kinds of activities you wish to engage in and to stick to those limits; to learn to take control of her sexuality; to overcome the fear of sexuality that tends to pervade many people's lives; and to think critically about sex, power, and love, and how she wants to put these explosive and powerful elements together (after all, there are so many rewarding ways to live).

On the other hand, stripping is still stigmatized work, which means that it does involve personal challenges that should not be glossed over—there will always (at least in the current climate) be those individuals who see strippers as "trash." Stripping is also physical labor: it can be grueling at times, dirty (literally, not figuratively), exhausting, and downright boring. But so can waitressing! Doing physical and menial labor is the fate of many teenagers, and such work is accompanied by the benefits of low personal investment, flexibility, a lack of required skills and training, and low competition. Some of us find stripping to be far preferable to taking orders all night and delivering burgers and fries to surly or amorous customers. Stripping, of course, is also premised on appearance. Girls are hired at other jobs for their appearance, or are successful in them because they have a particular kind of middle-class, girly look. In some ways, the explicitness of stripping can be a relief from some of the more covert ways that women are sexualized at work and elsewhere.

Categorizing women as Madonnas or whores, "girls you date" or "girls you sleep with," good girls or sluts, has a long and unfortunate history that will not be overturned without a struggle. And women who strip or work in other realms of the sex industry will likely continue to find themselves fighting against these kinds of labels and the judgments that accompany them. But one hope that I would have for my daughter, and yours, is that she could grow up in a world where some women are not highly valued at the expense of other women, and where a woman's sexual desire, interest, experience, pleasure, or mistakes are truly her own.

KATHERINE FRANK, PhD, is a cultural anthropologist and the author of *Plays Well in Groups: A Journey Through The World of Group Sex* and *G-Strings and Sympathy: Strip Club Regulars and Male Desire*. She is also a coeditor of *Flesh for Fantasy: Producing and Consuming Exotic Dance*. See Katefrank.com for more information.

HOT TOPIC:
PEOPLE WHO DATE SEX WORKERS

Peter, Natalie, Allen, Bob C., and Fred

ISSUE 1.4 (2006)

A few years ago, I was in a relationship with a woman who was escorting, and it permanently altered the way I look at the world. Before that experience, I only had a vague sense of how the sex industry worked, and how big it was. Now I can't walk down the street without wondering how many people around me have secret lives as johns or escorts that no one in their life knows about.

Most of my friends didn't know anything about sex work either. So just by being involved with someone who was escorting, I was forced to be an advocate for sex workers. That awakened me to the pervasiveness of anti-sex work attitudes, even among people who call themselves feminists and leftists. I knew I was in the right, but it made me angry to feel like I was being judged just for giving my love and support to a woman who was working as an escort. If I really loved her, people suggested, I wouldn't let her do this work.

Of course, dating a sex worker wasn't all stress—it had its own special thrills, too. It was a turn-on to know that, with all the men who were paying her big bucks for her body, I was the only one she wanted to sleep with for free.

—*Peter, Queens, New York*

I was in a nonmonogamous relationship with an online stripper. She invited me to hang out at work with her many times, and I only went once. I was shy. I think I wanted to compartmentalize her life in order to better understand/handle the situation. There was her work, and then there was us. And I thought I was comfortable with that. The fucked up thing about that was, I was comfortable as long as I didn't really know what she was doing.

The work was really hard on her relationship to her sex life. She found it difficult to make distinctions between performance of pleasure and real pleasure, and I found it tough because she talked about her clients often as being creeps, and I was scared of being someone she perceived as being a creep for desiring her. It was hard to be honest about my fears and insecurities related to her work, because I really wanted to be 100 percent pro-sex work, no doubts about it.

—Natalie, Canada

I dated a call girl/madam several years back. I started out as her client and quickly became a regular (once a week). She started asking me to go out to dinner, stay the night. I really didn't catch on that she was interested until one of her coworkers gave me a heads up. Soon she cajoled me into a foursome with her, another lady, and the lady's male client who was bi. Next thing I know, I am working for my loving girlfriend! I later realized that, by setting this and the later encounters up, I could not hold against her what she chose to do for a living, for I also did it!

—Allen, New York City

My mother did not raise me to be the partner of a sex worker, and yet here I am. I believe that sex work has no business being illegal and that sex workers serve a valid social function. In choosing this relationship I have had to accept that my political beliefs conflict with cultural conditioning and to face personal fears.

One lesson was that those things that I judge in my partner mirror the parts of myself where I carry sexual shame, do not allow myself to feel my full sexuality, or restrict my full sexual expression. So now when I feel judgmental, I look for which part of myself is being denied. I choose to reclaim these aspects of my sexuality instead of trying to control the uncontrollable in my partner when it scares me.

Secondly, when my partner is drained by her work and does not want to play sexually with me, it used to be easy for me to make this about her work. Now I see other explanations: After an intense workweek, anyone is likely to be tired and have a lowered libido. She might be feeling angry with me at the moment. There are natural cycles in relationships and she might just not be there for me in this moment. I have learned to trust that she loves me. After all, in the end, she consistently comes back to me. We share rich passion and a depth of understanding love that is profound.

—*Bob C., Santa Cruz County, California*

It's about forty-eight hours before Barney's wedding when Wilma tells me she can't go. "He was in the club," she says. "Just sitting there at the bar. He was joking around, pretending to cover his eyes, and laughing." About forty-eight hours before we're supposed to be at his wedding on the Jersey shore, with the car rental and the hotel and his friends and all that.

He'll think it was about me. That I put a ban on the place because Wilma works there. That I'm pissed about him checking out my girlfriend's tits. Which I have to admit makes sense, but it's all wrong. It's about how, sitting on that barstool, he was telling Wilma that the relationship between them wasn't peer to peer but client to sex worker. A stripper doesn't go a customer's wedding. A customer is not a friend.

Barney chose one relationship over the other, and Wilma's a little bit heartbroken over what he decided.

When you've been in love with a sex worker for a while, things like this seem fairly obvious. You forget that other people tend not to grasp a lot of these dilemmas, mostly because they've never had to consider them. Somebody like Barney doesn't even get that the person he needs to work this out with is Wilma, not me.

We don't work it out. We don't even talk about it. There's a huge conceptual divide here, and in the brief window of time available, nobody seems to know how to bridge it. Needless to say, we don't show up at the wedding. A couple weeks later, I get an email from Barney telling me I'm dead to him. At least I know where I stand.

—Fred, Brooklyn, New York

I (HEART) AFFECTION, AND OTHER FORMS OF EMOTIONAL MASOCHISM

Hawk Kinkaid

ISSUE 1.2 (2005)

I always found managing clients to be easy. I established a system so structured and well timed it felt like sleepwalking. From the phone call or email to the front door—stripped, sexed, soaped, and summarily rewarded—explaining myself wasn't even a necessary part of the engagement. My rules were straightforward; all limitations and expectations turned to the Ten Cock Commandments and were carried up the mountain.

But it was my heart that wanted to kill me.

Perhaps it was something about the off-hours, the free time, or the idea of being in "time out" that gave me too much room to contemplate and to play out alternate scenarios or to think about what others would think about what I was doing. I found that when I was most free, I kept caging up my own thoughts about escorting, porn, and why I was glad so few knew. Like many guys working in the business, I hit the bars just to be somewhere else. Not only were they some of the only places gay men could socialize (and still are), but they were the loudest and the must ruckus spaces where my attention was diverted faster than a wardrobe malfunction at the Super Bowl.

When someone makes a commitment to becoming a sex worker, whether it is placing an ad, getting a second cell phone or screen name, or just making a regular client list, he also takes on a weighty repertoire of consciousness that is hell-bent on drowning him in the malaise of traditional morals and propaganda. It is easy to say it doesn't bother me, but I'd be lying if I said I didn't pay some attention to the rife indignation. After all, it is the right of all Americans to be indignant, even if it's to ourselves. To live or work within Main Street, USA, means finding a way of talking to it, negotiating with it, and sliding past when no one is looking.

I always wanted to dismiss the weight of John Q. Public's anti-prostitution convictions, and there were moments when it was easy enough to think of the world as being filled with people who could not claim their own bodies and who lacked the responsibility to own them, use them, comfort them, and fuck with them as they wanted. In my thoughts, pleasure did not equal shame: those rules were made by men seeking to control other men. I was a self-touted intellectual and activist and I could throw off that guilt on a dance floor or street side, a poetry reading or a night fucking someone of my own free will.

And that was often the route I most liked to explore: lost among the skins and the hairs, the names often too common to remember or guess accurately, the terrain of escape often shaped like an anus, a towering phallus, a kiss, or even the wink of an eye. There were no appointments. If there was negotiation it often went on wordlessly between lips. From bathrooms to park walks, adult arcades to discotheques, it was sex that took my mind off of . . . well . . . sex. I mean, how could I possibly be thinking of the social injustices done to gay men while some distracting tongue was working against me? What freedom it was to celebrate a new set of curves on the arch of another's foot. I was absolutely intoxicated and busy.

And work continued as always—I saw regulars and visitors, the inexperienced and the overzealous. Once, I came eight times in a day to satisfy seven clients (such a large tip warranted an extra "go") and at the end of the day, I still wanted more as I headed toward a bathhouse. Once there, I wandered around, looking past open doors and toweled military men and down to the next corner, where I would turn and continue walking. At the next corner I would continue until I had practically played out a masturbatory marathon, thinking of absolutely nothing at all. I realized that I was not there for sex.

I imagine that people who spend their entire workday pushing buttons and fumbling numbers don't spend a lot of time at home doing the same thing. Instead, we have TV, beer, professional wrestling, and toy train collections. Sex might fall into the category of obscure and popular entertainment; a drug of some sort or a recreational habit, the main benefit being the momentary shift of focus from the big picture to the tiny silver skin screen.

I learned to cope this way while others turned to booze and narcotics. Some relied on shopping therapy, blowing a week's worth of earnings on the trends and tailors that would promise the most impact on the Saturday night of dancing they had promised themselves, but often abandoned early for a call in order to make rent. Others had practical rationales for their guilt—they would allocate dollar figures in the place of crucifixes and Hail Marys, determined that the light at the end of the tunnel would eventually make them smarter and happier than the others they competed with. This house, that job, that degree: all of these things were logical ends for the means they had chosen to explore.

Regardless of what we did, society and its confidence stuck all around us. This just made some of us push that much harder to be that much more outrageous. And even though I was never ashamed of my behavior, a wild word out of place or the sprinkled hints in conversation always left me with one ear upturned to see if a possibly new sexual prey—romantic or otherwise—was paying attention, making a judgment, or stepping backward. As I waited for them to run, in my heart I was secretly testing them with the promise of disguised bravado.

Like all of the guys I knew—the ones I passed in clubs, the clients who paid, the others who did not—I wanted to be loved. In my head, I had this ongoing mantra, which undercut even the harshest attitude I would take and the most

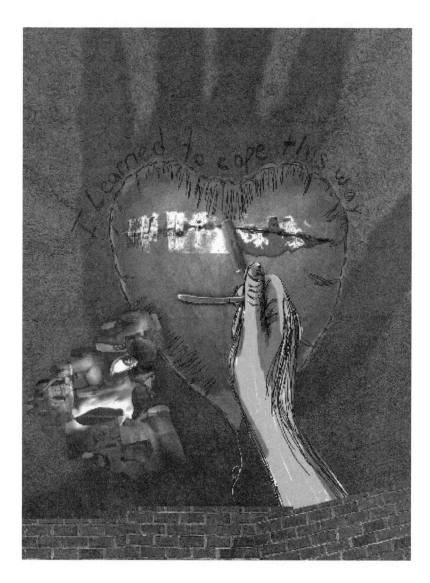

Illustration by author.

practical self-talk I could offer. I knew without a doubt that, like everyone, I wanted not only to be adored, but to be important to someone. One night, I would make promises to commit myself to one person who could really love me and the next I would remember that loving me was impossible and, as I took three men into my mouth, that one person could never be enough.

Still, I was generous to these men who carried my amour. I was even generous to those who showed the slightest hint of wanting it, to those who were attentive, and particularly to those who simply gave me the time of day. In my own life, I'm certain that I was looking to reconcile a gross error in my own calculation, which led me to believe that I was never to be the attractive one in the waiting line, the one someone jerked off to, the fantasy that is harbored from a distance. And so when they wanted something from me, I was willing.

Hell, I was eager to be liked.

Many other working guys I have talked to have shared this dichotomy, the one that whispers in one ear that it is important to be loved, and in the other that there is so much of us to share, how could we possibly hold it all in or confine it to one person? I was a balloon, a time bomb, an unopened bag of popcorn: in the evenings after the hardest days at work I was freedom looking for a cage to open. And this isn't just true for guys in the business, but also guys I know who work day jobs and fuck nights at group sex events—the right hand couples who don't know what their left hand is doing. The country is populated with glory holes looking for love.

So, a client said he loved me. This one guy I'd been seeing for a week said he loved me. There was a guy I knew only through a friend who wanted to love me. He knew he would, he just needed the chance. When these words popped out of people's mouths, whether in the throws of passion or in the sincerest expressions, they seemed so fragile.

I knew that I wouldn't know what to do with love if I had it. Sex, yes. Cash, yes. And I have liked and loved much in my lifetime, but the exchanges of affection were frequent and happenstance, ordered like pizzas and accomplished on schedules. My sentiments were often faked and occasionally sincere, like the clients who were charmingly sad or simply ineffably brilliant, certain what they wanted, or simply needing to talk. Some of these were lovers' moments, and I respected that. These moments made me envy lovers and reminded me that I was not one. I would feel the need to emphasize my sexual and professional choices, as if my extreme certainty were not a small, obvious gray doubt perched on my forehead.

It's when someone loves us, tells us they love us, or we think they might love us that we become unhinged. In one way, I believe it is because we have drawn such clear boundaries with our clients that we don't pay much attention to rules when we are giving it away.

The truth is, few of us ever spend time drawing a separate set of boundaries for the men we fuck in our free time, and consequently, many of us have let romantic or play partners get away with things we would never tolerate from clients. The great walls of the heart and even the skin surrounding our asses require a certain amount of care. When someone was paying me, I found it easier to demarcate limits on their advances.

For those of us who give in so easily because we fear that we'll be turned away upon disclosing our choices, there must be a reminder that who we are is worth more than the world's ignorance would have us believe. Love is not the occasional slap across the face. Love is not the acceptance of frequent untruths. Love is not the sacrifice of our own skin for the sake of another person. There should be Post-it notes and small alarm clocks, e-vite reminders and voicemail messages that tell us that protecting ourselves is not just about locating the nearest exit and notifying friends of where we are. It is also about considering how reasonable our choices are and remembering that respect is a requirement and not a matter for discussion—that includes self-respect.

For sex workers, it is crucial to think of how our work affects all parts of our lives and to think through how it might affect introducing ourselves to other people; coming out to each person in a new way once we feel safe and comfortable. It is also important to understand how we react to withholding sensitive information, and to decide what information is best to hold onto and how we can cope with it, because the cash comes quickly. The process develops into a simple pattern, but the heart can't be always understood—it's too easy to try and outrun it, and when we do we fall to pieces.

HAWK KINKAID is the founder and current president of HOOK ONLINE, the American-based harm reduction nonprofit project by, for, and about men in the sex industry. HOOK ONLINE produces Rent University, an education series for sex workers. Kinkaid is a former sex worker, current writer and spoken word artist, and lifelong harm reduction activist. His writing has appeared in many anthologies and collections, including *Hos, Hookers, Call Girls, and Rent Boys* and *Johns, Marks, Tricks and Chickenhawks*.

THE COLDEST PROFESSION

Eliyanna Kaiser

ISSUE 1.3 (2005)

Just like the northern lights with which we are more familiar, the southern lights (aurora australis) dance furiously over our planet's southernmost region, Antarctica. Perhaps they shine with a slightly red-tinted hue over Ross Island. Eight hundred miles away from the South Pole, this little island is home to the Adelie penguins, where scientists Dr. Fiona Hunter (Cambridge) and Dr. Lloyd Davis (University of Otago), have observed a zoological first: a monogamous bird species engaging in extramarital sex explicitly in return for material items.

That's right: hooker penguins.

In the world of the Homo sapien, it is scarcity that creates the conditions for commercial prostitution. Prostitutes seek to acquire finite resources—money and goods—while clients seek increased access to willing sexual partners. It really shouldn't be surprising that life in the rest of the animal kingdom isn't so different.

Mating pairs of Adelies make their elaborate nests on a raised platform built from stones, where each female will lay two eggs per mating season. The structure keeps the eggs away from the ice and the freezing spring runoff. But the stones are hard to come by. The male penguins have to dive for the pebbles and bring them to shore one at a time, and without a sufficient number the chicks won't hatch.

The researchers witnessed females, who were already

Illustration by Cristy C. Road.

paired, soliciting males for stones in exchange for sex. Often the penguin clients were so happy with this service that they allowed their girls to help themselves to more stones later.

Hunter and Davis even observed some particularly sly penguin gals getting stones without putting out, just by going through the courtship ritual (lap dance, anyone?). One female teased sixty-two stones from a single male this way, without him getting any tail.

The researchers don't think that the males are simply after sex for its own sake but that they are hoping to impregnate the female penguins. They also don't believe that the females are solely after hard currency. There is a possible evolutionary advantage for them in this practice, since sex with multiple males helps ensure "genetic quality or variability." Additionally, if their mate dies, they have already established a relationship (of sorts) with another male.

Hunter and Davis are planning another trip to Antarctica's red-light district for further research.

ELIYANNA KAISER is a former executive editor of *$pread* magazine. She is currently raising her two children in Manhattan. In her spare time, she writes fiction.

CRISTY C. ROAD is a Cuban-American illustrator and writer. Road published a zine, *Greenzine*, for ten years, and has released three novels tackling queerness, mental health, cultural identity, and punk. Her most recent work, *Spit and Passion*, is a graphic coming-out memoir (about Green Day). She's currently working on a tarot card deck, and her punk rock band The Homewreckers. Road hibernates in Brooklyn.

HELL'S KITCHEN: GROWING UP LOVING A WORKING MOTHER

Syd V.

ISSUE 5.2 (2010)

When I tell people that my mother was a stripper and a professional dominatrix, and at one point owned her own escort service, I usually get the "Wow, that's so cool" response, or a blank stare and an "Oh shit, really?" By the time I was born, my mother, at twenty-six, had been stripping for eleven years, but after all this time I'm still figuring out how I feel about the memories and experiences I had growing up. It is cool when I can call my mother and get help with a paper that I'm writing about sex work or kink, but it's painful when I think back on the economic hardships we faced, the problems she still faces, and the evenings I spent wishing my mother was at home reading me a bedtime story or making me dinner instead of spending time with strangers.

Like most children of single parents, I spent much of my time with babysitters in the evenings watching soap operas. My babysitter, Meche, was an elderly woman who I suspect was surviving off the little money from all the single mothers in the building who could afford to pay for a sitter. I remember crying and running after my mother with my plastic Tina doll in tow down the hallway of our prewar building in Hell's Kitchen in the early 1980s, begging her to stay home and put me to bed. The flickering hall light above reflected a greenish tint over my mother's face as she tried not to cry for fear she would ruin her makeup.

By the time I got to preschool, we had moved into my

grandmother's apartment on the Upper West Side because we could no longer afford rent in Hell's Kitchen. There in our new apartment I watched my mother getting ready for work, intently examining the way she would burn the ends of her black Revlon eyeliner, and how she would pout her lips to apply her reddish-orange lipstick. Something about the routine was comforting for me. I would sit on the toilet seat, my knees up to my chest, and move my lips with hers, feeling excited. When I told my mother I was writing this piece a few days ago, I reminded her of the fascination I had with watching her get ready. Over the phone, my mother explained to me that whenever she would get ready for work, I would cry because that meant it was time for mommy to leave.

Sometimes my mother let me play dress up with her mostly handmade costumes. I would get all dolled up in her deep blue sequined robe and slinky dresses and parade around the house in her heels like I was a famous dancer. My mom once told me she used to dance ballet and regretted stopping. I always wondered, aside from the need for quick money to support us, was dancing on a nightclub stage as close as she could get to that lost dream? Did receiving all of that attention somehow make her feel special, beautiful, or important?

I remember going to work with my mother on two occasions. The first time was when I was about four and she had arranged for Linda, another dancer who lived above the club, to watch over me. I either managed to convince Linda to bring me downstairs or I snuck down by myself so I could peek through a door by the right side of the stage to see my mother dressed in a beautiful costume and dancing provocatively. She didn't see me and I was probably only there for a moment, but I did see plenty of men in the audience watching her. I don't know what I thought then. I probably missed her and was curious about what she was doing so I decided to find out. I know that I always thought she looked beautiful, no matter what she was wearing.

When I told this same story to a friend in college, he began laughing and asked me if I had ever seen *Striptease*. When he told me about the scene when Demi Moore's daughter sneaks upstairs to peek through golden foil and watches her mother dancing, I knew I had to watch it.

The second occasion was the first time in my life that I ever danced onstage. It was during the daytime, but she had taken me with her to put in some dancing shifts at this little club in Jersey. I don't even think it was a bona fide club. There were windows everywhere and it was daytime so the place was brightly lit. As I was enjoying my second Shirley Temple of the day at a table near the bar and waiting for my mother, a Madonna song came on the jukebox and I ran up on stage and started dancing like a little girl might do to a song she knows. I wasn't shy and loved attention. I danced the whole song, and by the end of it I guess the owner or a customer made a joke that I should be paid for dancing. Someone gave me a few dollars. The next day, my mother took me to the bodega near our apartment and, with my hard-earned money, I bought my first set of Crayola bathroom chalk. To this day, my mother is terrified that if I write about this someone will arrest her twenty-five years later for the one afternoon she let me dance like a little girl onstage to Madonna.

Once I began going to school, my mother stopped dancing, but she continued to work in bars. She would work late, come home, usually drunk, and sleep in. I would get ready for school by myself most mornings or my grandmother, who we still lived with, would help out. On the weekends, I would go downstairs and get my mother the usual (a liter of ginger-ale, a pack of More cigarettes), come home, and make her a cup of coffee.

When I was about eight years old, the fantasy world I had created of working in clubs came to an end and I began to resent both my mother and her work. I had learned how to make up stories about her profession. I worried the kids at school would ask what my mother did for work, and if they did I would lie. I would stay home from school on Take Your Daughter to Work Day. I was already one of the only kids in my group of friends who was being raised by a single mother and I surely didn't want to add to the stigma by admitting I had a barmaid, ex-stripper mother who came home drunk

Illustration by Sadie Lune.

and angry most nights. I wanted to be like everyone else who lived on the Upper West Side of Manhattan in the late 80s. I wanted the artist mother, the blue-collar working father, the life that so many of my friends had.

It wasn't until I was in my teens, when my mother became a professional dominatrix and owned her own escort service, that I began to really hate her job choices. This was not something my mother was excited about either. She took the gig purely out of desperation. I myself had already been exploring my sexuality, having first slept with a female friend of mine when I was twelve, and spent many late nights on rooftops, doing too much perhaps too soon. I always knew more about sex than most of my friends, probably because my mother told me when we had one of many "talks" that I shouldn't wait until I was married to have sex. "What if the person you choose is bad in bed? Then you'll never know what good sex is." With that, I marched into adolescence ready to find good sex, whatever that meant.

At the age of fourteen I partied at the S/M club where my mother eventually worked, and my best friend dated the owner's son. I came to know, even before my mother was working there, how to flog someone, about suspension and piercing, and that certain older men enjoyed spanking young girls. Even before then, at the age of thirteen, I had my tongue, nipples, and navel pierced and knew which clubs in the East Village would let me in. My mother did not have to be a domme for me to know these things; growing up in New York City was enough. What I did learn from living with her was how to hide her employment.

She once took professional photos for the domme job and told me the photos would be in the back of newspapers where all of the other sex ads were. I imagined my friends flipping to the back of the *Village Voice* to look at the half-naked women (what most adolescents do for kicks) and seeing her suited up in leather, holding a mini crop. I was terrified that they would recognize her and call her a hooker. But what was I going to do at that point? I was already angry that my mother hadn't gotten her shit together, but I loved the fact that I could talk to her about anything and it wouldn't faze her. When friends' parents asked at the dinner table, "So, what does your mother do?" I just made up elaborate lies about my mother being a real estate agent (which she did dabble in) and hoped that the truth would never get out.

Not surprisingly, throughout all of this, I became my mother's confidant more than her daughter. In the morning, over coffee, my mother would go over her encounters with her clients in detail. I quickly learned the difference between submissive and dominant, since my mother made it a point to remind me she would never be a sub. She could never let someone tell her what to do, but: "Kick the shit out of some guy: Why not?"

It was creepy imagining that my mother was now working in a club I had hung out in, or that I had been high on ecstasy in one of the rooms where she tied people up. I squirmed when she told me about one client who liked to be peed on and another who liked to pick condoms out of the trash with his mouth. She would talk with disgust about these men, some of whom were married and had kids, were teachers or politicians, and would then get into how much I needed to use protection and condoms when I had sex. What a strange way to be taught sex ed. At the time, I didn't even understand fetishes. All I could imagine was my biology teacher being hog-tied and whipped by my mother.

When she ran the escort service out of her apartment in Inwood (I was living with my grandmother at the time), I learned a tremendous amount about sexual stereotypes and the dangers call girls faced. I saw pictures of the girls or my mother would describe them and they each fulfilled a very racialized and hypersexual woman. I realized men fetishized different ethnicities. My mother then called it "picking your flavor" and explained that each girl she employed had to be able to fulfill some kind of stereotype. They had to be the thin busty blonde or the caramel Latina with an accent but, as customers would often say, "not too ghetto."

I met some of the girls when they would stop over at the apartment while I was there. All of them were really sweet, some a little ditzy, and most were either going to college or trying to just get by. My mother also explained to me that each girl went out with a driver who had a pager. They would page the driver a certain number if everything was OK with the customer. If the driver didn't hear from them within five to ten minutes he was supposed to try to contact the girl or get into the building. This safety system was unfortunately too costly and eventually mom shut it down.

My mother explained that she was trying to run a business where the girls were being paid fairly and protected. She said her "being a feminist didn't work for sex work." The only way she could make money in the business was to exploit the girls and pay them less in order to pay the drivers, or cut the drivers out and offer them no safety. Both were out of the question for her and so the business ended.

After my grandmother passed away, I eventually had to move back in with my mom, still struggling to make ends meet. We fought constantly. I was experimenting with drugs but my mother always knew where I was, who I was with, and what I was doing. We had built a strange trust. I would probably never do anything more stigmatized than she had done, so I could tell her anything.

Seeing what my mother went through all those years—the late nights, the drinking to please customers, the frustrations of never making enough money to support me, and her hardened attitude toward life—lead me to choose against going into sex work. But as I went off to college on scholarship and jumped into sociology, gender studies, and sexuality studies, I began to make sense of mine and my mother's lives. I read Annie Sprinkle's *Post-Porn Modernist* and *Live Sex Acts* by Wendy Chapkis, and I began to understand that my mother was not alone and that what she had done for a living had a place in meaningful discussions. I learned that I did not have to be ashamed of her work. I began to find a community where I felt safe to share my stories with people who I thought could understand.

While I find power, control, and erotic beauty in the positive sex and sex worker communities, a part of me still wonders about those women out there who don't blog extensively about their customers and experiences, who didn't get to go to college and become an empowered sex worker. I'm thinking of the women out there like my mother, who did sex work to survive and did not really enjoy it, who would have rather been a ballet dancer or engineer or teacher.

The relationship I have with my mother is complicated, as you can imagine, and my memories are only pieces of a much larger story. My mother taught me to be critical of institutions but compassionate to individuals and their circumstances. I now keep a copy of the photo of my mother in the leather outfit that was printed in the *Village Voice*, framed in my living room. As complex as my feelings are about sex work, I will never feel ashamed about my mother's profession again.

SYD V. works with young adults around issues of gender, race, class, and sexuality through the use of social media, advocacy, teaching, and youth/adult partnerships to promote healthy, pleasurable sexual lives and social change. She is a photographer, writer, feminist, educator, activist, daughter, femme, lesbian, Latina, sister, and lover interested in youth-led research, photography, sexuality education, media, female empowerment, and all things that come from the ocean. Find her current work at Taintedlenzphotography.com.

SADIE LUNE is a multimedia artist, sex worker for over fifteen years, and pleasure activist. She has won awards for her films and performances, appeared in feature films and queer porn, exhibited explicit whore-positive work in venues from a former army barracks latrine to the SFMOMA, and shown her cervix internationally. She is currently coediting *WhoreLover* (forthcoming), an anthology of writing by the romantic partners of sex workers, with P. Crego. Sadie lives in Berlin with her baby.

CLIENTS

INTRODUCTION

Sarah Elspeth Patterson

This job would be great if it wasn't for the fucking customers.
                                        —Randal Graves, *Clerks*

Like any intimate encounter, the relationship between a sex worker and her client is a complicated and layered one. The stories in this chapter expose some truths about these relationships. Each piece brushes up against what's hard (pun very much intended) about human interactions. For the client, it may be a need for physical touch, a secret sexual desire, or an impulse to get off. In the case of the worker, the money usually comes first, and other desires may follow.

Negotiation plays a vital role. *$pread*'s editors created the regular column "Indecent Proposal" to provide a space for sex workers to answer the question, "What's the weirdest or funniest thing a client has ever asked you to do?" In "Bento Bitch," Miguel describes his evening with a client who paid him to eat sushi, while Audacia Ray's "Tiny Town" describes a client's highly structured and scripted giantess fantasy. As these stories illustrate, sometimes the negotiation itself can be enough to make the work feel fun.

Not every client is a benevolent or safe one, however. Because of the isolated, stigmatized, and often illegal nature of their work, many sex workers find themselves in risky situations. Dorothy Schwartz and Eliyanna Kaiser provide a practical breakdown of how safe sex practices and sex work may interact and sometimes conflict in "Healthy Hooker: Condoms 101," including advice for what to do if a client refuses to wear a condom. In "The Last Outcall," Fabulous describes her escape from a client who pushes her boundaries too far.

Expanding on the question of what it means to be a "good customer," Chanelle Gallant examines the relationships between Thai sex workers and their Western clients and boyfriends in "Empower: In Defense of Sex Tourism." Gallant dissects the ways in which racism, sexism, and colonial narratives shape Western assumptions, and shows that Thai sex workers understand their experiences better than well-meaning outsiders.

In "Cher John," Mirha-Soleil Ross celebrates how a sex worker can be both a caretaker and friend to a client. She reminds us that, while sex workers ultimately do it for the money, empathy plays a role. Exploring empathy from the perspective of a very devoted client, Jimmy Bob waxes poetic in "Haikus for Mistress Octavia."

A very different viewpoint is offered up in Kristie Alshaibi's "Honest John," an interview with Caveh Zahedi about his film *I Am A Sex Addict*. The interview explores the problems the filmmaker has with his family and relationships because of his addiction to soliciting street-based sex workers. Meanwhile, three sex workers grapple with the ethics of the worker/client relationship as they answer the question, "Would You Steal from a Client?"

Presenting a range of experiences, these stories are fascinating representations of what clients can mean to sex workers, and indeed, what sex workers mean to their clients.

SARAH ELSPETH PATTERSON, MD, is the cofounder and executive director of Persist Health Project, a New York City-based health organization that provides care coordination, health services, and workshops by and for folks involved in the sex trade, while educating the providers that serve us. Sarah worked at *$pread* from 2005 to 2007 as a staff writer and media columnist.

CHER JOHN (DEAR JOHN)

Mirha-Soleil Ross

ISSUE 2.3 (2006)

Alexandre, Camille, Abel, Sacha, Simon, Raoul, Jean-Pierre, François, Mathieu, Angelo, Kwan, Mohamed, Alain, Miguel, Gabriel, Rafael, Eduardo, Kori, Benoit, Thomas, Said, Gilles, Maurice, Albert, Réjean, Cédric, Carmine, Sylvain, Philippe, Carlos . . .

And of course I shouldn't forget Johhhhnnn!

How easy it is to stereotype millions of men when they are all referred to as John. Might as well call them Dick.

Sexist hypocrites cheating on their wives. Horny brutes willing to buy women's bodies. Ugly bogeymen in trench coats objectifying women.

In my book: a bunch of mostly nice guys whose invisibility is perhaps the political missing link to the obtainment of prostitutes' rights.

As prostitutes we too often focus on the few bad tricks: the abusive ones who sneak through our screening process, the jerks who set up appointments and never show up, the clumsy twits who squeeze our tits too hard, the ones with cheesy dicks and the foul drunks and the ones who purposely take more time than they paid for to come. Those make for vivid stories at dinner parties and at performance art events.

And feminism has had squat shit impact on these guys. All feminism ever did is make the sweetest of my clients feel guilty, and make me have to spend extra time playing political therapist, having to reassure them that no, they are not hurting my sense of self. That if I feel exploited at a hundred and fifty bucks an hour I need a serious reality check, and that yes, they should continue seeing me, 'cause otherwise I'll be stuck with only stinky assholes as clients. I don't know if it is because they stand in such extreme contrast to the way they are portrayed by feminists but there is something in my clients, in their tenderness and gestures toward me, that I find deeply moving.

It's in their voices when they finally get a hold of me on the phone. It's in their smiles when they open the door and invite me in. It's in the sparkles of light I see in their eyes when I say: "First I collect my money and then I tickle your nipples." It's in the way they tense their bodies and hold their breath when I very gently put my lips on those neglected areolas and start sucking on them. It's in their shivering skin when I slowly work my way up to kiss their tight necks. When I start rubbing my body against theirs, it's in these few seconds when it feels like we're suspended in time and they hold on and hold on and hold on as long as they can before finally allowing themselves to release decades of repressed desires. It's in their nervously shaking moist hands trying to caress me with the intentions of the best lovers. Then it's in their goose bumps and gluttony and giggling and growling and glowing and glory. It is also in less poetic moments when they say things like: "Those are beautiful tits!" while caressing my implants, which actually feel about as delicate as a pair of five pin bowling balls. For the most part, it is in their courage to see me, a transsexual woman, again and again, because yes, in this culture, it takes courage for a man to get so close, so intimate with an individual whom a large percentage of the population considers a freak.

My clients constantly remind me that with reclaiming prostitution as a fundamental and legitimate service comes responsibilities. I recently met Claudio, a very attractive, fit, thirty-eight-year-old Italian man, one who had a lovely penis—the kind I like—with enough foreskin to wrap all of next year's holiday season presents. Things were going quite well, we were both enjoying each other but he somehow seemed

Illustration by Molly Crabapple.

uncomfortable with his body. At one point he even interrupted our session to take a little break. He wanted to hold me in his arms and caress my hair, but while doing so, I noticed him examining his penis and looking quite perplexed. Just as I thought "Oh no, not another one who wants to know if I find it big enough!" he asked in the most innocent, childlike voice: "Am I circumcised? Because I really don't know."

Whether I am working with a 600-pound disabled man who can't reach his penis to masturbate or an intersex guy whose genitals are nothing like the ones you're used to dealing with, or simply the average Joe Blow who wants to start under the blankets 'cause he's too shy, the men I meet force me to be sensitive to a certain reality: that I am not dealing with objects here but with complex and vulnerable individuals who can be stricken by as many body image problems, self-concept issues, and fears of sexual inadequacy as anyone else.

Some of my clients are married men, but it becomes clear when speaking with them that they love their wives very much, enjoy their companionship and, in most cases, want to spend the rest of their lives with them. It's just that sexuality has become limited, lifeless, or is absent from the relationship. And every so often I meet a man whose dedication to his wife I find particularly commendable.

Anthony is one of them. He started seeing me years after his wife fell ill due to multiple sclerosis. Every time we'd get together, he would update me on her deteriorating condition and on his struggle trying to keep his family above water—working two jobs in order to afford a private nurse so that his wife wouldn't be locked up in a hospital room for the rest of her life. Last time I saw him he said she was completely incapacitated and no longer cognizant. He told me with tears in his eyes that he saw prostitutes because the idea of seriously dating any woman while his wife was still alive was emotionally unbearable. And *that*, I thought, brought true meaning to the word "commitment."

Ali is a man I have been seeing for years. He works for minimum wage at the coat check of a restaurant. He's been fighting for over a decade with the immigration system, spending thousands of dollars in legal fees trying to have his wife—of whom he speaks with so much love—join him here. When I found out how much he was earning an hour and about his costly ordeal with immigration, I felt concerned, so I told him that maybe he should reconsider spending money to see me. "Don't worry!" he insisted—rightfully offended— adding that it was all budgeted and that all his meager tips were set aside just to see me. "If I didn't spend a few minutes of joy with someone, anyone nice, every couple of months," he concluded abruptly, "I'd probably kill myself!"

Michael is a man I saw only once. He called me for an appointment and mentioned that he was sexually inexperienced, that he had been with very few women in his life, never with a transsexual, and that he felt very intimidated. It was a busy day, I was high on Jolt Cola, juggling prostitution with a million chores related to my "political" and "artistic" life, so I said in a sales-pitch tone, "I'll be right there to take good care of you." He was a tall, handsome sixty-year-old who spoke and moved with the grace and grounded serenity of James Earl Jones. Our rendezvous unfolded perfectly, so before we parted he said "Thank you!" which they always do, so I replied very mechanically, "You're welcome!" But he took my hand and held it over his heart; he gave me the sweetest "bisou" on the left cheek and said: "I mean thank you!" I could tell there was more to this "thank you" than simple gratitude for activating his vas deferens so I asked why. He told me that he had been with his wife for forty years, that she had died two years earlier, that he had never been with anyone other than her in all these years, and that he thought he'd never again feel at ease being intimate with someone, until he heard my French accent on an escort service line.

These are times when I feel like revolting against this system that is ready to condemn and even jail us for caressing, kissing, and holding each other. These are times when I rid myself of all the fears and anxieties I have about the long-term ramifications of being a prostitute, a social pariah. These are times when I feel like it's worth growing into an old, tired, bitter, dried-up whore. These are times when I feel like there was, indeed, a higher calling for me to sacrifice my personal reputation, comfort, safety, social status, and even my freedom for a greater good.

MIRHA-SOLEIL ROSS is an interdisciplinary artist, writer, translator, and social justice activist. She is widely known for her work in video, performance, and theater as well as for her critical contributions to transsexual and sex worker political movements and cultures. "Dear John" is taken from *Yapping Out Loud: Contagious Thoughts from an Unrepentant Whore* (Buddies in Bad Times Theatre 2004-2005 season, Toronto). She performs a powerful version of the text in her French-Métis mother tongue as part of *Les Criminelles*, Québec mainstream filmmaker Jean-Claude Lord's new documentary about sex worker rights.

MOLLY CRABAPPLE is an artist who has been called "equal parts Hieronymus Bosch, William S. Burroughs, and Cirque du Soleil" by *The Guardian*. She's covered hotel rooms with art-induced madness, drawn class warfare allegories on the walls of the world's most depraved nightclubs, and created art for *The Wall Street Journal* and Occupy Wall Street. Her published books include *Discordia*, *Devil in the Details*, and *Week in Hell*.

INDECENT PROPOSAL: BENTO BITCH

Miguel

ISSUE 2.4 (2007)

"Suck that red tuna like you'd suck my big, brown dick, bitch." Wait—did I really just compare my penis to a tuna roll? I wonder. Oh, the things a New York City boy will do to pay rent.

Of course, working as a fetish-focused pro-domme for years, I'd found myself in peculiar situations before. But this date surprised even me. Here I was in dirty jeans and beat-up work boots at the trendy Sushi Samba, spitting kinky demands involving seafood at my trembling client.

His name was Lucas and he was the ideal trick: submissive, reliable, loaded. After chatting online for weeks, I demanded he fly down from his native Toronto to bring to life his greatest fantasy: to stare at me while I ingest copious amounts of sushi.

I explained that, once in the city, he would find me standing on East 64th Street, somewhere between Madison and Third. "But how will I know it's you, my king?" he whimpered.

I had a simple solution, "Tape a piece of paper to your chest, and write B-I-T-C-H on it."

"But, no, I can't, I—" he cried. "Yes, bitch, you will."

That night Lucas did precisely as told. I greeted him by hurling a nasty loogie on his cheek and hailed us a cab downtown to Sushi Samba. I felt out of place among the restaurant's Park Avenue crowd, not just because of my ratty jeans and oversized football jersey, but because of the dark sunglasses I refused to remove even past midnight. (Worried I might run into an acquaintance, I always insist on shades.)

Once seated, Lucas ordered nearly everything on the menu, from yellowtail to lobster tempura. Five plates arrived and he began diligently mixing soy sauce and wasabi, preparing each morsel for me to devour. And devour I did. The more raw fish I brought to my purple lips, the hornier he got. "I'm so hard, Papi," he cooed.

After minutes of teasing him, I gave him what he really wanted: a taste fresh off his master's tongue. I took a big piece and inserted it into my mouth. Without masticating, I held onto the sushi with the chopsticks for a moment, removed it and tossed it onto his barren plate.

"Eat it, Pussy!" I ordered. He whimpered and fidgeted. I repeated, "Eat it, Puto!" His eyes watered. He looked scared. "Put it in your mouth, chew, and swallow, cunt." He was in heaven. I watched, delighted, as he touched the tuna to his quivering lip, moaned, and rolled his eyes to the back of his head.

I repeated this scenario throughout the night with only slight variation. We finished dinner and I received a hefty sum for my time. I thought to myself, was dinner that much of a turn on? The monstrous bulge in his slacks showed me it was.

Our trysts continued for nearly two years before the spark sadly died. In those years, however, I visited the finest Japanese dining rooms in Manhattan, skillfully eroticizing everything from mackerel sashimi to a BBQ Chilean sea bass roll. And although I now chuckle to myself every time I think back on how aroused Lucas got by our scene, I never told him that the funnier thing was that it always got me hard too.

MIGUEL is a New Yorker with a penchant for the kinkier, more off-the-beaten-path side of sex work.

EMPOWER:
IN DEFENSE OF SEX TOURISM

Chanelle Gallant

ISSUE 4.2 (2008)

It's Friday night and I'm sitting in a noisy dance bar in the northern Thai city of Chiang Mai with three local sex workers. Hip-hop pounds out of the speakers. The bar is filled with mostly Western tourists and a few Thai folks. My three friends are students in the English class I've been teaching for Empower, a national sex workers' support organization. We drink our whiskey and sodas, yell over the music, dance to the latest Rihanna hit, and scope the crowd. Sex workers frequently work in regular bars and tonight my friends may or may not be working, depending on whether they see any clients they find desirable. So I ask P. if she thinks anyone at the bar is cute. *Yes actually!* she says. Smiling, she points to three young English men, dancing in a manner I can only call erratic. They're all drunk and dancing with their sunglasses on. *Indoors.* I look at her incredulously.

"*Really?*"

"Yes!" She nods enthusiastically.

"*Those guys?!*"

"Mmhmm!"

Another woman in our group shakes her head and tells me she doesn't like the young men. She prefers men with white hair and points to an older guy, in his late 60s, sitting with a pretty young Thai (working) woman. She thinks they're more handsome *and* better clients. You mean one of those guys that everyone thinks is a horrible sleaze for hooking up with twenty-somethings? Yep! That's the one she's referring to!

I'm stunned and even more amazed by my own assumptions: where exactly did I get the idea that Thai sex workers must dislike or resent foreign clients?

Sex Tourism

I came to Thailand packing 250 condoms donated by Toronto sex shop Good For Her and sex work agency Maggie's, in full support of Thai sex workers and thrilled to be working with them. But when late one night I saw a white guy with a buzz-cut wearing a sports jersey bearing the number sixty-nine that read "Sex Tourist," I felt ambivalence. Even though they are a minority compared to Thai clients, foreign clients are one of the most controversial elements of the industry, disdained by Thais and Westerners alike.

Without exception, every non-sex worker I've met in Thailand assumes the worst about "sex-pats." Not a day has passed where I don't hear a disparaging comment about the men we see daily, walking around hand in hand with their pretty new Thai girlfriends. They're seen as sleazy, misogynistic losers, "fat, old white guys" who aren't able to "get a woman" at home so come to Thailand to use the advantage of their relative wealth to exploit poorer Thai women.

But this isn't how they are seen by the women *here*, many of whom have boyfriends they met via sex work. They painted me a much more complicated (but also simpler) story about foreign clients. Just like Western sex workers, the distinction they draw isn't between foreign and Thai clients (and the vast majority of clients are Thai) but between good and bad clients.

So what gives? How have foreign clients come to be perceived as jerks out to exploit a poorer nation's sex workers? In working with Empower, I came to see how stereotypes about sex work, racism, and fat-phobia have blinded many Westerners from seeing a realistic picture of the relationships between foreign clients and local working women.

The "Poor Victimized" Thai Woman

Every story about the supposed exploitation of Thai women starts with the Western assumption that "Asian" women are submissive. Liz Cameron, one of the organizers in the Chiang Mai Empower office, summed it up: "It's racism underlying the mistaken idea that sex tourists exploit Thai sex workers. Westerners think that customers get an easy time with Thai women because they are so poor or so desperate that they can't set boundaries. But really, underlying this, there is also the belief that Thai women are submissive and simply don't know how to be strong and capable."

Sex workers everywhere are assumed to have reluctantly entered the industry. In Thailand, this is compounded by the racism that allows a Westerner to envision Thai women as submissive and pliant. Occasionally more educated (non-sex working) Westerners compare the Thai sex work industry unfavorably to Amsterdam. Because *there*, they assure me, women are safer (read: smart and capable enough to take care of themselves). But these same Westerners don't know a thing about the industry in Thailand and are shocked to learn that sex workers here frequently refuse clients, are often out to their families, and *of course* will not have unprotected sex on request. Even when Westerners are trying to be supportive, they often reveal outrageously racist assumptions. Like the middle-aged French woman who said to me, "*Ze Thai women, zey are very clever, even ze prostitutes.*"

It doesn't help that the only English books published by or about Thai sex-working women portray them as victims. Books like *Miss Bangkok* or *My Name Lon* allow the Western reader to voyeuristically peak inside the life of an unhappy sex worker and confirm their established prejudices—that sex work is awful and no one does it voluntarily. Just like anywhere, there are sex workers in Thailand who are sick of their jobs, women and men who want to do something else but stay because the money is great and they have a family to support. Of course, this doesn't necessarily make it any different from driving a taxi or nursing the sick. There are also women like Thanta (aka Ping Pong), a worker-owner at the collectively owned "Can Do" Experitainment Bar, who told me "I did twenty-one jobs before this one, so I know it's the right one for me. Even if I move onto something else, it will always be my hobby." Like most workers I've met, Thanta uses her real name with clients and is completely out about her work. "Why not? We're confident about what we do so there's no reason not to be open." But Thanta's story doesn't fit the stereotype, so you won't hear it in the mainstream media.

Som, who manages the Bangkok office, puts it simply: "Foreign clients aren't all good or all bad. We welcome them if they are good clients. Bad ones, we don't want." By bad clients, she means those who are cheap, who steal from workers, who use date-rape drugs, or who want sex all night long. When I asked Lek, another worker-owner at "Can Do," what message she wanted to send to North American sex workers, she said, "Send us your customers!" On the second floor of the "Can Do" Bar, full of offices and classrooms, they have a male mannequin they call The Perfect Customer. Mr. Perfect sports an Empower T-shirt, a full wallet, and a single red rose. He packs his own condoms and is dressed sharply. In short: supportive of sex worker rights, pays well, is presentable and a little bit romantic. What more could a working girl ask for?

Customer/Funder/Boyfriend

In fact, many women long for a customer who becomes a boyfriend/long-term financial supporter, a man with whom she can pursue a relationship that provides both love and financial support. If she's lucky, a woman won't have to work too many years before she finds one. She may keep working or not, depending on the level of support she receives, her financial needs, and her interest in the business. The tourist biz is fickle and low season can be hard on a woman who is raising kids (the majority of sex workers have kids and, according to Empower, are supporting on average of five to eight family members including their parents). Regular support from a boyfriend can ease that burden.

Another stereotype Westerners often have of Thai sex workers is that they all want to get out of Thailand for a "better life" in the West. In fact, I met few who wanted to relocate permanently. Rather, if a woman finds the right guy to settle down with, she may pursue a dream to open a small business not far from her family with the money invested by her boyfriend.[1]

I met one such couple in Chiang Mai. Together they'd opened up a little flower shop outside of the city that was doing quite well. She managed it year-round and he visited a few times a year. He happened to be in town the night I joined in for the weekly outreach in the city's bars. He came with us, sitting alongside us all on the truck ride into the neighborhood with the highest concentration of sex work bars, praising his girlfriend for her work with Empower. "She's always helping people!" he beamed. In fact, relationships between Western men and Thai women that began through sex work are some of happiest relationships I've seen. Not all, of course, but they serve as a reminder that the two people involved in a sex work relationship are perfectly capable of figuring out an arrangement that serves them both well.

FAT Is Still a Four-Letter Word

"Oh, but I just couldn't . . . with *him*." Just about every sex worker has heard that one, and it brings us to some of the more visceral reasons for opposing sex tourism: Non-sexworking Westerners think the clients are gross. They whisper about how wrong it is to see older, fat white men with beautiful, young, slender Thai women. It offends their sense of the order of the universe. They don't deserve it—they're not

1. In the 2007 Survey of Sexual and Reproductive Health of Sex Workers in Thailand, only 3.4 percent of women surveyed would like to live overseas after leaving sex work. 67 percent said they'd like to start a small business. The survey can be downloaded for free at www.ipsr.mahidol.ac.th under "Publications."

beautiful enough. Fatness and age are *always* mentioned as the qualities that make the clients unacceptable. The two are not evenly matched, according to Western standards.

Empower recently released a Bad Girls Dictionary where they take the reins over the language that has long been used to define and marginalize them. In it, they have an entry for the word Fat: "Many fat old men are very respectful, kind, entertaining, generous, and polite customers. We don't discriminate." Accepting and desiring a wide variety of bodies is a skill that sex workers across the world bring to their jobs.

Hiring a Sex Worker Is Like Sunning on the Beach

What is a "sex tourist?" Am I a "massage tourist" because I've gotten about half a dozen Thai massages while I've been here? The women of Empower reject the division between so called sex tourists and regular tourists, describing sex tourism as "when tourists visit our workplace at nighttime, though they may visit other places, like temples and palaces, during the day time" and "a form of tourism that creates jobs for many of us." So-called sex tourists come to Thailand for the same reasons that non-sex tourists do: a tropical country, wonderful people, delicious food. Non-Thai folk want to learn about another culture, roast on a beach while it's minus five in Munich, go snorkeling, learn how to cook Thai food, or get a Thai massage. In short, they want things they can't get at home—either because they don't exist or are too expensive.

The same goes with so-called sex tourists. They want to do all of the above *and* spend time with a sex worker who offers services that are more abundant and affordable than those in the West. For example, workers here often offer a service called "long time." It means she is offering to be your companion from anywhere from overnight to a few months. If you'd like, she (or he) will show you around the city, take you to the major tourist destinations, translate, and introduce you to Thai life and food. Essentially, be a fun and expert guide, a friend as well as a sexual companion. What's not to love?

The cost varies but—as Lek put it—"whatever it is, it's less than a North American sex worker makes." So Thailand offers services not readily available at home at prices a middle-class guy might be able to afford. I interviewed one gay male client, a Thai-American painter in his late twenties who told me that he found Thai sex workers more fun, less into drugs, and of course, more affordable—an important factor for a working artist. But to the majority of folks I've spoken with, enjoying a beach side bungalow for seven dollars a day in December is perfectly acceptable, but spending time with a Thai sex worker is not.

We Are All Customers

Global tourism is complicated. It is made possible by the massive wealth disparities between the global north and south—and it is precisely through the theft of the South's resources that the north is wealthy. Some see it as a matter of rich people coming to culturally "consume" another culture and in the process turn a distinct culture, economy, and environment into a cultural Disneyland. On the other hand, many people I meet in Thailand wish more of us would come—and bring our money with us.

I'm not arguing that tourism is politically neutral—just that "sex tourism" is subject to the same critiques as tourism in general. Everyone in the tourist industry wants *good* customers. Some tourists are considerate and thoughtful of the country they are visiting. Some are asshole yobs with imperialist attitudes. While sex tourists are no better than non-sex tourists, they aren't any worse either. It's our responsibility to ensure we learn how to be good customers and make thoughtful choices about how our visit is going to impact the country (e.g. environmental impact, animal rights, observing religious and cultural mores).

Trafficking! Coercion! Child Abuse!

In the West, we're regularly inundated with horror stories about women being tricked or sold by their families to human traffickers, made into what are salaciously referred to as "sex slaves." The problem is that in general, Western media ignores the difference between a migrant worker and a trafficked person—and it's easy to do so when this story lines up so nicely with the popular belief that no one really chooses sex work. Just because a woman is working without documents does not mean she was tricked or forced into working.

If women in Thailand were being coerced into working, you wouldn't see hundreds of them heading to and from work on the bus, chatting with friends on their cells, munching on green mango. Coerced means "locked-in." It means unable to leave of your own volition. According to Empower, there have been "locked-in" brothels in Thailand, but most of them disappeared in the late nineties after new legislation was introduced that substantially reduced penalties against adult prostitution (a thirty-dollar fine and no jail time. In Bangkok, littering will net you a heavier fine) but heavily penalized hiring underage or undocumented workers. Once the owners of regular brothels were no longer willing to pay bribes to police (why, when fines are a pittance?), the police switched to extorting those with undocumented or underage workers. Suddenly it was no longer economically advantageous to hire the workers normally used in locked-in brothels—trafficked and migrant women—and the practice all but stopped.

And as for the grisly stories about girls sold by their families? Here's what Som and Tuk, both Bangkok sex workers with years of experience, had to say: "Yes, twenty to thirty years ago, girls were pressured by their families to come to Bangkok to work and make money for the family. But now, no. Now girls decide for themselves if they want to work. No one can control you. Before girls didn't know [anything about sex work], they were scared. Now they come to Bangkok and they've already had a boyfriend, they have been to school and studied. They decide for themselves."

Of course, when trafficking does happen, it's an atrocious human rights violation. Since 2001 though, the United States has pushed for trafficking to be treated as a crime and not a human rights issue, which means overlooking issues related to the rights to travel and to work safely. Even the UN's anti-trafficking protocols make no distinction between voluntary cross-border migration for sex work and situations where force or coercion are employed. Incredibly, consent to engage in sex work is described as "irrelevant,"[2] meaning that resources are wasted on search and rescue raids on voluntary sex workers.

With increased policing comes increased risk. In April of this year, fifty-four Burmese people were found suffocated to death in the back of a truck crossing the Thai border. According to one Empower source, "All the trafficking border control stuff is doing is making it more dangerous. People used to come across the border in open trucks but now they keep them closed to avoid detection. People used a footpath that's now being patrolled, so instead they have to use landmine fields. And as for deporting women to Burma? For fuck's sake thanks for all your help! Everyone is busy looking for imaginary victims because it's tied to aid money."

By the Thai government's own figures, they "rescued" 900 workers from forced labor situations last year. But looking more closely at the figures, 800 were from one shrimp factory and fifty-eight women were from two karaoke bars. They spent thirteen million baht (over $400,000) to send 900 people to be locked up in "rehabilitation centers" or deport them back to dangerous situations. Empower helps 5,000 to 10,000 women per year and no one gets locked up or deported in exchange.

A more accurate picture of the situation in Thailand is provided by the 2007 Survey of Sexual and Reproductive Health of Sex Workers in Thailand, conducted in part by Service Workers in Groups (SWING), a sex work organization that works with male and transgendered workers primarily. In their report, they found that the average sex worker is twenty-eight and entered the sex industry at twenty-three, typi-

2. Janice G. Raymond. Guide to the New UN Trafficking Protocol, 2001.

cally after a marriage broke down and she suddenly became responsible for providing an income.

This confirms what Empower reports about the sexual abuse of children—that it is happening but well outside the sex work industry in Thailand. (I spoke to an NGO worker in Cambodia who confirmed that this "trade" has moved to Cambodia.) And please, let's distinguish between children and the adult Thai women that Westerners often perceive as minors. One woman told me a story about two Italian journalists at the "Can Do" bar who guessed two workers ages as sixteen and seventeen. Everyone had a good laugh—they were twenty-four and twenty-six.

Sex workers should not have to constantly defend against assumptions of trafficking and child exploitation—these are issues affecting many industries but only the sex industry is relentlessly and inaccurately perceived as a major offender. With regard to the concerns that Western sex workers have for the safety and well-being of sex workers in Thailand, the message I heard over and over was this: *"Thanks for your concern, but we're all right!"*

Thai sex workers do not need our help—as women, as Thai people, or as sex workers—but they could do with our solidarity. So if one of your (good) clients is heading to Bangkok for business, don't hesitate to suggest he pack a phrasebook, a wallet full of baht, and some condoms and head over to Patpong or Pattaya beach to enjoy the company of one of Thailand's lovely and friendly sex workers. He just might end up a flower shop owner.

CHANELLE GALLANT is a white, working-class, queer femme-inist activist, writer, and educator. Her jam is lifting up the leadership of those most directly impacted in queer and sex working communities. She is the cofounder and editor of the prison abolition site Everydayabolition.com.

HAIKUS FOR MISTRESS OCTAVIA

Jimmy Bob

ISSUE 3.3 (2007)

A chance to serve Her:
"Take earrings to Tiffany's."
Silent ecstasy.

No playtime this week.
Pretend to be indifferent.
It does not fool Her.

Wife: "Be my partner!"
Mistress: "On your knees, loser!"
Slave: "I'm in deep shit!"

Interrogation.
Will She accept my answers?
She pries open souls.

Naked and prostrate,
I rely on Her kindness.
Her tortures are sweet.

Scarlet, grim dungeon.
Shackles and sharp playthings.
Her smile; my cold sweat.

JIMMY BOB wrote "Haikus for Mistress Octavia," which was published in *$pread*, Issue 3.3.

HONEST JOHN:
AN INTERVIEW WITH CAVEH ZAHEDI

Kristie Alshaibi

ISSUE 1.3 (2005)

I recently saw an interview in which a popular epic filmmaker stated that a good film is one that you continue to discuss at length after walking out of the theater. Judging by that criterion, Caveh Zahedi's newest movie, *I Am a Sex Addict*, is truly great. I left the theater feeling uneasy and agitated, and was unable to pinpoint the reason for this reaction until much later.

As a sex worker, my immediate desire upon watching this film was to do what I consider a large part of my job: to help Zahedi gain some acceptance of his own sexual fantasies. It's an incurable instinct that stems from more than five years of having sex with, and hopefully helping, many shy, shamed, and guilt-ridden men. Caveh's self-deprecating humor and conflicted sexual psyche unexpectedly brought out the super-whore in me, in a context to which I was previously unaccustomed. I suddenly felt a surprising urge to impose my own brand of carnal openness on a person who seemed to be very willfully turning away from it. Suddenly I began to see myself as less of a healer and more of a sexual fascist. It was unsettling.

The movie is a combination of video diary, documentary and re-enactment of real events. This true-to-life narrative is propelled by Caveh's persistent attempt to rid himself of his obsession with prostitutes. It is structured by a number of strategies to "get it out of his system," from masturbation, to talking to prostitutes, to acting out his darkest fantasy. It all begins with a French prostitute who looks just like his now-ex-wife Caroline (both played by French porn star Rebecca Lord). From there he engages in a habit that he just can't seem to break: cruising hookers and occasionally paying for sex. What he believes to be a harmless fetish becomes a real problem as the acts, and his unrelenting honesty about them, begin damaging his romantic relationships along the way. His first two marriages end in divorce, due in part to his need for extramarital explorations.

Caveh effectively conveys the thrill of merely approaching a woman and asking her, "Will you suck me?" Every woman in the movie responds with a performance of slapstick, simulated fellatio, except for actress Emily Morse, who plays Caveh's girlfriend Christa. She is shown voicing her objection to this act in the movie's self-reflexive parallel narrative about the process of making the film, which is a common aspect of Caveh's work. He often documents much of what really unfolds during the course of creation and almost seems to be attempting to allow the movie to tell its own story, to direct itself. This lets the viewer in on fascinating details, like the remarkable parallel lives of the actors and their real life counterparts. For example, Rebecca Lord, who is a makeup artist in the movie (while playing the role of wife), is, in actuality, not only a porn star but also an escort and makeup artist.

Caveh Zahedi is what I refer to as an exhibitionist soothsayer. He can't help but expose his honesty to anyone who cares to pay attention. His films on the whole are intimate, confessional dialogues with the voyeur. One effect of this is that Caveh's own revelations may incidentally open the possibility of catharsis in his viewers. It's an admirable pursuit in a culture full of shame and guilt.

I met Caveh at the Tribeca Film Festival where his movie recently premiered, and he later agreed to do an interview for $pread.

KRISTIE: When you spoke at the Tribeca Film Festival you mentioned that you began working on *I Am a Sex Addict* more than ten years ago. Can you tell me a little more about that process, and when you got the idea to make this movie?

CAVEH: I got the idea for the film the night that I went to my first Sex Addicts Anonymous (SAA) meeting. I was blown away by the honesty and vulnerability of the other men in the room, and realized that I had never in my life heard men talking openly and honestly about their sexual problems before. I immediately realized the healing potential of making such a film, and decided that I wanted to do for other men what these men had done for me.

KRISTIE: What do you think makes your "prostitute fetish," as you so appropriately named it, an addiction rather than just a misunderstood hobby?

CAVEH: SAA defines an addiction as not being able to stop doing something that you don't want to do. A hobby is something one wants to do. As long as one isn't trying to stop and finding that one can't stop, then it's not an addiction. If you can stop smoking when you decide to, you're not addicted. If you're trying to quit, but find yourself unable to stop, then you're addicted.

KRISTIE: I noticed in the movie that you solicited mostly street prostitutes and went to massage parlors. Did you ever try calling an escort? If not, was it for economic reasons, or did you just prefer something in particular about picking a girl up off the street?

CAVEH: I did have sex with escorts, but escorts were typically much more expensive. Also, a lot of the acting-out ritual involved cruising, which doesn't really happen when you call an escort service. Typically, I would go cruising, just to experience the rush of talking to them, with no intention of actually having sex. And then occasionally, my desire would get the better of me, and I would find myself giving in to the temptation, even though I hadn't planned to do that.

KRISTIE: Your parents are from Iran, correct? Has your ethnic background had any effect on your own sexuality?

CAVEH: My parents are from Iran, correct. I think my ethnic background has had a definite effect on my sexuality. First of all, Iranian culture is extremely puritanical sexually, and I definitely inherited that sense of shame and repression. Secondly, being an ethnic minority (as an Iranian American) is hard sexually, because one always feels marginal to the culture's notions of what is sexually attractive. For me, the result was a compounding of sexual shame and a feeling of sexual inadequacy.

KRISTIE: As a sex worker I've always been asked the question, "Does your family know what you do?" So let me ask you a similar question. I've seen two of your movies so far (this one and *In the Bathtub of the World*). They are extremely personal and even confessional. Do members of your family watch them? If so what kinds of reactions do you get from them?

CAVEH: Well, most of my family members have seen enough of my work to know that they don't really want to see any more. I think it's disturbing for them, and they'd rather not think about it. My youngest half-sister is a big fan, though. She likes all my movies a lot. Still, it's embarrassing for me to have her see them.

KRISTIE: In the movie you list a number of strategies for "getting it out of your system" ("it" being your preoccupation with prostitutes). I noticed you never mentioned role-playing. Did you ever ask your partner to pretend to be a prostitute?

CAVEH: That's a very good question. There was a scene in the film that involved role-playing that got cut out, for pacing reasons. But yes, I did try that as a strategy. It never worked for me because I was much too shy and felt much too guilty to be able to role-play very effectively. The truth is I still have tremendous shame about my sexual desires, and role-playing is something that requires a certain amount of courage and self-acceptance. I have courage, but I lack the requisite self-acceptance.

Movie still by Caveh Zahedi.

KRISTIE: Are you still tempted to solicit prostitutes? Is the desire still as strong? Have you ever "slipped?" Do you still go to meetings for sex addicts?

CAVEH: I do still get tempted to solicit prostitutes, but only rarely, and less and less often. Basically, I get tempted when I'm extremely angry or upset. And for a variety of reasons, I seem to get less angry and upset than I used to, so the desire is not as strong as it used to be. I did "slip" several times after I started going to meetings, but I haven't slipped in about eight years. And no, I no longer go to sex addicts anonymous meetings. I went for several years, and found going extremely helpful, but at a certain point, it became a case of diminishing returns.

KRISTIE: At the Tribeca screening someone asked you about your current opinion of monogamy, given that you used to view it as a form of ownership. You said that you now believe in it. You also said something to the effect that other people may have non-monogamous relationships, and that's fine, but that your wife isn't into it. If your wife were into it, would you be as well? Or do you find that monogamy personally suits you better than alternative types of relationships?

CAVEH: I have nothing against non-monogamy morally speaking, but for me it never worked very well in practice. I personally find that the deep intimacy required to make a relationship work is severely compromised by the incredibly primal feelings of abandonment that come up whenever one person becomes sexually involved with a third party. Relationships are so much about trust, and trust is incredibly difficult to build. So, for me, why jeopardize something as delicate and fragile as trust? I've never met anyone evolved enough to be truly happy and intimate in a non-monogamous relationship, and I'm certainly not that person. But if someone were that evolved, I think that would be ideal. I used to be an idealist, and believed I could become that person, but as I've gotten older, I've gotten to know my own limitations, and this is one of them.

If my wife was into non-monogamous relationships, I

suppose I might give it another try, but I would be suspicious of her reasons. I suspect that a lot of interest in non-monogamous relationships is the result of dissatisfaction in one's primary relationship, and that getting involved sexually with other people is inherently destabilizing to one's primary relationship. I think the solution is to look deeper into the roots of one's dissatisfaction rather than to look outside the relationship for fulfillment.

KRISTIE: And finally, what are some the most interesting or unexpected reactions you've gotten to this movie?

CAVEH: At Tribeca, all of the janitors and ticket-takers and popcorn-makers snuck into the screening and wanted to shake my hand afterward. They were visibly sincerely touched. I was surprised that people who would never relate to any of my other movies (which are all decidedly on the artsy side) were so profoundly enthusiastic about this one. I think there's a huge thirst among men for this part of themselves to be given a voice, free from the shame-based moralistic ideologies which have made them feel guilty for having normal sexual desires. Our culture has a false notion of what is "normal," and a lot of suffering ensues from that. I think people really appreciate it when someone speaks out against the rampant dishonesty in our culture and tells it like it is.

KRISTIE ALSHAIBI has participated in many illicit occupations, including running a BDSM studio, escorting, and organizing the Z Film Festival in Chicago. She owns the production company Artvamp, LLC. Kristie's alter ego, Echo Transgression, appeared on MTV's "Sex2K" and is also the central character of her film *Other People's Mirrors*. Kristie also produces her husband Usama's films, including the feature-length movie *Profane*. Her photography is published on Nerve.com. She now lives in Boulder, Colorado.

HOT TOPIC: WOULD YOU STEAL FROM A CLIENT?

Moxy, Violine Verseau, and Jessica

ISSUE 4.4 (2009)

As a former klepto, the decision of whether or not to steal from a client has been quite the predicament for me. A few years ago, before my life as a whore began, I had a friend who lived by the motto, "Do only one illegal act at a time." I thought this theory was brilliant, but years later I found myself rummaging through Jerome's jewelry box, which allegedly belonged to his ex, and snagged the sweetest pair of earrings. Now these hooker hoops are my good luck charm. I wear them every time I turn a trick, and Jerome never even noticed.

Being a righteous whore is a constant aspiration of mine, and I'd hate to taint my name before it's truly made. After all, I love what I do, and I think stealing from tricks is unethical. I want clients to trust me and keep their fantasies coming, not give them a reason to turn away. I detest and reject "hand job handouts" for johns, and I'd be a complete hypocrite to implement a five-finger discount for myself.

I don't think I'll steal from a client again, but I admit I quite enjoyed the rush of dirty luxury.

—*Moxy, New York, NY*

It was Hanukkah, and Dave had just cooked us a meal of lat-kes and eggplant parmesan. No cash appeared on the immac-ulate glass coffee table, and indeed no money was spoken of. This was a longtime, if prodigal, client, so I dropped a diplomatic hint:

"Dave, why did I bring the sexy Santa costume over?"

"Yeah, why did you bring the sexy Santa costume over?"

"Because you wanted a session, and I know how you like your costumes."

"Oh, I told you I wanted a session? I'm sorry. I really just wanted to get together and reconnect . . . Why don't you give me an energy healing? I don't want to pay for IT any more."

I wanted to heal the manipulative, pitiful hole in his ethics with grand theft auto of his Lexus. But I don't drive, so I ran reiki on him in a pristinely slutty Santa suit and watched HDTV in his Twin Peaks condo for six straight hours until he saw fit to drive me back to Oakland. En route, I demanded that he stop at an ATM and take out everything he had.

". . . for my time."

He withdrew $200. "That's all I've got."

"Can you write me a check for another hundred, at least?"

"I won't have that 'til the middle of January."

I could have stolen from Dave that night. But I didn't, even though I felt entitled, even though I knew where the valuable things were, even though I saw the painting he had bought as a gift for me hanging in his mudroom. Not because of karma—shit, my time was worth his money—but because I didn't want to steal from myself.

—*Violine Verseau, Oakland, CA*

Kaylani was the first dancer I knew to outright steal from a customer. She found the resident alcoholic, grabbed him by the shoulders and shoved him off the wagon by plying him with drinks. After a few hours, she brought his debit card to the bar, took out $500, got dressed, and left.

He found out after waiting for her in the VIP for an hour.

With that as a reference point, stealing from customers is really not my style (nor is taking advantage of alcoholics). It's not so much that I can't imagine how it would happen—customers frequently trust me with their credit and debit cards. But I could never take advantage of an overly trusting schmoe. I'd feel guilty; it would be letting myself down.

However, there are the customers who are such misogynistic douchebags that doing them dirty would not eat away at my conscience. If I wouldn't feel bad about charging them extra for a lap dance, or lying about the existence of a two-for-one, could I take it any further?

Nah. In the end, ganking their cards or their cash would only make me feel like I stooped to their level. I have to retain my sense of self, and winding up with something that wasn't really mine would be a very quick way to lose it.

—*Jessica, Tinseltown Tease*

INDECENT PROPOSAL: TINY TOWN

Audacia Ray

ISSUE 2.3 (2006)

When I was first trying to find my place in the sex industry, a girl I knew told me all about a client of hers who had a giantess fetish and was always looking for bespectacled girls like myself.

Peter lived on the Upper East Side of Manhattan—a neighborhood where, before I became a sex worker, I only ventured to when the desire to visit museums struck me. The area's inhabitants seem to be neatly divided into little old purple-haired ladies and their minute dogs, families with more money than anyone should rightfully have, and quirky, rich singletons like Peter. When my friend told me about Peter's fetish I thought I understood. He liked big women—not fat ones, but giant ones, women who could crush cities with their heels.

On my visit to Peter's apartment, I'd been told that I'd be paid handsomely, fed dinner, and allowed to keep the outfit Peter provided. The man was quite a fan of the color brown, and when I arrived he ushered me from his hallway of extravagant woodwork into a cool, beige marble bathroom where a schoolmarm-ish outfit was laid out. Brown pumps, nude hose, brown tweed skirt, brown sweater. He was really excited about my glasses and even more excited when I told him how strong my prescription is.

Also laid out in the bathroom was a script. I flipped through the three pages briefly so I could get a general idea of what

Illustration by Fly.

he wanted and then emerged from the bathroom. Peter's eyes sparkled at me, and he took me by the hand and led me into the living room, where he had painstakingly set up an entire little city with three-inch-high buildings, tiny people, tiny trees, and tiny cars—all to scale, naturally. He hurried to the other side of the room, crouched down and pressed his cheek to the floor.

"Would you like to get comfortable?" I asked—universal escort-speak for "Please get naked now."

"I am comfortable," he said, not lifting his cheek from the floor. With that, I understood that it was time to start the scene.

I was to play a librarian who had awoken to find herself a giantess and was very angry about it. Actually, there was a nuanced bit to the acting—I was to be confused first, then angry at my situation, taking that anger out on the city by smashing it. The smashing of the library was the climax—a kind of liberation from books and knowledge. There's nothing like being paid to make a mess and destroy things, and I got good and carried away, decadently grinding the entire city to dust. When I finally got to the library, I shook my fist at the sky and ad-libbed, "Why? Whhhhhyyyy?"

Proud of myself for my creativity, I looked to my benefactor, who seemed as if he was going to cry. He sat up on his heels and said softly, "You should be more careful next time. The script is very important."

AUDACIA RAY is the founder and executive director of the Red Umbrella Project (RedUP), a peer-led organization in New York that amplifies the voices of people in the sex trades through media, storytelling, and advocacy programs. At RedUP, she publishes the literary journal Prose & Lore: Memoir Stories About Sex Work and she has taught media strategy workshops for sex workers in New York, San Francisco, Las Vegas, and London. She is the author of Naked on the Internet: Hookups, Downloads, and Cashing in On Internet Sexploration and has contributed to many anthologies. She joined the $pread staff in 2004 and was an executive editor from 2005 to 2008.

FLY has been a Lower East Side squatter since the late 80s. She is a painter and commix artist, illustrator, punk musician, sometimes muralist, and teacher. A collection of her zines and comics, *CHRON!IC!RIOTS!PA!SM!*, was published in 1998 by Autonomedia. *PEOPS*, a collection of 196 portraits and stories, was published in 2003 by Soft Skull Press. Fly was a recipient of a 2013 Acker Award for Excellence Within the Avant-Garde. Fly is currently working on a multi-media project called *UnReal Estate; a Late Twentieth Century History of Squatting in the Lower East Side*.

HEALTHY HOOKER: CONDOMS 101

Eliyanna Kaiser and Dorothy Schwartz

ISSUE 2.4 (2007)

Condoms are the only form of protection that, when used properly, stop the transmission of sexually transmitted infections (STIs) like HIV as well as preventing pregnancy. But as simple as they seem, there are a lot of things people don't know about condoms. And sex workers who have sexual contact with their clients need to be verifiable experts on condom use!

Choosing the Right Condom (and Lube)

If you don't have an allergy, latex condoms are the best choice for both protection and convenience. Using lube along with your condoms is a good idea—they prevent breakage (more about that later) and increase comfort during a session.

Remember you can only use water-based lubricants with latex. Although some condoms come prelubricated, this wetness can run out quickly. If you don't have lube on hand, you have to stop right away and put on a new one so it won't dry out and break. Disrupting your session is likely to frustrate your client—and you, because then he'll take longer!

Lots of people have latex allergies. So even if you're not allergic, it's important to carry an alternative in case your client is. One alternative is polyurethane, which is more durable than latex anyway. The only drawback is that these condoms are pricy. Male and female polyurethane condoms can be used with either water-based or oil-based lubricants like Vaseline or baby oil.

In general, stay away from lambskin condoms. They are porous, and while they are effective at pregnancy prevention, they are much less effective against sexually transmitted infections.

Flavored condoms are great for oral sex, but don't use them for vaginal or anal sex—they aren't built to last like non-flavored condoms.

Sometimes a more snug or larger fit is required, so make sure you have a variety of sizes on hand. A very loose condom can slip off and a very tight one can break. If a regular client is picky about condom size, tell him to shop for a custom fit at a store like this one: www.condomania.com/TheyFit/.

Avoid condoms that are packaged with Nonoxynol-9. It was originally released on the market as a spermicide, but has since been shown to increase the risk of HIV transmission and is a major irritant to the mouth (it tastes awful) and vagina. It can even damage the inner lining of your ass. Condoms with Nonoxynol-9 are also more likely to break.

Female condoms are another option, and are especially convenient when your client isn't hard enough to wear a male condom. These condoms are made of polyurethane, which causes fewer allergic reactions than latex and is more durable. Because they stay in place, female condoms can be inserted hours before use. Not sure how to put it in? Don't be discouraged by the unfamiliar two-ring structure. Ladies, if you've inserted a tampon, you can handle this one. Just pinch the smaller ring and use it to guide the condom into the vagina. If you're using it for anal sex, just remove the smaller ring before you insert it in your ass. After using the female condom, just twist the outer ring to close up the condom before pulling it out.

Storage and Expiration

Always check the expiration date on a condom's wrapper before use. Also, never store a condom in your wallet or car—the combination of pressure and heat accelerate the degradation of the condom, making the expiration date meaningless. Consider any condom that's been stored in heat or under pressure "expired."

When to Use a Condom

This should be obvious, but we'll say it anyway. Please, don't put a condom on a non-erect penis. Mr. Floppy can easily break a condom as he morphs into Mr. Happy. Wait until he's erect!

Opening the Condom Package

Tear the package open at its corner using the manufacturer's perforated edge. Never open a package with scissors and be careful not to tear the condom itself with your fingernails or teeth.

Putting the Condom On

Putting two to three drops of lube (not more!) into a condom is a good trick. It will increase the man's sensation while decreasing the chance of the condom tearing due to dryness.

Don't trust a client to put a condom on correctly. Make putting on the condom your job, and make it fun so he lets you do it! He's horny and excited and this is about your safety.

Remember, there's a difference between putting a condom on a circumcised and uncircumcised penis. If he has foreskin, you need to pull it back before you put the condom on him.

Cover the head of his penis with the ring while pinching the tip (or, for a non-tipped condom, pinch enough of the top to hold the ejaculated semen) with your free hand. As you unroll the condom to the base of his penis, avoiding any stray pubic hairs, keep pinching the top until the condom is completely unrolled.

What's that, the condom won't unroll? You fucked up and put it on backward. Now THROW IT OUT and start over. The outside of that condom is covered in pre-come and potential STIs.

Putting the Condom on With Your Mouth

Same rules essentially apply. But the trick here is to hold the condom so that the reservoir tip is in your mouth and the ring of the condom is either (a) between your teeth and lips or (b) outside your lips. It's OK to roll the condom down partway with a little deep throating, but don't leave it like that. Make sure that the reservoir tip isn't filled with air like a balloon (pinch it and stroke downward along the penis shaft to get the air out of the tip). If air is left in the reservoir tip, it will come under pressure and is likely to pop.

Changing Positions

Any time you change positions and his penis leaves your body, hold the ring of the condom against him, so that it doesn't slip off. Also, if you change between vaginal, anal, and oral, start again with a new condom. Take these moments to reapply lube. Passing bacteria between your mouth, vagina, and ass is a really unhygienic, unhealthy practice.

Mouth to Ass

And we all collectively cringe. But seriously, your best bet here is a dental dam. And if you don't have one, you can use a condom to make one in a pinch. A lot of people tell you to use scissors, but they aren't advising sex workers. Sex workers should never bring a potentially lethal weapon into a session with a client. It's a bad idea. Without scissors, use your teeth to loosen the condom's seam that runs down its length. After you pull the condom apart by the seam, you'll have a rectangular dental dam with two ends to hold on to, the condom's ring, and the reservoir tip, which you can hold with a thumb. Pretty cool, right? Practice at home to perfect this one.

After He's Finished

It's important to pull out before his erection is gone. Hold the condom's ring against his body as you pull out, so that the condom doesn't end up inside you.

Disposal

Who cares, right? Wrong. There's a lot to consider here. If you're a street worker remember that the number one factor that will influence whether or not the police crack down on you is "quality of life" complaints from local residents. Littering an area with used condoms is a sure way to piss off the neighbors and ensure a police visit. Use a trash bin and wash your hands afterward with soap and hot water.

Anyone who works in an establishment or in their own home needs to use good disposal practices too. Many guys flush their condoms, out of some strange Neanderthal habit. Don't let your clients do this. Condoms, especially a very impressive number of condoms, are very likely to block your toilet and cause expensive, embarrassing plumbing issues.

Worst Case Scenario: Without a Condom

If you're in a situation that you can't safely get out of and you don't have a condom, or the guy won't wear one, or if you make the extremely risky decision to see a client without using a condom, here are a few things to keep in mind to minimize risk:

- Say "No" again. And keep repeating it as long as it's safe to do so.

- Avoid obvious problem spots. Do a visual check and avoid contact with any sores.
- Get him off quickly. More foreplay will make the sex act shorter. Time is risk.
- Clean toys. It's best to boil silicone sex toys between uses or to wipe down toys with an alcohol solution. At the very least, try to use hot water and soap. Remember that you can get a serious infection if you put a toy that's been in someone's ass in any other orifice.
- Stay wet and stay relaxed. It's really important to stay well lubricated, but that's really difficult to do when you are scared or upset. If you are dry, you're more likely to tear your ass or vagina, increasing your risk of infection. If you don't have lube, use saliva. If at all possible, try to relax your muscles to avoid tearing.
- Avoid his bodily fluids. Especially, don't take semen or pre-come in your mouth, vagina, or ass. A good trick is to pretend that it really turns you on to have a guy come on your chest, tits, or back.
- Get immediate treatment. After rape, sexual assault, or any trauma, we often want to keep to ourselves. *Don't.* Get to a doctor immediately. Treatments and tests are available that can reduce the risk of pregnancy and certain STIs (including HIV) but they lose their effectiveness over time. And if you were raped or assaulted, get a rape kit done. You can decide later if you want to press charges. Once the evidence is gone, it's gone for good.

John's Excuse/Healthy Hooker's Reply

I don't have any STDs.
You have unprotected sex with prostitutes and I'm supposed to buy that? And how do you know I don't?

This is not what I thought I was paying for.
You must be a first timer. Condom use is standard. Everyone who hobbies knows that. Ask around.

You didn't say anything about condoms in your ad or on the phone.

Why would I make any reference to illegal activity on my ad or on the phone? You could be a cop!

I'll pay extra.

No amount of money is worth it. Sorry. But I can give you something worth tipping for if you wear it.

I can't feel as much with a condom.

Maybe this way you'll last longer or go more times.

I won't stay hard with a condom on.

I'll put it on with my mouth. That'll keep it hard. OR I'll use a female condom so you don't have to worry about that.

I can't get off if I use a condom.

Let me get you started other ways so you'll be ready to come before we have sex.

I don't have a condom.

No problem, I do!

I'm allergic to latex.

Lucky me, I have polyurethane.

Condoms don't fit me.

Lucky me, I have all sizes.

But I'm a regular.

And I like you. Why are you messing with a good thing? If you put pressure on me, I can't trust you.

This column is for news reporting only and is not a substitute for medical advice.

ELIYANNA KAISER is a former executive editor of *$pread* magazine. She is currently raising her two children in Manhattan. In her spare time, she writes fiction.

DOROTHY SCHWARTZ is a proud supporter of sex worker rights as human rights who did outreach work with street-based prostitutes in New Brunswick, New Jersey, shortly after graduating from Rutgers University. She was honored to work alongside the talented women and men of *$pread* as the financial director and Healthy Hooker columnist. After working in health education in the New York City area, she found her calling as an ER nurse. She currently works as an ER nurse in Los Angeles, California.

THE LAST OUTCALL

Fabulous

ISSUE 1.2 (2005)

I just started working at a new house—a new house for me, anyway. I've never turned tricks out of a house before. This house is actually a three-bedroom apartment in a gigantic apartment complex, a new development in a commuter town full of convenience-driven corporations. You know the type: Target, Home Depot, Bed Bath & Beyond, and your friendly corporate brothel for the commuter on the go. I call it a condo in my ads. Sounds kinda classy, don't you think?

So it's my second day on the job, and so far the sessions have been fairly uneventful, meat-and-potatoes kind of guys. There was a tall, middle-aged Spaniard with soft eyes and a thick, uncut cock who had been window-shopping at Old Navy and stopped by after visiting the new, high-end strip mall down the street. He didn't say much, just wanted a quick hand job and a light Swedish massage. Not in that order. It gets kind of scary when you can't remember the details, but honestly, why bother? I have a friend who, when she sees four or five guys in a day, can't even remember the first one.

Anyway, on my way home I get another call, just as I'm about to walk through my front door. After much haggling I agree to a $160 massage outcall, which is outrageously low, frankly, considering the risk involved in going to his house, but right now I'm feeling like I need to work, work, work. Plus, the economy is terrible and work is harder to come by when you have an "alternative look," so I agree.

Once I get off the phone I have to move quickly. I'm trying to get someone to come with me for security, redoing my lipstick, brushing my teeth, stuffing some leftovers into my mouth and getting directions over the phone. Of course, I am still running late—I usually am—but luckily Billy is around and willing to come with me, so we scramble into my rusty pickup and head down the freeway toward the South Bay.

I call the john, Mike, from the road to get more directions, and he seems pretty understanding. A frustrating series of directions leads us over some train tracks and into a small strip of houses, but I don't see the place so I call again. I'm next door to the address he gave me but it turns out he's in a back cottage. Strange, I think, as I try to parallel park, but my driving is terrible and I'm backing into things as I reverse, so Billy hops over and quickly trades places with me.

We drive around to the back of the house and I knock on the screen door. Mike is in his mid-thirties, tall, olive complexion, chiseled jaw, lean body, and muscled face, and he's wearing a black sleeveless shirt and G-string. I'm not kidding. His tightly bound buns peek out at me as he fries an egg on his stove. The first thing he says as I drop my stuff on his couch is, "Hey, I do the same thing you do. I'm an escort too."

Wow, I think, he must be kidding. I've never had a client tell me that before and I'm kind of fascinated. I've gotten unsolicited career advice from clients, and inquiries as to how they might become escorts themselves, but never this. Actually, I sort of believe him, with his cut off sleeves, G-string, and slicked-back hair.

"You want a drink?" he asks.

"Sure," I answer, and try to find out more about the whole escort thing. "So, you're an escort, huh? For who? Who are your clients?"

"Oh, older ladies mostly, I show them a good time."

"That's great. I bet they love to have you around." It's always good to stroke the old ego before starting a session. He offers me a cocktail, then a line. I accept the drink, but coke before a session? Before a sensual massage? I'd be tense and irritable after half an hour. "So let's do the business stuff before we start, OK?"

The house is an old, wood-paneled mother-in-law, filled with cheesy bachelor crap: a framed furry print of a tiger, some nautical paraphernalia, and a big, lit-up, tropical fish tank. There are coasters on the coffee table and a glossy dark wooden bed with a burgundy comforter. I follow him into the kitchen, and he shows me a card from his friends, with a few twenties attached. The scrawling handwriting says things like, "She sounds like just your type," and "Enjoy her buddy. All the best, Steve."

"My best friend and brother called you tonight. You're a present from them," he confesses.

"Oh, really?" I say. This is quite a night for surprises.

I count the money attached to the note. It's short—really short—only half of what I agreed to, which was small anyway. This is getting frustrating. But I'm already here, and my security, who also needs to get paid, is waiting in the car. And I had to pay for gas on the way. So I decide to stay. I tell him I need more money and he gets pissed.

"Geez, great present!" he spits and proceeds to call his brother, telling him he needs to come over and give me the other half of my payment.

"Look, I'm already here, so let's start the session, but since there's only half the money here, I'll only work for half the time," I suggest. "Hopefully your brother will show up between now and the time we're done so I can finish you off." In retrospect, this was a really bad plan. It meant that if he did show up, I might be in a semicompromising position with another guy there, and if he didn't, I might need to leave before this coked-out trick got off.

We proceed to his bedroom. At this point, I haven't yet realized that he's a total asshole. In fact I'm sort of having fun with him, duding it up. Talking loud and feeling comfortable with myself, I order him onto the bed spread eagle and proceed to massage his back. He still has his T-bar underwear on and I dig for more information about his job as an escort. He says something about "the ladies" and how he rubs them and massages them and licks them until they come. What a stud! He finds them at his electrician job at a computer programming company. Apparently someone pointed him out as the guy to call and his number just got passed around among the lonely divorcées. So the whole time I am massaging him he keeps talking about how he wants to see how I do it, you know, 'cuz he's an escort, too, and he really wants to experience my special technique. Basically he wants to see if I can get his coke dick off.

Time is ticking and his darling brother isn't showing up. I turn him over and start massaging his limp cock, which gets even limper when I ask where his brother is and remind him that I can't stay the whole hour if he doesn't get here soon. When his dick is greasy with lube, my new friend insists I blow him. Now, that doesn't even come with a full, hour-long sensual massage, let alone this half-paid half-hour, which is quickly coming to a halt. I sort of laugh at the absurdity of it all, and that, of course, pisses him off even more.

Sitting there, rolling my eyes in his wood-paneled bedroom, my sweaty cocktail glass wetting a circle on his dresser, I feel like I'm in some weird 70s porn flick that's slowing before my eyes. This is frustrating for both of us. I want him to come just as much as he does—it makes my job easier, and by this point I just want to get out of there and cut my losses—but unfortunately his limped out coke dick will just not allow it. He's getting more and more pissed off, baiting me with phrases like, "You're the professional, why can't you get it up?" and "I could do a better job than that. Show me what you're made of." I feel like a magician trying to pull a rabbit out of his crotch.

By this point it's become all too obvious that this guy is never going to be erect in my hands again and that his friends are not arriving anytime soon. (Is this for real? Or did this guy sign the card himself?) I try to figure out how to make my exit gracefully.

Illustration by Cristy C. Road.

"Well, Mike, this is obviously not happening. I think I'll be on my way!" "What? I didn't even come yet!"

"I know, but your half hour is way up, and where's your brother?" "He's on his way!"

"Well, I don't know. He's still not here. What am I supposed to do?"

"You bitch! Are you ripping me off? You didn't even give me a blow job! Give me some money back!"

I check him out and decide to fork over a ten.

"A blow job doesn't come with a massage, but here you go. Well, I gotta go."

I hurriedly stuff my greasy lube bottle and massage oil back into my itty-bitty backpack and scurry toward the front door. He's instantly at the door, blocking my way, eyes bugging out and chest puffing up. I'm shocked, and for a minute I don't know what to do, then I realize I can cry out: "Billy! Billy!" It's the first time I've ever had to use the security I bring along for anything other than help with navigation and late-night gossip.

As Billy runs toward me I'm able to edge my way into the night air. Mike is huffing and puffing at us, surprised to see someone else at his door. He starts screaming at me as I jump in the truck.

"You bitch! You ripped me off! Gimme back my money! Gimme back my money!"

"Whatever dude, I gave you a massage, just like I said I would." I bark at him as Billy guns the engine.

"You bitch! I'm calling the cops."

I can't help but laugh.

"What are you going to tell them?"

"You didn't even give me a blow job, that's what, you rip-off!"

"Well, I saw you try to deal us coke and rape my friend," Billy butts in. "I was in your apartment this whole time and saw the entire thing."

I feel sort of shameful. But I wasn't raped, I think. It hurts my ears to hear it. And anyway, there's no physical evidence of that on me.

Mike jumps behind the truck and starts pushing it forward, phone in hand, as we're trying to reverse our way out of there. Wow, I think, is this guy for real?

"You better give me back my money or I'm not letting you go. The cops are on their way."

"Good," Billy says, as I sit there, horrified.

I'm in shock. What the hell is this guy gonna do when the cops get here? I know I'm not legally obliged to blow him, but what the hell am I supposed to say I'm doing there, lube and condoms in tow? Dealing with this situation is the last thing I want to do. And what about my partner, the worst part of the fiasco: A simple security job turned into pimping and pandering charges? We need to get the hell out of there, and we need to do it now. Mr. Man isn't making this very easy with his Incredible Hulk act, straining at the back of the truck. I agree to give him more money back, and as he reaches toward me for the two twenties, we're able to do a clumsy three-point turn out of there.

"Forty bucks?!" he shrieks, as we stare back at him, wide-eyed. I hand Billy a twenty, put the other one in my bra and moan in agony over the injustice of it all.

On the way home I'm nervous and skittish, obsessively imagining sirens all the way to the on-ramp. I can just see the headlines: "Call Girl Gets Busted for Not Keeping Dick Hard," or "Stingy Prostitute Refuses to Blow." Is this what it's coming to? This is the last one, I tell myself. The very last outcall I will ever do.

FABULOUS is a San Francisco native, queer femme working class ho, director of the SF Sex Worker Film and Art Festival, and brainchild of the Whore's Bath, a spa and healing day for sex workers. She also works at Homobiles, a safe ride service for people of all stripes and alternative sexualities. She lives with her cute little dog in sunny Oakland, where she dreams of someday starting an urban/rural trailer park for aging queers and hoes.

CRISTY C. ROAD is a Cuban-American illustrator and writer. Road published a zine, *Greenzine*, for ten years, and has released three novels tackling queerness, mental health, cultural identity, and punk. Her most recent work, *Spit and Passion*, is a graphic coming-out memoir (about Green Day). She's currently working on a tarot card deck, and her punk rock band The Homewreckers. Road hibernates in Brooklyn.

VIOLENCE

INTRODUCTION

Brendan Michael Conner

I picked prostitutes because I thought I could kill as many of
them as I wanted without getting caught.

—Gary Ridgway, aka The Green River Killer

The paradox of the "violent victim" determines how the
public casts sex workers as both perpetrators and victims of
violence. The "victim" is a homeless fifteen year old; a mother
of three in shackles; a migrant in debt bondage. She is someone's daughter. She is light-skinned and from a broken mid-
dle-income home, or a country in Southeast Asia. Her fate
is arbitrary detention and rehabilitation. The "perpetrator,"
on the other hand, is a predator, pimp, crack whore, "female
impersonator," or junkie. She—or he—is from a low-income
background and is probably Latin@ or of African descent. She
spreads disease and lowers property values, strolling outside
elementary schools leaving a trail of condoms and needles in
her wake. His fate is incarceration, deportation, loss of social
benefits, and humiliation. Neighbors operate sprinklers to
drive her out like a stray cat. Police march him and his peers
in chain gangs to the city limits after collecting them on
street sweeps and stings.

The narrative is different, but the approach is the same:
state violence in the form of targeted raids, brutal street
sweeps, arbitrary detention, sterilization, forced labor, mass
incarceration, and license to murder. The violent victim paradox endorses a schizophrenic reality in which people must
be punished as they are saved, shamed as they are pitied,
condemned as they are declared innocent.

Cha Cha illustrates the stereotype of sex workers as perpetrators of violence in "Paradise Lost, Paradox Found," in which she details her intimate experience with Louisiana's since-repealed Crimes Against Nature law. The victim stereotype, meanwhile, is exploited in the cases of migrant sex workers and those from the Global South to justify another form of violence: regressive anti-immigrant laws. In "Bodies Across Borders," Juhu Thukral and Melissa Ditmore examine how the anti-trafficking movement peddles sexist assumptions about female migrants' capacity for choice, leading to arbitrarily arrest and deportation of migrant sex workers and survivors of trafficking.

Exclusion from social and health benefits is another form of violence. In "Epidemic of Neglect," Mack Friedman discusses how discrimination has led to a criminally high prevalence of HIV and AIDS among transgender sex workers. Similarly, the Thai sex worker outreach organization Empower reports on how sex workers were denied international aid in the aftermath of the 2004 tsunami.

The violence that sex workers face at the hands of clients is often compounded by the state. Catherine Plato discusses a case in which a man arrested for raping a sex worker at gunpoint had his charges reduced to "theft of services" by a Philadelphia judge. Indeed, societal acceptance of violence leaves the sex worker community to take care of our own. In "The Unicorn and the Crow," Prin Roussin uses a traditional First Nations storytelling form to depict the haunting years in which a serial killer murdered dozens of women, almost all of whom were First Nations and sex workers. Roussin reminds us all "to make sure our sister and our brother are protected, because if we do not protect each other and ourselves, no one will."

Suffice it to say, violence against sex workers is institutionalized. Politicians push "quality of life" policing, resulting in fines and incarceration for minor conduct. Police use vague and far-reaching laws to harass sex workers and cycle them through the criminal system. Killers lurk in the dark, taking advantage of workers' isolation. The few who report crimes are usually assumed to be deserving of violence. And the media greases its distribution with yearly bloodlettings of Jack the Ripper headlines, where "Hooker Murdered!" is just a placeholder. Workers are not considered mothers, sons, brothers, cousins, or even neighbors, just bodies to be murdered and moved, whether to prison or as dismembered body parts in the trunk of a car. In the pages of *$pread,* sex workers counteract this dehumanization by documenting both the violence against and the resilience of our communities.

BRENDAN MICHAEL CONNER—also known by his pseudonym, Will Rockwell—is a former escort and *$pread* editor. He currently works as a police misconduct and prisoner's rights attorney for people in the sex trade and street economy in New York City. Brendan has also worked both independently and as a research editor with Avrett Consulting for organizations such as Safe Horizon's Streetwork Project, UNDP, USAID, the HIV Young Leaders Fund, and the Open Society Institute.

PARADISE LOST, PARADOX FOUND: OR, DON'T GET CAUGHT SLIPPING IN THE BIG HYPOCRO-EASY

Cha Cha

ISSUE 5.4 (2011)

I fell in love with New Orleans simply by listening to Labelle's "Lady Marmalade" at the very impressionable age of ten. The lyrics, about a Creole sex worker, eventually inspired my "Gitchy Gitchy Ya Ya Ya" wishes and "Voulez-Vous Coucher Avec Moi" dreams. I was further lured to this charming Old World city by talking to other girls who claimed that they made a fortune there and accrued several very sweet sugar daddies.

Four months after the devastation of Katrina, I decided to venture into the Big Easy and live out my wishes and dreams. My wishes were granted for a hot minute but my dreams quickly turned into nightmares when I crossed paths with America's most corrupt police force, the NOPD, and an archaic law from 1805, punishing "Crimes Against Nature." Throw in a little racism, some good ol' boy politics, and a justice system mired in its own bureaucratic mindlessness, and my nightmares went viral.

I have to admit that I fell in love with this city at first sight. But to love New Orleans, one has to know it in the context of all its idiosyncrasies and ironic histories. The study in contrasts and paradoxes is staggering. Only in the French Quarter can you walk into a bar and see a rich best-selling author toss a few back with his drinking buddy, an indigent street-level drug dealer who has been recently released from prison. In New Orleans one can only expect the unexpected.

Maybe a brief tour of Big Easy history will elucidate why New Orleans is a paradise lost and a paradox found.

The French Quarter gained infamy first as the area where enslaved Africans awaited auction in Congo Square and later as the place where slavers and the gentry housed their mixed-race mistresses and their illegitimate children—often referred to by the derogatory terms "quadroon" and "octoroon." These terms were supposed to indicate the proportion of African blood an individual was deemed to carry under the "one drop rule," which ensured that any person who had an ancestor of African descent, regardless of white parentage, nevertheless remained enslaved. The slave masters housed their respectable white families on one side of town, while they quartered their mixed-race enslaved families on the other. The same women who were considered only good enough to work the fields and clean their homes were also good enough to be raped to produce mixed-race concubines for their pleasure.

These same women, the products of slavemaster rape, supplied the notorious "Quadroon Balls" which served Frenchmen wanting to meet available young women, whom they often sexually exploited. Historians and writers can romanticize and sanitize this era as much as they like, but time does not wash away the ugly truth. This class of women was more or less bred by a racist society to be mistresses for members of a gentry class who were trapped in loveless arranged marriages. Even though this travesty was masked by the "respectability" of mothers who attended the balls as chaperones and negotiated the terms of how these men would support their daughters, it was still tantamount to organized exploitation. In essence, both before and after the formal abolition of slavery, Louisiana society set up structures that reduced black women to enforced sexual availability, on a spectrum from enslaved women forced to perform sexual acts as well as labor, to nominally "free" women who society's structures relegated to positions of sexual availability, to the pseudo-legitimacy of what were called "Left Handed Marriages."

Now the irony and hypocrisy come into play when this same society that sanctioned "left handed marriages" also deploys an arcane law imposing harsh penalties for commission of "Crimes Against Nature," which was amended in 1982 to add a provision imposing heavier penalties against anyone who solicits anal or oral sex for a fee than a person who is charged and convicted of prostitution would receive. Adding insult to injury, since 1992, once convicted under this law, an individual is labeled a "sex offender" and subject to all the goodies that come with that label: postcards that alert your neighbors that you are a convicted sex offender and a "Sex Offender" imprint on your state driver's license or ID. Those most overwhelmingly singled out for charges for the "offense" of soliciting a "Crime Against Nature" are African American women, including transgender women.

Perhaps the worst consequences are the difficulties resulting from having to show your ID with the "sex offender" label on it to prospective landlords and employers, and restrictions on your ability to do something as simple as drop your children off at school or obtain quality childcare for them. And what if another natural disaster is imminent and you need to go to a shelter? Guess what? You won't be able to! That's right. You will have to fend for yourself with the "real" sex offenders, pedophiles, and people who ostensibly have done serious harm. Getting a decent job is out of the question, so that means you will have to do whatever it takes to survive, i.e. selling sex. This usually means more arrests for solicitation and eventually, with enough "Crimes Against Nature" convictions and the wrong judge, you could face a sentence of five to twenty years in prison simply for asking the wrong person, "Voulez-vous coucher avec moi?" The really disheartening part is that many of the victims of this law are women with children.

I got caught in this nightmare by working for an escort service. One night the owner and I went on an outcall to an uber luxury hotel on Bourbon St., which unbeknownst to us was also NOPD vice central. The undercover cop wanted Shannon[1] and I to do each other while he watched. We agreed,

1. Not her actual name.

and his buddies came out of the woodworks and arrested us. We posted bond and flew back to our respective hometowns. I had a family emergency so I paid a prominent but unscrupulous New Orleans attorney to get me a continuance for a later date. He told me I was in the clear, but warned me not to come back to the Big Easy. I thought this was strange but didn't give it another thought.

I continued my "Escort Tours" to other cities, where I had a few run-ins with local police but always prevailed against criminal charges. Never at any time did a warrant from the NOPD rear its ugly head. This gave me the courage to return and to continue living out my "Lady Marmalade" fantasy. Hey, what can I say? I'm an eternal optimist. Besides, I had plans to start a clothing line and eventually to open up a Cajun/Caribbean fusion restaurant—and what better place to do so than in one of the major culinary capitals of the country?

However the turn of events that occurred after my return took me on a legal odyssey that not only put my fashion and culinary plans on hold, but also led me down a different path; a path of genuine advocacy and activism against a justice system gone awry. Not long after my return, I got arrested in another sting and the warrant popped up. Languishing and awaiting trial in the "Tents," a makeshift detention facility for the Orleans Parish Prison constructed right after Hurricane Katrina, I began listening intently to the stories of other inmates.

An ugly and disturbing pattern began to emerge. The majority of those incarcerated were black and impoverished, and also unaware of their constitutional rights. Their attitudes toward the system were totally fatalistic. They believed this was their due and that nothing could be done to alleviate their situation. The prevalent attitude was "They are going to do what they want to do!"

A few freely admitted to selling drugs or stealing. The vast majority, however, were basically fodder for the gristmill because the police had to meet their "arrest quotas" to create the illusion that they are cleaning up the streets. A lot of them had been arrested either for "loitering for prostitution"

(LFP) or "trespassing." Both of these are "nuisance" laws and they leave too much discretion for overzealous and corrupt police to abuse their authority (which most do). You can end up in jail while walking to the store if you happen to have a prior arrest record of solicitation and run into a police officer with a quota to meet.

I was charged with crimes against nature, and could have faced, among other things, years of paying hundreds of dollars to annually register as a sex offender, and to mail postcards to my neighbors. However, I put up a fight and did not plead guilty to this charge, and instead ended up pleading to a misdemeanor. I believe that I avoided the felony charge in part because the particular judge to whom my case was assigned happens to hate the crimes against nature charge and apparently throws it out any time it comes up in his courtroom.

My troubles with NOLA's unjust criminal system did not end there, however, and I soon was struggling directly against the "Loitering for Prostitution" statute, which is so often used by abusive police to target people of color. I placed an escort ad on Craigslist.com and the same undercover police officer that had arrested me two years ago, Sgt. Anthony Baker, invited me to come back to the same hotel for another rendezvous. I declined. Two weeks later, after partying in the Quarter, I was standing on the corner waiting for a cab to take me to the airport. A police cruiser drove past me and then backed up. Two police officers jumped out and handcuffed me without any explanation. When I arrived at the Royal Street police station three minutes later I asked Sgt. Baker why I had been subject to this baseless and unlawful arrest and he replied that it was "for advertising on the Internet."

I requested that he please show me that charge and the statutes. He ignored me. I was once again being confronted with the familiar "Loitering for Prostitution" charge. My only saving grace (besides God) were two very altruistic, diligent, and noble public defenders originally from New York—Thomas Nosewicz and Grania O'Neill. Without their intervention, I might still be caught up in that system. I immediately called

Tom after I got booked and he got me released without bail.

Tom's and Grania's strategy was to put the law itself on trial. We hoped through the trial to challenge the entire LFP statute. Two months and two continuances later, I got the good news/bad news call from Tom. The district attorney had decided to drop the LFP charge, but we did not get to challenge the constitutionality of the statute. This meant that the NOPD would continue to use the LFP as a tool to harass innocent citizens and effect bogus arrests.

The city attorney joked that if this law was struck down, they would have to step up arrests for marijuana possession to make up for the shortfall for the revenues they got from the fines levied on the LFP arrests. This sinister revelation hit me hard and everything I heard in jail and experienced firsthand led me to a disgusting conclusion: what fuels the majority of the arrests in New Orleans is tantamount to a corrupt system of extortion that targets poor black citizens and relies on constitutionally unsound laws in order to conduct illegitimate arrests. Putting impoverished New Orleans residents in the untenable position of having to either pay a fine or remain in jail sounds like a piss-poor way for the city to generate revenue. Either way, the city profits and individual citizens lose.

In between my bogus arrests I began to align myself with several citizens' rights advocacy groups such as Critical Resistance, Women With A Vision, and Brotherhood Inc. I also got the word out to the other girls (both cisgender and trans) and told them to call Tom and Grania instead of pleading guilty to the LFP charge so that we would have another chance to challenge the law.

I also did public speaking engagements for *Left Turn* magazine, a very important force in the community that is working toward getting the "Crimes Against Nature" law repealed. They are not alone. Deon Haywood, founder of Women With a Vision, a great organization that assists sex workers and low-income women, is also extremely instrumental in exposing and eradicating this biased and degrading law, which punishes impoverished women, and particularly trans women, of color. She is now involved with a crack legal team of civil rights attorneys and activists imported from New York. I spoke with her recently and, though she was not able to divulge much because of the risk of jeopardizing their hard work, she did say they were making headway. How encouraging![2]

I no longer live in New Orleans, but I still adore it. It has taught me a lot and made me stronger and wiser. I have also met people whom I will treasure and appreciate forever. It is not because of all I've been through with the police. Never that! Hey, I'm a tough nut to crack and I love a good fight—especially when it is about righting a wrong or helping those who cannot help themselves. I now live in Houston, Texas, where there are many opportunities for launching my fashion career. I have also made many new friends and I am about to make some new enemies because I am aligning myself with struggles here to stop injustices that I see impacting the transgender population (especially African American transgender people). I plan to be wherever injustice is and, in between my battles, I hope to get Saphires Sealiscious (my restaurant) and Kiss My "A" (my clothing line) off the ground. The "A" is open for interpretation: Attitude, Audacity, Ass. With me, it is all three.

CHA CHA wrote "Paradise Lost, Paradox Found," which was published in $pread, Issue 5.4.

2. Editors' Update—As a result of Women With A Vision's efforts, a legal team including Center for Constitutional Rights, police misconduct attorney Andrea Ritchie, and the Law Clinic of Loyola University New Orleans College of Law filed a federal lawsuit in February challenging the Crimes Against Nature Law as unconstitutional.

TSUNAMI REPORT: SEX WORKERS IN SOUTH THAILAND

Empower Foundation

ISSUE 1.1 (2005)

Thai sex workers' advocacy organization Empower is working with sex workers, bar owners, brothel owners, *tuk tuk* drivers, customers, landlords, and other members of the sex worker community in areas hit by the December tsunami. The organization hopes to begin to create a way to find solutions for all those affected by the disaster. It will be a slow, sad process that will require a lot of human resources.

Our current data estimates that over 2,000 sex workers were killed in Thailand on December 26, 2004. More than 2,000 families lost a daughter, a sister, a mother, or a provider when the tsunami struck the south of Thailand. Two thousand friends are gone.

"There were about fifty brothels in this area, small shantytown type shacks. Each brothel had at least ten workers who lived and worked in the brothels. Everyone was sleeping when the tsunami hit. There are no women or brothels left."

"I was on the beach massaging a customer when the tide went out really fast. I saw my workmates and many other people running down, laughing and picking up the fish and prawns left stranded on the sand. Then the huge wave came. I ran away and I haven't seen the others since."

"By law, bars need a license to open. How can I go and report that I have lost three workers when my business and their work is illegal?"

The labor of entertainment workers such as ourselves

has long been denied recognition as a valid form of labor, despite huge economic contributions to Thailand. Prior to the tsunami, other migrant workers had the opportunity to register as workers and be protected under labor laws that prevent them from being subject to deportation. However, sex workers are not protected under labor laws or by government social security assistance, which includes sickness and unemployment benefits, and disability allowances do not apply to us. Many sex workers cannot pay into the public social security or health schemes but we pay taxes on all the goods we buy and most pay some form of unofficial "tax" as part of our work.

"We pay one hundred baht every day to be able to give massages on the beach."

"Every woman here (in Ranong) paid immigration and police 200 baht every month. Will police or immigration look after us now?"

Recognition of sex work as work would have given us the same chance of survival, after the tsunami, that many others now have. The affected provinces, which are major tourist destinations, receive nearly six million foreign tourists a year, half the national total. Phuket alone normally receives about 1.5 million tourists during the holiday season. The tourism business generates about 100 billion baht in foreign exchange in these areas. Tourists come to visit the natural beauty of the islands, relax in luxurious resorts, and be entertained by sex workers employed in hotels, bars, and massage parlors. Local and migrant sex workers have long been part of the attraction of these provinces and have generated billions of baht for Thailand.

"I hear the (Thai) government is offering 2,000 baht compensation for each person affected by the tsunami. But for women like us, who have no proof we work and come from other provinces, it would be impossible to get this compensation and it would be a huge hassle to even try. If I can work I don't need it. It can be used for those who really need it."

As Pi Noi of Empower put it, "living people need some way to bring back their lives. They want houses, boats, fishery tools, jobs, materials, and equipment for earning income. Fishermen need boats, venders need stalls, dancers need music, housekeepers need hotel rooms, service workers need restaurants, taxi drivers need cars, massagers want to return to the mats on the beaches."

Sex workers and all other people affected by the tsunami in Thailand have said very clearly that their priority is to get back to work. However, finding work is proving difficult. Entertainment places in all areas affected by the tsunami are mainly still closed. Bars are beginning to reopen on the main tourist strip near Patong Beach, Phuket, but there are very few customers. Even in those areas where entertainment places were not directly affected by the tsunami, working has become impossible. In many of the affected areas, most of the customers of migrant sex workers were other migrant workers, e.g. construction site workers or seafarers. Many of these men were also lost in the tsunami, and most of those who survived have since been arrested or are now in hiding to avoid arrest.

Some workers are committed to waiting it out and staying and some are beginning to talk about moving to find work in other places. Usually, we ask our friends whom we trust when we consider moving. We usually have the luxury of time to think about it and make plans. The situation now is different in that women will need to make rushed decisions. Empower is exploring ways of collecting information about living and working in other areas and giving sex workers easy access to that information. Our experience tells us that communication within our sex workers' community is best when delivered in person via the sex worker grapevine and backed up by distributing brochures with clear, useful facts. Once again, this will be a lengthy process.

Trafficking and the Tsunami

We have been very disappointed and alarmed to see the ongoing rhetoric about "traffickers and the tsunami." Prior to the tsunami in Asia we were already being flooded with misleading information about trafficking and harmful anti-trafficking responses.

One international NGO working in affected provinces had previously adopted an anti-trafficking perspective and actively participated in the US-recommended practice of "raid and rescue." Their main focus is on offering health services to documented and undocumented migrants from Burma, which should include undocumented migrant sex workers. We contacted them to ask about the situation of sex workers in one of the affected areas, but because of their previous participation in a "raid and rescue" at a brothel in the areas, they had established bad relations with the community and were unable to help. So, in this time of crisis, not only had sex workers been without regular services for three months, but the only international NGO in the area was unable to help.

There is an urgent need for those working with migrant populations to establish practices that don't create situations where migrants are isolated from the services they need. Groups working with marginalized populations like sex workers or other migrant workers need to have strong roots in those communities in order to make sound judgments about actions and possible consequences.

In order for sex workers to have access to social services, there would need to be recognition that sex work is, in fact, work, and that migrating to do sex work is a legitimate option that should be supported with work cards, visas, etc. This is essential in enabling sex workers to migrate legally, independently, and safely. We fear that instead we will see an even greater decline in the accessibility of independent migration and safe, fair work.

EMPOWER FOUNDATION is a nonprofit organization that fights for the rights of sex workers in Thailand.

EPIDEMIC OF NEGLECT: TRANS WOMEN SEX WORKERS AND HIV

Mack Friedman

ISSUE 2.1 (2006)

We call them *hijra* in India, *waria* in Indonesia, *katoey* in Thailand, *travestis* in Brazil. They've been plying their trade for thousands of years, since male slaves were sold wearing face paint at ancient Roman auctions. Here in America, we've come up with other vernacular through the centuries: man-monsters, fairies, transvestites. Academia has settled on the cumbersome term "male-to-female transgender individuals engaged in transactional sex" to define people who were born male but express a female gender identity when sex-working. That's a little rocky to read, so I'll use tranny sex workers from now on.

The first American report of tranny sex work that's been found was recorded in 1836 in a New York tabloid, when Peter Sewally (who used the aliases Eliza Smith and Mary Jones) was arrested for rolling a trick in a Manhattan alleyway. (She got five years in prison for running off with the man's bankbook.) Tranny sex work is not a new phenomenon, but I'm not here to oil you down with the lubricious history of nancy boys (you can read my book, *Strapped for Cash*, if that's what you're looking for). I want to talk about what's happening right now, because our tranny street sisters are in serious danger all over the world, and it's hard to find anyone who's doing anything about it.

We're talking, of course, about HIV. When we think about HIV infecting certain populations, tranny sex workers may not be the first group that comes to mind. We might think about pregnant women in South Africa, over a quarter of whom are infected. Or intravenous drug users in Moscow, almost half of whom are living with HIV.

But tranny sex workers have been shown to bear HIV rates from 15 to 81 percent in the two dozen studies conducted since 1987. Eighty-one percent is one of the highest rates of HIV infection ever recorded anywhere, and it happened right here in America, in Georgia. Incredibly high HIV rates among tranny sex workers also have been discovered in a number of other countries, as we will soon see.

In the twenty-five-year history of HIV, only four HIV prevalence studies among tranny sex workers have been conducted and published in the United States (in peer-reviewed journals). In Atlanta, San Francisco, and Los Angeles, hundreds of tranny sex workers were tested for HIV; in each case, they had infection rates above 25 percent.

A sociologist named Jackie Boles analyzed the findings of a study based in Atlanta. Comparing two main strolls, Foggy Bottom and Midtown, Boles found HIV prevalence rates of 81 percent and 38 percent, respectively. These differences were the first warning that HIV could be very dangerous for tranny sex-working ethnic and racial minorities throughout the world. "Foggy Bottom," wrote Boles, "is characterized by extreme poverty, racial segregation [all participants from this locale were black], and a deteriorating physical environment." On the other hand, the trannies working in Midtown were more likely to be white (56 percent) and less likely to have been paid for receptive anal intercourse. Because the Atlanta studies were conducted in 1987, we can view their results as a cross section of the time when the first wave of HIV was peaking in the United States.

But why were trannies getting the virus at such high rates? Boles points out that the high prevalence found in Atlanta might indicate that the tranny sex-working community was "ghettoized . . . an oppressed minority within an oppressed minority" and subject to a variety of negative social factors that quickly made the community a reservoir for HIV. In most of the world, including the United States, transgender people face serious job discrimination. When you are being interviewed as a woman named Denise, and your state ID lists you as Harold, potential employers might get confused and angry and refuse to hire you. But that's just the edge of the blade. When you factor in the high school dropout rates among trannies (getting made fun of and beat up in class would make anyone not want to go to school anymore), and the inevitable gaps in the résumé (can't exactly put sex work on your CV, can you?), employers don't always have to work too hard to find reasons not to hire transgender people while still abiding by the non-discrimination laws that some progressive cities have enacted. The difficulties transgender people encounter when looking for legal employment force many to engage in sex work in order to survive.

And when they do engage in sex work, trannies generally find themselves at the low end of the totem pole in terms of prestige and power. They have been found to make less per trick than non-transgender male and female sex workers, and they are more likely to work the streets than in bars and clubs. In addition, researchers have found that the strolls that tranny sex workers occupy are less desirable than the strolls available to non-transgender sex workers. Taking this one step further, the strolls that are available to tranny sex workers of color tend to be less desirable than those available to whites. What does this mean? More competition; price-gouging; less ability and economic incentive to negotiate safe sex with tricks. Less patrolled strolls can attract violent clients and lead to physical and sexual assaults; more patrolled strolls leave trannies subject to high visibility and greater incarceration rates. All of these reasons and more contribute to the finding that tranny sex workers of color in Atlanta were six times more likely to have HIV than their white colleagues.

In the late 1990s, after HIV had peaked in most American populations, Dr. Tooru Nemoto found that an alarming 47 percent of sex-working African American transgender sex workers in San Francisco were HIV positive. Among white trannies, unprotected receptive anal intercourse was taking place primarily between primary and casual partners, not commercial partners. But this was not true for the African Americans Nemoto studied, who were five times more likely than whites to get paid for unsafe sex. In Dr. Paul Simon's study, 44 percent of African American tranny sex workers were HIV positive, compared with 16 percent of whites. Dr. Cathy Reback later analyzed Simon's data, and found that sex work "was not directly associated with HIV infection," although she found it was "associated with the other factors that related to HIV seroprevalence." These other risk factors included unsafe needle use, higher numbers of non-paying partners, and substance use during sex. Nemoto noted that "paying for drugs can increase financial strain and dependence on sex work for income." And, as many of us know from personal experience, tricking can increase the demand for drugs in order to cope with emotional and physical stresses that often ensue from engaging in unpleasant, forced, or unsafe sex.

Economic coercion seems also to heighten HIV risk among American tranny sex workers. Many of us have been in a situation where a client offered us twice as much cash (or more) to have unprotected sex. Dr. Boles reported that johns comparison-shopped, finding the individual who would "perform the desired sex act for the least money," and that African American tranny sex workers generally were paid the least per act. Dr. Nemoto agrees with these pressures. His focus group findings suggest that "economic pressure compelled many to compromise their condom rules and engage in unsafe sex for increased money." Clements-Noelle writes that "many male-to-female transgender persons turn to sex work because they face severe employment discrimination," and that this might account for the "high numbers of sexual partners and prevalence of sex work" among study participants. Because American sex work is illegal and underground, there is not always room for a sex worker to negotiate. In addition, tranny sex workers frequently work on their own, independent of pimps and procurers who might find a john that wasn't playing by the rules and set him straight.

But even in countries where sex work was legal, HIV rates among tranny sex workers soared in the 1990s. There are fifteen relevant international studies, and each of them corroborates our limited US evidence of very high HIV rates among tranny sex workers. HIV prevalence trends within the global tranny sex work population are remarkably consistent, showing a sharp peak of infection in the late 1980s and early 1990s in Western countries (infecting 57 to 81 percent of street-based sex workers surveyed), and gradually decreasing since then to its current level of 11 to 26 percent. Smaller cities with less immigration, like Antwerp and Rotterdam, tended to have the lowest HIV rates, while larger ones with more immigration, like Rome and Sao Paolo, had higher rates. Both domestically and internationally, one-third of all tranny sex workers tested for HIV have come up positive.

These international studies also corroborate American findings of racial minorities bearing the highest HIV rates in the tranny sex work world. In Milan in the 1980s, 76 percent of South American foreign nationals tested positive compared to 38 percent of Italian natives. Typically, male sex worker HIV prevalence rates have been considerably lower, more in keeping with the gay male community: 18 percent in New Orleans, 12 percent in Long Beach, 4 percent in Jakarta. And compared to female sex workers, tranny sex worker HIV rates have been exponentially higher: working girls had less than 1 percent HIV prevalence in Montevideo, Amsterdam, and Madrid, and a range in HIV prevalence from less than 1 percent to 6 percent in Rome, Barcelona, London, and other European cities. Meanwhile, tranny sex worker HIV rates have been five to thirty times higher throughout North America and Western Europe, and have approached rates seen previously only among female sex workers in sub-Saharan Africa. Transgender sex workers have been significantly absent from the world's scientific literature (if not from the planet's sexual awareness). This is perhaps best described by the authors of a Thai study on drug-using men, who note that their participants often paid *katoey* (Thai "ladyboys") for sex. "This cultural pattern has been remarkably little studied," they concluded. "A Medline search (on February 12, 2005) on the term '*katoey*' yielded no scientific publications—a google search on the same term (on February 12, 2005) yielded 25,600 results, including bars, clubs, cabaret shows, dating services, and chat rooms dedicated to Thai *katoey*. Although HIV and sexual health research may have overlooked *katoey*, the sex and tourism industries have not."

The scarcity of HIV prevalence studies here in America indicates a more systemic bias in this country's research funding structure. If HIV prevalence rates in the four studies conducted here are any indication, corroborative studies should have been done in every major city in America. Instead, there is zero published data for HIV prevalence among tranny sex workers in New York City, Miami, Philadelphia, Boston, or Seattle, and no HIV prevalence research available on midwestern populations where substantial transgender sex work takes place, such as Chicago and Minneapolis.

In the United States, there is serious scientific stigma attached to lesbian, gay, bisexual, and transgender (LGBT) health research. Nemoto's group at the University of California-San Francisco Center for AIDS Prevention Studies was recently audited by the Department of Health and Human Services; Nemoto was one of several research scientists whose work on LGBT and sex work-related issues was targeted for audits. Dr. Emilia Lombardi, one of Dr. Simon's collaborators, made a recent Congressional "hit list" for her interest in transgender research. "Studies of gay men, prostitutes come under scrutiny," headlined a Science article in February 2005 in response to a Congressional inquiry on government-funded research in sexuality and health. The Association of Reproductive Health Professionals kindly warned researchers against using "sex work" and "transgender," among several other terms, in government grant applications. The message: your research won't get funded if it has anything to do with transgender sex work.

This de facto censorship of American public health has both direct and indirect elements and consequences, and clearly deters researchers from examining health conditions in tranny sex work communities. It is difficult to get tenure if you cannot publish your research; it is difficult to publish when the journals are squeamish about your research focus; and it is tough to get funding from a government agency that refuses to consider grants involving the population you want to research. My own public health professors have suggested I focus on something more "practical," for instance. (One in particular listened to me talk about this problem, and then asked, "Why should I care?") Other well-meaning advisers have suggested that I could still apply for grants by focusing on faith-based initiatives to help people escape prostitution. While I look absolutely stunning in my cape and boots, I have chosen to leave supernatural interventions to the Ghostbusters.

Crack and heroin research czar Dr. James Inciardi points out that barriers faced by our researchers aren't limited to America. Discussing Brazil, he writes, "Doctors who work with street people, prostitutes, and transvestites in Rio de Janeiro, for example, report hostile reactions on the part of their medical colleagues as they themselves, apparently through guilt by association, come to be seen as sources of contagion and risk." This has had the effect of squelching relevant research as well as diminishing necessary access to care.

There are no solid estimates for the number of transgender people who live in the United States, and no health data is collected routinely on transgender people in surveys administered by the US Census or the National Center of Health Statistics. In none of these large government assays is "transgender" even a gender category to choose from. Local research centers, erstwhile academic studies, and community-based organizations are by default the only realistic mechanisms by which to collect tranny sex work data.

In the studies we have cited, minority ethnicity consistently compounded already high HIV risks for tranny sex workers.

Ethnic and racial minorities were found to be marginalized even within tranny sex-working communities. Their magnified HIV risk can be seen as a reflection of extraordinarily limited social agency and grave economic coercion: when you're that low on the totem pole and you can't get a job, you have to make money somehow. Being transgender can often lead to severely reduced legal employment options via job discrimination. Racial and ethnic minority status (and/or foreign national status), while also contributing to job discrimination, has the effect of reducing one's market value within sex work. Being underpaid compared to male and female sex workers leads to reduced sexual safety within the sexual economy both by price constraint (having to turn more tricks to make as much money as non-minorities and non-transgender sex workers) and increased customer leverage (having unsafe sex to meet sex client demands or risk losing the client). Many of these studies cited violence (including frequent murder sprees) as another major occupational hazard faced by tranny sex workers.

What can we do about this? First, we can insist on conducting our own research, getting degrees and grants, and doing it right. We can help established researchers gain interest in this community by alerting them to these criminally high infection rates and the massive health care costs associated with them, bills footed mostly by taxpayers—when was the last time you saw a tranny sex worker with a health insurance plan besides Medicare? Second, we can keep reading, educating ourselves, and voting for politicians and ordinances that promote smart, targeted social services and expand employment rights of transgender people (as well as sex workers as a whole). Third, we can get out onto the streets and into the chat rooms and talk to the working girls and the johns, to remind them how risky unsafe sex work can be. And finally, we can keep doing our own research on the economic costs of managing health problems among sex workers instead of solving them. Ultimately, I bet it's cheaper to give a gal her own apartment, a day job, and health insurance than foot her ER bill when she gets stabbed or raped or has an overdose or a staph infection from the used needle she injected hormones with. When we can convince narrow-minded public health professors that it makes economic sense to do the right thing, then we can convince the narrow-minded public, too.

MACK FRIEDMAN has extensive experience conducting community-based participatory research and programming with sex workers, and is a critically acclaimed writer and performer. His popular history, *Strapped for Cash: A History of American Hustler Culture*, was a Lambda Literary Award finalist in LGBT Studies. His novel, *Setting the Lawn on Fire*, won the Publishers Triangle Award for Debut Fiction. He is currently spearheading a project intended to decrease the stigma that sex workers endure.

THE UNICORN AND THE CROW

Story and photos by Prin Roussin

ISSUE 3.2 (2007)

Many years ago, in a land not all that different from our own, a great hardship had plagued the world and all the creatures living in it. Among them, there lived a unicorn and a crow who had become the best of friends.

Like many who lived through such times, they worked in what some have called the oldest profession, working day and night down by the old train yard, they kept careful watch to make sure the other was always safe and protected.

One day, while the crow was keeping watch, something caught her attention: a shiny flash out of the corner of her eye. She flew away to find what had distracted her, forgetting all about her dear friend, if only for a moment.

When the crow realized that she had left her friend working alone, she quickly returned. She searched high and low around the old train yard, cawing loudly, but alas, the unicorn was nowhere to be found.

The unicorn was never seen or heard from again. She was thought by most to be gone, but the crow never stopped searching for her friend. It is said that she still waits in the old train yard for any sign of her dear friend, and there she will wait until the end of time.

Editors' Note: This is a fairy tale about the sex workers of East Vancouver, Canada. In 2002, Robert Pickton was charged with the murders of twenty-seven women, most of whom were sex workers, street-involved, and/or First Nations. Pickton likely killed many more of the sixty-two people on the list called "Vancouver's Missing Women." In the shadow of the Pickton trial, we are reminded about how fragile our lives are and how vulnerable we all are, especially if we are isolated and criminalized. "The Unicorn and the Crow" is a reminder to us all to make sure our sister and our brother are protected, because if we do not protect each other and ourselves, no one will.

PRIN ROUSSIN is a sex worker and artist working in the Coast Salish Territories of Vancouver, Canada.

ESCORT RAPE CASE CAUSES UPROAR IN PHILADELPHIA

Catherine Plato

ISSUE 3.4 (2008)

A man arrested for gang raping a prostitute at gunpoint had his charges reduced to "theft of services" by Philadelphia judge Teresa Carr Deni. According to reports, the twenty-year-old single mother who worked for a Philadelphia escort agency negotiated to have sex with nineteen-year-old Dominique Gindraw on September 20, 2007. He responded to the woman's Craiglist ad and agreed to give her $150 in exchange for an hour of sex. They arranged to meet at a location in North Philadelphia, which she believed to be his house, but instead it was an abandoned property. Upon their meeting, she agreed to have sex with one of Gindraw's friends for an additional one hundred dollars.

When Gindraw's friend arrived, he was reportedly carrying a gun and no money. Two more friends arrived, and Gindraw forced the woman at gunpoint to have unprotected sex with all four men. A fifth man was also invited, but when he arrived he noticed the victim was crying. Rather than joining in and raping her, he helped her get dressed and leave. Gindraw and his friends were arrested and charged with rape and assault.

When the case was presented to Philadelphia municipal court judge Deni on October 4, 2007, she dropped all sexual assault charges and charged the men with "theft of services." According to Jill Porter of the *Philadelphia Daily News*, Deni justified her decision by stating: "She consented and she didn't get paid . . . I thought it was a robbery." And though being forced into sex at gunpoint by four men seems about as violent and coercive a case as possible, Deni doesn't believe the victim suffered from "true" rape, stating to Porter that the case "minimizes true rape cases and demeans women who are really raped."

In response to this deeply insulting decision, based on Deni's personal moral judgment rather than Pennsylvania law, more than just the sex worker community has rallied in support of the victim. According to the *Daily News*, assistant district attorney Rich DeSipio accused Deni of "rewriting her own laws," stating that the legislature defines rape as sex by force—regardless of the victim's profession. While the woman did consent to protected sex with two men for a negotiated fee, her having unprotected sex with four men, under the threat of violence and with no compensation, was not consensual. And is nonconsensual sex not rape? The Philadelphia Bar Association states that Deni's ruling was a miscarriage of justice, demonstrating "clear disregard of the legal definition of rape and the rule of the law."

Beyond questions of judgment or compassion for the victim, Deni's allowing Gindraw to get off with only theft charges meant that a dangerous, armed sexual predator was free to strike again. And four days later he did. Gindraw was charged with an identical crime involving a twenty-three-year-old victim, according to DeSipio. The women did not know each other. Shocked by Deni's ruling in the first case, DeSipio refused to present the second one, stating that he didn't want to demean the victim. In addition to showing deep disregard for state law and citizens' safety by allowing a serial rapist to roam free, Deni's decision to reduce the charges to "theft" is baffling in light of the fact that the services in question are illegal.

To state that Gindraw's chief offense was not paying a prostitute is to show a certain acceptance of the woman's occupation. If it is possible to "rob" a prostitute of her illicit service by raping her and not paying, then it seems logical that the prostitute should be entitled to any damages that she would be awarded in any legal industry, including direct damages for the service "stolen" from her, in addition to medical and counseling costs and any lost earnings during the legal proceedings. Given the nature of the prostitute's profession, however, it is unlikely that this will come to pass. Deni's decision was demeaning and irresponsible, as well as illogical in a society where the services were illicit to begin with.

Despite criticism from local press, the district attorney, and the Philadelphia Bar Association, on November 7, 2007, Deni won a retention vote. She will serve another six-year term.

CATHERINE PLATO is a former editor of *Curve* magazine and *$pread*, and a founding member of the sex work blog TitsandSass.com. She currently works as a freelance writer, editor, and stripper in San Francisco and Las Vegas.

BODIES ACROSS BORDERS: EXPERIENCES OF TRAFFICKING AND MIGRATION

Melissa Ditmore and Juhu Thukral

ISSUE 2.4 (2007)

When people think of "human trafficking," they generally imagine "sex slaves:" women and children, usually from Eastern Europe or Asia, forced into prostitution by a heavy who beats them and takes their money. This image conjures strong emotions and eclipses the reality, which is that people, including men, are trafficked into many labor sectors—construction, cleaning, manufacturing, sweatshops, agriculture, and sex work. People who leave their homes to move to another country are usually ambitious and are often the "go-getters" of their hometowns. Some anti-prostitution activists look at all migrant sex workers as trafficked, even when they don't identify as trafficked themselves. Conceptualizations of trafficking have traditionally reflected sexist assumptions. The discussion often centers on the category of "women and children." The UN has protocols both on "smuggling people" and another on "trafficking in persons." At meetings to discuss these laws, it became clear that "trafficking" was the term used to discuss women and children, while "smuggling" was used to refer to men. The gendered agenda is clear in the title of the trafficking protocol, United Nations Optional Protocol to Prevent, Suppress, and Punish Trafficking in Persons, Especially Women and Children. There is no gendered coda on the title of the Protocol Against the Smuggling of Migrants by Land, Air, and Sea.

These stereotypes—of women and children who are victims who need to be protected, in contrast with men who are self-motivated agents—get in the way of the real issues: migration within and across borders, travel restrictions, economic opportunity, and taking advantage of one's situation. Media reports add to these stereotypes with salacious stories of girls forced into the sex industry, giving far less attention to other forms of trafficking.

Recent Trafficking Cases

An activist from Cambodia recently described being duped and forced to work in a brothel the first time she left her family. Her story is common. "When I came back to Koh Kong with the owner, they forced me to put my thumbprint on paper to say that I borrowed money and that I owe an amount that I didn't even know . . . They sold me to a brothel in Srae Ambel [a place known for crime, near the Thai border and not far from the beach resort of Sihanoukville]. My friend was also sold to another brothel. We both had to work hard day and night to send back money to the owner. If we had clients, it was OK, but if we had no clients, the owner beat us and blamed us and said 'you cannot find money for me.' Even if we were sick, they forced us to have sex with clients . . . Whenever I went outside, there was always a guard who followed me. I knew only that house in the whole year I lived in Srae Ambel."

In one recent case here in the United States, an elderly Eastern European woman was brought to the United States by a relative. Upon arrival, the relative took her passport and then tore up her return ticket. The elderly woman was forced to be a domestic slave for the relative, who also found under-the-table outside work for her and kept all of her money. This case was exposed when the relative who enslaved her died after a long illness through which the trafficked woman cared for her. Because the trafficker died and there is no one to prosecute, the government does not want to help the trafficked woman stay in the United States. In the United States, a trafficker brought two teenage girls into the country claiming that he would help them get jobs and reunite one of the girls with her mother. He won their trust by creating personal relationships with both girls: he told one that he wanted to marry her and acted as a boyfriend, and created a platonic "older brother" friendship with the other. Ultimately, he sexually assaulted both girls and forced them to work against their will in a brothel. They were helped to escape by other sex workers: they then found someone on the street who spoke their language and assisted them.

Some Central American men involved in construction work in the United States are here illegally. An acquaintance from their hometown lent them the money for transportation to the United States and arranged for clandestine travel. When they arrived, they worked for his construction company for a few years without pay. They are in debt bondage and do not know how long it will take to "earn" their freedom. None of them have been willing to speak to police or press charges against the person who arranged their travel and work. Many keep working and do eventually earn money to send home to their families. Such remissions have vastly improved life in their hometown, making the trafficker a hero. This makes it even more difficult to confront this abuse.

Government Response

The conservative movement in the United States and the current administration are prioritizing trafficking as an important human rights issue, and the United States is promoting anti-trafficking legislation around the world. However, this campaign against trafficking is really a campaign against sex work. All US government funds for anti-trafficking activities are given only to organizations that pledge not to support sex workers organizing. The majority of trafficking cases in the United States do not involve sex work, yet US government rhetoric on trafficking consistently focuses on it. In fact, policies that are ostensibly aimed at eliminating trafficking in persons adversely affect all sex workers around the world, the overwhelming majority of whom are not trafficked. This is part of a larger government campaign against sex outside of heterosexual marriage and is shown in the government's campaigns against abortion, reproductive rights, condom promotion, and gay marriage.

One critique of the US strategy on trafficking comes from the government itself. In a July 2006 study, the US Government Accountability Office (GAO) found that all current estimates of the number of people trafficked into any kind of work, including sex work, are questionable: "The accuracy of the estimates is in doubt because of methodological weaknesses, gaps in data, and numerical discrepancies. For example, the US government's estimate was developed by one person who did not document all his work . . ." The questionable numbers are also hard to compare. While the US government estimated that 68 percent of cross-border trafficking in 2003 involved commercial sex, the International Labour Organization estimated that 43 percent of cross-border and internal trafficking from 1995 to 2004 involved commercial sex. Moreover, girls, children, and trafficking itself were defined differently in each case. It is through this lack of clarity that some policymakers and advocates have been misled by these unreliable estimates into the belief that human trafficking and sex work are inextricably linked and that all sex work is coerced. The reality is very different.

Anti-prostitution rhetoric cannot be used constructively to address the issue of trafficking. Much research on sex work is widely viewed as flawed and inaccurate. Studies in radical feminist literature consistently violate the canons of objectivity in conducting social science research. In evaluating anti-prostitution literature, experts find that "[a]necdotes are generalized and presented as conclusive evidence, sampling is selective, and counterevidence is routinely ignored." In light of the poor quality of research, scholars attribute government agencies' use of anti-prostitution findings to political connections rather than academic integrity.

There is dubious or little indication that increased criminalization of sex work and clients decreases instances of abuse of sex workers. Treating human trafficking as the same as prostitution ignores the large population of victims trafficked into labor such as manual labor and domestic service. Defining sex work as identical to trafficking into sex work negates sex work as a voluntary choice, further criminalizes sex work, and exaggerates the negative conditions that harm sex workers. In most places, people who identify themselves as victims of trafficking to the police may be assisted, while those who do not are treated as criminals. This is an artificial distinction, forcing people to "choose" to be a whore or a victim.

Migrant Sex Workers in New York City

In 2005, the Sex Workers Project released a report, *Behind Closed Doors*, in which we presented data from interviews with fifty-two sex workers who lived in New York City and worked in gang clubhouses, bars, hotels, nightclubs, and dungeons, as well as through the internet and other sex workers. Twenty-one of these fifty-two were migrant sex workers from countries in Asia, Latin America, the Caribbean, and Europe. These sex workers spoke openly of their reasons for doing sex work. Their stories highlight the wide variety of reasons for entering the sex industry.

Thirteen of the twenty-one sex workers from other countries who took part in the study had some form of legal immigration status, although not all were authorized to work in the country. Eight of the twenty-one were completely undocumented and had no legal status in the United States. Most entered the country legally with tourist or student visas, which they overstayed, while one, Maria, entered the country with no documents at all "by running across the border." Four of the twenty-one migrant sex workers were trafficked into sex work, meaning they were coerced into working in prostitution.

Reasons for Coming to America

Sex workers offered a wide variety of answers to the question of why they left their home countries, ranging from a lack of economic opportunities to enjoying greater freedom by avoiding discrimination and stigma based on gender, gender identity, and sexual orientation. Luciana said, "I had a friend from Brazil in New York City [who] told me to come here, that I could make good money. I was looking for change after my parents' passing." Transgender women and gay men reported that their families were ashamed and that they were discriminated against in their home countries. Scarlett came to the United States "for a new life" and to be accepted for "the way I was." Grace said that "people didn't understand that [I am] gay." She added that her family would kill her and themselves if she had remained in the country as a woman.

The United States is a destination for immigrants from around the world, including migrant sex workers. When asked why they came to the United States, Connie and Emiko referred to the "American dream" and Maria said that "in the US . . . people have everything." Some said that the "American dream" is inextricably linked to jobs and financial opportunities. Others referred to sexual freedom in the United States. Emiko came to the United States with a student visa—she talked about cultural forces making her want to leave Japan. For example, she felt too old there to be a single woman.

Twelve of the twenty-one immigrant sex workers described having some assistance during the migration process, ranging from consulting firms that arrange for visas, to people like "coyotes" who smuggle people across borders. Keiko said, "I applied to school and they [the consulting firm] issued the F1 Visa. They said they have some residence, so the first month or two you don't have to worry about anything. If you pay this consulting it's very easy." Rita came to New York to escape from an abusive husband. It was her husband's aunt who helped her arrange her visa and passport. The trafficked women came to the US through arrangements made by the people who trafficked them.

Involvement with Sex Work

Sex workers interviewed for this report generally became involved in the sex industry for monetary reasons. Some turned to the sex industry out of desperation, such as Keiko, who said, "I didn't know anything about how to make money, but I knew I needed to find out how to make money." Others made a decision to utilize the sex industry rather than struggle in employment that did not pay them a living wage. Yoko said, "I was already working as a hostess in Japan, so I just started looking for it naturally in the US."

The decision to enter the sex trade was not always an easy one for these migrants. For respondents who did not have legal immigration status or proper documentation, the ability to settle, find housing, and support themselves was compounded by fear of deportation and a lack of employment authorization. This led some participants to look at sex work as their best economically viable option. Respondents in this situation discussed the fact that they could work out of their apartments independently without involving an employer. In addition, many escort agencies and brothels do not check for legal immigration status.

Connie spoke of being "afraid to give fake papers" to a potential employer, saying that sex work seemed to be a better option than that kind of fraud. She was essentially weighing one unlawful act against another. This reflects an unexpected ethical decision in opting to enter the sex industry.

In making her decision, Connie also considered sex work to be more lucrative than other jobs available to her. Immigrant and undocumented respondents often spoke of the need for "work papers" and "a green card." For example, Maria spoke of limited employment options, saying that "with papers, I could go more easily to school and apply for other jobs." Grace worried that she "can't find a regular job because [I'm] illegal . . . Can't have health insurance." Scarlett has a B.A., but says "I can't get a job because of my [undocumented] status."

Luciana spoke of her ambivalence about engaging in sex work to support herself: [I started] when I met Regina. I was a dog walker at the time. I was afraid at first and took a month to decide. I'd stripped before and worked in a restaurant/bar. I was a sex worker for a month, then didn't do full service and started stripping again, but [it was] not enough money and too much talking/objectification, so I returned to sex work. I don't do full service, only touching and blow jobs, everything but penetration and intercourse. I made a lot, $200 from no full service, so I wouldn't go back to full service because I didn't make more money doing it. I'm not comfortable with full service and I think guys prefer non-full service because it's safer.

Perhaps one of the most significant findings among the immigrant respondents in the sample relate to the relationship between their motivation to engage in sex work and the remittances that they send home to their families in their countries of origin. Eight migrant sex workers reported sending money home to their families. Having immigrated to the United States for economic reasons and often having the pressure of supporting family members at home, a number of participants mentioned that sex work was the only work that would support their daily needs in the United States while allowing them to save enough money to send home. Because legal work was unavailable or did not pay enough to allow for this, a number of respondents turned to sex work for employment.

Violence and Coercion

The four trafficked women spoke of experiencing coercion and slave-like conditions. Two of these women thought that they would be involved in other types of work and did not know that they were going to be involved in prostitution. The other two had worked as prostitutes in their native countries and knew that they were to continue as sex workers in the United States. However, they did not realize that they would be beaten or threatened, and have their money taken from them. For the women who did not know that they were going to be prostitutes, the act of engaging in prostitution itself was a violent one because they were being forced into having sex with customers against their will.

The sex workers who were not in abusive situations were very concerned about violence from customers, but the violent experiences that affected the trafficked women more deeply were the threats and assaults from the traffickers themselves. The women told of being threatened, beaten, raped, and having their money withheld by the traffickers as a means of keeping them in line. Belinda did report that occasionally johns "would get a little rough," a sentiment echoed by Raquel. However, they were predominantly concerned with violence from the traffickers.

Thirteen of the twenty-one sex workers who were not US citizens described having concerns about their participation in the sex trade, especially worries about immigration policies and agents. This fear reflects a greater stress on sex workers who lack citizenship because they worry not only about police interference but also about the immigration consequences related to their work. In addition, Louise makes an important point, saying, "I worry [about immigration authorities] when I'm working, but it's not my biggest concern. Safety is always my biggest concern."

Migrants in the sex industry—like other migrants—pursue their dreams and make decisions that they hope will lead to financial opportunity and security for them and their families here and abroad. Trafficking in persons is a serious problem, but it by no means afflicts all migrant sex workers. Many migrants, including sex workers, speak of economic need and the desire to support their families, often in situations that offer them few options for financial freedom. US policies on migration and trafficking undermine security for all sex workers, including those who have been trafficked, rather than achieving their stated goals.

MELISSA DITMORE writes about gender, development, health, and human rights, particularly as they relate to marginalized populations such as sex workers, migrants, and people who use drugs. She edited the *Encyclopedia of Prostitution and Sex Work*. When her piece in this anthology was written, she was the coordinator of the Network of Sex Work Projects.

JUHU THUKRAL is a leading expert on the rights of low-income and immigrant women in the areas of sexual health and rights, gender-based violence, economic opportunity, and criminal justice. She is director of law and advocacy at The Opportunity Agenda, and is a founding Steering Committee member of the NY Anti-Trafficking Network. Juhu was the founder and Director of the Sex Workers Project at the Urban Justice Center in New York City.

RESISTANCE

INTRODUCTION

Bhavana Karani

I write these words to bear witness to the primacy of resistance struggle in any situation of domination . . . to the strength and power that emerges from sustained resistance and the profound conviction that these forces can be healing, can protect us from dehumanization and despair.
—bell hooks, *Talking Back: Thinking Feminist, Thinking Black*

Resistance is usually thought of as the counterpoint to oppression and violence. So why a separate chapter about it? What is resistance on its own terms?

Resistance is transformation. Beneath the immediate ways that individuals and communities respond in moments of crisis and conflict, the struggle against oppression includes how they grow, build, and change. Just as solitary seedlings grow vast underground networks of roots in order to thrive, resistance is as much a web of interconnections as it is visible moments of assertion.

Trading sex in a world that routinely undermines the possibility of doing it safely makes survival alone a form of resistance. The stories in this chapter illustrate the tenacity and creativity with which sex workers survive, struggle, and thrive, and how, during these battles, many sex workers seek justice for a collective whole.

In "The Cutting Edge: On Sex Workers, Serial Killers, and Switchblades," Sarah Stillman shares the story of Tonya Richardson, a sex worker in Daytona Beach who made local news defending herself and colleagues from a serial killer. Stillman explores how sex workers and their communities stay safe while also demanding "a world where safety is considered a sex worker's basic human right."

"2 Young 2 B 4Gotten" was jointly written by four different organizations serving young people in the sex trades across the United States, and draws out the connections between the needs of individuals and the structural oppressions that impact them. Noting that "one of the most positive ways girls heal or fight back against violence is by relying on their own communities," this piece highlights how the most effective resistance does not come from outside, but from within communities.

Taking care of ourselves is also a form of resistance. In "B is for Bobbi," Morgan Ellis explores the importance of boundaries for sex workers. Erin Siegal's "Fashion With A Function," shows how art can embody resistance when a platform heel is modified with an alarm system and GPS tracking.

The act of fighting for one's life is undeniably an act of resistance. In "I Have Nothing to Say," Lynne Tansey describes struggling to stay alive and killing her attacker in self-defense. In the legal aftermath, she is charged with murder and her sanity is questioned. Although she was denied compensation as a victim of violence, her case would come to have a positive impact for other sex workers.

Creating spaces for sharing stories is itself a powerful form of resistance that can defy and complicate stereotypes about those who have for too long been denied voice. As you find your way through this chapter, I hope that bell hooks' words resonate, that these pieces serve to inspire, heal, and protect through the resistance demonstrated by each—and in the act of sharing and reading them.

BHAVANA KARANI worked at *$pread* from 2009 to 2011 as subscriptions coordinator and Race Issue editorial collective member.

I HAVE NOTHING TO SAY:
A STORY OF SELF-DEFENSE

Lynne Tansey

ISSUE 2.4 (2007)

It was a hot and sticky evening in the summer of 1976. I was talking to my prostitute colleagues at our usual spot on the corner of Union Street, Plymouth [England]. We always did this to confer and relate information about clients and to see if anyone had been in trouble that day.

I hadn't been there long before a huge guy approached me. At seventeen stones (250 pounds) and well over six feet tall, he seemed quiet and well mannered. None of the other girls had met him before. After our usual introductions (we had to move quickly in our appraisals, because of the police), we agreed to go back to my place for business. I lived with two other prostitutes and usually at least two of us were there at the same time, but that evening I was alone.

We had settled on a price and were getting down to business when suddenly, as he was on top of me, he threw back his fist and smashed it in my face.

The shock was overwhelming. There had been no previous indication of violence. I threw myself off the bed. He was crawling all over me and trying to strangle me. The bedside lamp had fallen on the floor, breaking, throwing us into darkness.

I tried to crawl into the kitchen, grabbing for the "lazy betty" switch (a long piece of cord attached to the ceiling light). The skin on my legs had been burned off during our struggles on the carpet. He managed to get to my throat again and throttled me so badly that I had the most terrible images flash through my mind. I thought of my children, my parents, and everyone who knew me. I saw an image of a newspaper headline saying, "Prostitute Murdered!"

What's really bizarre is that, to this day, I can still see that image in my mind. I really thought I was going to die that night.

All of a sudden a huge force overtook me, a hidden strength that I never knew existed. I heaved an enormous attack on him and managed to free myself for a moment; long enough to grab a carving knife from the kitchen counter.

By this time—and time by then had become static—we were standing facing each other in this small and surreal space. I had the carving knife in my hand and I warned him that if he attacked me again I would kill him. He had not uttered a word throughout the whole ordeal.

He didn't acknowledge my warnings and continued to attack me. I stabbed him in the stomach. He backed off momentarily, appearing shocked, but resumed his attack. I stabbed him again in the stomach, and again; he still kept coming. He reached out toward my weapon and grabbed the blade, saying nothing. I pulled the knife back toward me, severing his fingertips. He continued to attack, saying nothing!

Reality changed then. It seemed to shift sideways, and I no longer knew what world I was in. This was a monster, an inhuman thing that wanted to obliterate me, no matter what the consequences. I felt like I was watching myself and this man from a different height, like on television. I was separate from fear now, at least from fear in the sense that we know it. Survival was my only goal.

Still he attacked me.

By then I had stabbed him in the heart, the stomach, and the lungs. He still attacked. No blood came from this huge torso that was bent on destruction. Suddenly he managed to grab me and draw me close to him, crushing my small frame against his cold, white belly.

Illustration by Star St. Germain.

"Now," I thought, "is the time you are going to die, Lynne."

With that thought in my mind, I reached around his bulk and stabbed aimlessly into his shoulder. I thought of the place that would hurt him the most. I stabbed him in his temple. The blade ran down until it met the narrowness of his temple area. The blade stopped and my hand continued down the blade, practically severing it off.

He pushed away from me, turning around as if to take in the environment for the first time. The blood came then. He was like a colander: the blood shot all over the kitchen, on the walls, the ceiling, everywhere, mingling with my severed artery lifeblood.

Then he spoke for the first time. "I've had enough," were his last words to this world.

He walked into the bedroom and sat on the bed. I watched, fearful of another surreal attack. He urinated, and lay back to die. I watched him, hated him, feeling a cold anger and a creeping realization that my life would never be the same again. It was over for him, but not for me.

My screams and nightmares began that night, and it was many years before they stopped.

I ran outside, naked and bleeding, screaming for help. I had no telephone, but I knew there was a public phone some hundred yards down the road. At some point I collapsed, through loss of blood and shock. Nobody came, nobody helped, so I crawled the hundred yards down the road to the phone. I passed two sets of feet en route, male and female, a couple, but they just stood watching, offering no assistance, so I finished my desperate journey unaided.

The police and ambulance came quickly.

I nearly lost my arm from the elbow down, such were my injuries. I was black and blue from the face downwards, distorted and bloodied. I had several operations on my hand. The surgeons saved what they could, but some years later they had to amputate one of my fingers because my hand was curling inward and rheumatism was setting in. Despite my terrible injuries, I was still charged with the murder of a chief petty officer in the navy, a family man in a position of respect. I spent nearly a year in prison awaiting trial. I had had no previous convictions for anything, not even prostitution, and had never been in prison.

They gave me tests in a mental institution to see if I was responsible for my actions. They really tried to pin the murder on me, mainly because of the stab wound in his shoulder, which made them think I had initially attacked him from behind. But my QC and solicitor were brilliant, throwing out the first panel of jurors because of prejudice, and I was eventually found not guilty due to self-defense.

I found out that my client and attacker was a husband and father of two children. He also had two mistresses, who came to court unwillingly, under enforcement, and told their stories of a man who was occasionally violent to them. Apparently he had threatened to cut off the head of one of them with garden shears. His wife knew nothing about this double life, much like the wives of many other prostitute killers, who claim to be ignorant of their husband's atrocities. The Yorkshire Ripper comes to mind, since he was at-large at the time, much to the fear of prostitutes and other women in the country. I tried to claim criminal compensation for the injuries sustained, but failed because the Home Office decided that I "put [myself] in a position of danger," and was therefore "responsible" for actions taken against me! I couldn't appeal unless I paid for the appeal myself. My mother offered to remortgage her house, but I couldn't gamble with money that didn't belong to me.

Instead, I petitioned the government to acknowledge the human rights of prostitutes to claim criminal compensation. Eventually this was approved, too late for me, but not too late for the surviving victims of the Yorkshire Ripper, who some years later got their recompensation for the violence suffered at the hands of that man.

LYNNE TANSEY is a former sex worker, particularly a dominatrix and Sacred Whore, who has thirty years of experience in the sex industry. She set up an agency for homeless people and sex workers on the street in Plymouth, UK. Now she writes and uses her art to underpin her writing about sexual social issues and the psychology around sex. She is also an international adviser and advocate for the rights of sex workers. She lives in Tintagel, Cornwall, UK.

STAR ST. GERMAIN is a tornado disguised as a girl. She likes you a lot.

THE CUTTING EDGE: ON SEX WORKERS, SERIAL KILLERS, AND SWITCHBLADES

Sarah Stillman

ISSUE 3.2 (2007)

I remember how Ronnie, my third-grade playground crush, used to whisper that illicit little ditty from the top of the jungle gym as if it might be the secret password to the gates of American manhood: *"Lorena, Lorena, the nightmare wife . . . sliced her husband's hot dog with a butcher knife!"*

I remember, too, how it made me giggle hysterically—not just Ronnie's homespun folk song, but the deluge of cartoons, media wisecracks, T-shirt slogans, and weenie-whacking tunes that flooded my nine-year-old head in the months after John Wayne Bobbitt lost his penis to the glimmering knife of his then-wife, Lorena.

No one in the national press bothered to mention that the infamous deed had occurred only after John Wayne, an ex-marine with a history of domestic violence, allegedly returned from a drinking binge, raped Lorena, and then fell fast asleep in their bed. Between chuckles, no one read me Lorena Bobbitt's courtroom testimony, in which the Ecuadorian immigrant described the "beating, kicking, punching, shoving, slapping, dragging, [and] choking" she suffered at her husband's hand in the preceding years of economic dependency. Instead, I heard mostly of limericks and advertising gimmicks, like the radio disc jockey who offered free Slice soda and cocktail weenies with ketchup from a booth nearby the courthouse where Lorena was eventually acquitted of "malicious wounding" charges—not in the name of self-defense, but rather on a diagnosis of temporary insanity that required a stint in a mental hospital.

It was only a decade later, under the guidance of a wise feminist or two, that I discovered the bizarre story of John Wayne Bobbitt's rise—no pun intended—to stardom as an accused rapist-turned-pornstar. Following his debut in such hardcore hits as *Frankenpenis* and *John Wayne Bobbitt Uncut*, Mr. Bobbitt eventually moved on to an equally illustrious career as an evangelical minister. By then, however, he'd already taught me a valuable lesson about gender, sex, and knives: white men who use violence get to be porn stars and preachers (not to mention presidents), while women of color and low-income women who use violence get shipped off to the cuckoo's nest.

Recently, I've been thinking yet again about Lorena Bobbitt because I've been brooding even harder about a woman named Tonya Richardson. A self-described "working girl" with a Lara Croft air about her, Richardson walks the streets and jack-shacks of Daytona Beach, Florida, "specializing" in the notoriously bottle-strewn expanse of Ridgewood Avenue. She boasts a Southern twang that's just slightly more ass-kicker than sleep-walker—like a woman who's mastered Martin Luther King, Jr.'s famous art of righteous rage but who's starting to feel the wear and tear of it. She dresses in simple collared shirts. She warms to churchgoers. And, most relevant to the story at hand, she carries a sharpened switchblade with the intent to kill.

I first encountered Richardson on Florida's Local 6 nightly news, amidst reports back in March 2006 of a serial killer on the prowl. Three women, described in the press only as "addicts and prostitutes," had been murdered in the previous months near Richardson's Daytona Beach stomping grounds. As spring emerged, the silence enveloping their deaths thawed, largely due to fears that "innocent" spring break vacationers might now be at risk alongside their whoring counterparts. While Fox News dispensed footage of gyrating, bikini-clad college girls in reference to this possible threat—

as if the killings only merited coverage now that attractive state school students were arriving in droves—Local 6 had a very different story to tell.

"Daytona Prostitutes Hunting Serial Killer" read the title on the monitor. "Rather than run from the man police labeled a serial killer," Local 6 reporter Tarik Minor began, "street-walkers here in Daytona Beach along Ridgewood Avenue say they are seeking the serial killer out." As cameras panned the palm-lined street, Minor continued, "They believe the man responsible for murdering three women here is someone they have come in contact with."

Within no time, Tonya Richardson commanded the screen, framed in that familiar tight-angle crop of a politician or a spokeswoman for an international NGO. "We'll get him first," she declared of the serial killer. She nodded vigorously, "Yeah, we are going to get him first. When we find him, he is going to be sorry. It is as simple as that."

My jaw fell slack. It wasn't the extremity of Richardson's pledge that took me by surprise; her words fell miles away from "sugar and spice and everything nice," but her serious-ness matched the gravity of the threat she faced. Nor was it the melodramatic buzz of the broadcast that struck me, although it was certainly the stuff of a Hollywood screenwriter's wet dream. Instead, the straightforward way the details were pre-sented—right from Richardson's confident lips—brought me to a striking realization: never before on mainstream TV had I seen a story about sex workers' resistance told with this brand of matter-of-fact simplicity. Or even, come to think of it, told at all. This insight sparked my curiosity: How often have women like Richardson and her Daytona Beach cohorts taken up arms, and what kind of portrayals await them when they do? Where do sex workers and their allies turn in times of heightened violence—when a serial killer, for instance, is at large?

Since hearing about Tonya Richardson's case in the spring of 2006, I've set out to look for answers from those who know best: not news anchors or crime beat reporters, but self-iden-tified street-walkers, call girls, strippers, dommes, and sex workers of various stripes. And what I've collected over the past year are strategies for self-protection that run the gamut from the mundane to the no-holds-barred, the indulgently commercial to the intensely practical. Not far from my home in England, for example, I discovered a group of sex workers and their allies who took to the streets of Ipswich after a serial killer murdered five sex workers there in December: resisting national broadcasters' entreaties that women stay inside their homes until the "Ipswich Ripper" could be apprehended, the protestors stormed the area, chanting, "We don't need protection, we need a revolution." On the other side of the ocean, not far from a Canadian pig farm where more than two dozen indigenous sex workers were brutally murdered over a period of twenty-five years, I encountered a group of prostitutes in thigh-high boots who offered me a copy of their low-budget zine targeting johns, which, they explained, is meant to curb violence by communicating their standards for personal safety directly to the most relevant audience.

Street-savvy technologies and products seem to be the saving grace for many sex workers these days: everything from cell phones to bras with secret linings for hiding the evening's earnings. True, some examples are rather pricey and elaborate; a stripper named Veronica at the Catwalk in New Haven told me about a new kind of platform shoe for urban sex workers that has a built-in alarm system, a GPS receiver, and emergency buttons that signal both law enforcement and local sex workers' rights groups. But other ideas cooked up by women and transgender folks are more accessible to those with minimal resources at their disposal—from cheap rape alarms purchased in bulk to entirely cost-free practices like buddy systems. Some sex workers train together at firing ranges while others study non-violent strategies of conflict de-escalation; some rely on end-of-the-night text messaging while there are others still who have perfected the 100 percent free strategy of license-plate memorization.

More interesting than the individual, consumption-based strategies tend to be the collective ones. Groups like the Sex Workers Alliance of Toronto (SWAT) publish an annual "bad date booklet," where sex workers can anonymously report assaults, rip-offs, or harassment from clients (as well as from police, neighborhood groups, and stalkers) in order to help others avoid similar situations. Another Canadian initiative fights for "safe zones" in Vancouver—special areas of shops and buildings clearly marked with window stickers where sex workers of all gender identities can run if they're in danger, or if they simply want to use a phone or kick back with some coffee.

Then there are more broad-based co-ops like Nevada's Sex Workers Outreach Project or Seattle's Home Alive, whose mission is to fuel "a cultural and social movement that puts violence in a context of political, economic, and social oppression and frames safety as a human right." Founded in the wake of several brutal rapes and murders of women in the city, Home Alive organizes everything from self-defense classes and boundary-setting workshops to public chalking events and community conversations. In a single year, the non-profit offered more than one hundred presentations to schools, workplaces, and low-income housing projects and shelters. Their analysis continues to help place the struggle against sexual violence in a larger political framework. "We believe that debunking stereotypes grounded in sexism and racism is one of the keys to ensuring sex workers' safety," says Home Alive director Becka Tilsen. "This is why we advocate a community response to violence that targets all forms of institutional oppression, but also gives people the tools they need to defend themselves."

Returning to Tonya Richardson's story, it's worth noting that this, too, was an example of community mobilization and not an individual crusade. Richardson always spoke to reporters in the plural—"We will get him," not "I will get him"—and one doubts this detail was accidental. Some of the sex workers' commentary on the killer may have sounded individualist, like a woman cited only as Shalonda who told the *Orlando Sentinel*, "I don't go nowhere without my knife . . . [because] if nobody ain't gonna protect me, I gotta protect me." Ultimately, however, most women along Ridgewood Avenue took up arms as part of an informal communal strategy to both protect themselves and watch each others' backs.

And if it takes a village to thwart a serial killer, then sex worker allies in Daytona Beach have also played an important role in that task. Extremely problematic as the history of religious interventions might be, it's worth noting that the Halifax Urban Ministry's volunteers rallied to sex workers' defense with a streetwalking program of their own—going out to talk with sex workers about potential threats, providing space for them to brainstorm modes of self-protection, lobbying for better lighting on dangerous avenues, and reminding the wider community that the saintly Mary Magdalene herself was none other than a prostitute.

In each of the individual and collective examples of creative resistance I've cited so far, catching word of silenced stories is only half the battle. Next comes the challenge of representation. How do sex workers get their voices back into the public sphere, while also addressing difficult internal debates about, for instance, violent versus non-violent means of seeking change? On the one hand, sex workers' resistance is often ignored within or actively erased from our public records. On the other hand, it's sometimes scrawled in bright red ink on billboards and tabloids all across America: sexualized, sensationalized, glamorized, and repackaged for the highest bidder.

Nowhere is this truer than in Hollywood, where few things sell better or titillate more than the cocktail of sex, women, and weaponry. Directors often want to have their stories both ways: cashing in on the tear-jerking image of the helpless female victim, while also harnessing the energy of the hysterical whore. A clear case in point is that of Aileen Wuornos, a sex worker in Florida who earned infamy as "the first female serial killer" after murdering seven johns whom she accused of rape or attempted rape. In a searing documentary called, *Aileen Wuornos: The Selling of a Serial Killer*, Nick Broomfield shows how Wuornos's own lawyer showed more interest in auctioning off the film rights to his client's life than in saving her from death row. A decade later, when Charlize

Theron's portrayal of Wuornos in the Hollywood film *Monster* won her an Academy Award for Best Actress, more dicey questions about Wuornos's commodification arose. It was hard not to wonder what most gushing moviegoers who wept at Theron's on-screen demise and rallied to her character's imaginary defense were busy doing on the morning of October 9, 2002, when the "real" Wuornos was sent to her death by lethal injection.

On the rare occasions when women who employ extreme means of self-defense aren't depicted as stark-raving loonies, they still tend to be punished in the end—think *Thelma and Louise* or *Madame Butterfly*. Frankly, Pedro Almodóvar's recent box office hit, *Volver*, is the first movie I've seen in which a young woman's retaliation against sexual violence doesn't ultimately boomerang around to destroy her, too. But this plot anomaly is possible only because the doe-eyed teenage daughter with the kitchen knife in hand is not, in fact, a sex worker. To the contrary, she is still young and virginal enough to be considered an "innocent" victim—one who has not yet compromised her right to be surprised by male violence due to the clothes she wears, the streets she walks, or the hours she walks them.

Not true of Tonya Richardson. In a country of criminalized prostitution, in which women in Richardson's line of work supposedly forfeit their entitlement to safety, she demands it anyway, with a switchblade. And that's why I return to her story again and again, filled with a deep and contradictory swirl of emotions: My admiration for a woman and her colleagues who have stood up for themselves against a serial killer who "left three women with their pants down in a ditch." My surprise that a mainstream media source dared to cover their collective action so straightforwardly. My anger and heartbreak that a group of women—or, for that matter, people—would ever be placed in a circumstance where wielding a switchblade felt "necessary." Or, perhaps more inexcusable, where the burden of finding and restraining a person who wants to mutilate their bodies would be thrust on an already disenfranchised group instead of being considered a collective, societal priority. And of course, my awareness that, as a privileged white woman, I owe Richardson and her colleagues far more by way of solidarity than I've offered—pulling my weight in pursuit of a world where safety is considered a sex worker's basic human right.

SARAH STILLMAN is a staff writer for *The New Yorker* and visiting scholar at New York University's Arthur L. Carter Journalism Institute.

FASHION WITH A FUNCTION: THE APHRODITE PROJECT

Erin Siegal

ISSUE 3.2 (2007)

Originally inspired by a need to stay safe on the streets, the Aphrodite Project has created a stylish prototype platform sandal that just might save your life. "One of the main concerns of contemporary urban sex workers, even in areas where prostitution is legal, is violence," says Norene Leddy, who founded the project in 2000.

Photo courtesy of Nadine.

Each shoe will theoretically contain an audible alarm system, capable of emitting a piercingly loud noise to ward off violent attackers. The platforms will also be equipped with a built-in GPS (Global Positioning Satellite) as well as an emergency button to silently relay the sex worker's location to a chosen third party as well as emergency services.

"Where there are problematic relations [for sex workers] with law enforcement, like [in] most places, the shoes will relay the signal to sex workers' rights groups, such as PONY in New York, COYOTE in Los Angeles, or SWEAT (Sex Worker Education and Advocacy Taskforce) in South Africa. Because the shoes are specifically designed to help both sex workers and sex workers' rights organizations, I am speaking with sex workers and as many of their advocates as possible to assess the actual needs of these user groups in urban areas," Leddy notes.

ERIN SIEGAL is a senior fellow at the Schuster Institute for Investigative Journalism and the author of the books *Finding Fernanda* and *The US Embassy Cables: Adoption Fraud in Guatemala, 1987-2010*. She was *$pread*'s first art director from 2004 to 2007. She currently lives in Tijuana, Mexico.

2 YOUNG 2 B 4GOTTEN: YOUTH IN THE SEX TRADE

Brendan Michael Conner, writing as Will Rockwell

ISSUE 5.3 (2010)

$pread brings you the inside scoop on four service providers working with young people in the sex trade to address the perennial question: What is to be done for young people trading sex? We've included a range of organizations, from the cooperatively run Young Women's Empowerment Project (YWEP) to the Streetwise and Safe program hosted by the Peter Cicchino Youth Project at the Urban Justice Center. From Safe Horizon's Streetwork Project, a needle exchange and shelter, to Safe Space, which provides shelter and services for homeless and at-risk youth. While we approached abolitionist projects such as Girls Educational and Mentoring Services (GEMS) and the Standing Against Global Exploitation (SAGE) project's youth program hoping for an open dialogue around mandatory "rehabilitation" and in-custody services, our repeated queries were met with rejection. In the following profile pieces, we have included each organization's mission statement and a Q&A detailing their operations.

Safe Space NYC Young Adult Services, Project GAIN
Type: Harm Reduction Services and Drop-In
Location: Jamaica, NY
Demographic: runaway, homeless, and at-risk youth, twenty-four and under

Safe Space works with the city's most at-risk youth and families in order to prevent foster care placement, to build strong families, and to promote self-sufficiency. Our mission remains urgent: to protect kids, keep them safe, and help them grow. Safe Space serves nearly 10,000 youths and their families throughout Queens and Manhattan using an integrated system of innovative programs in three core areas: Children and Family Services, Young Adult Services, and Community Health Services.

Our programs aim to strengthen families and help them develop skills that lead to self-sufficiency and personal growth. Safe Space hosts several special events throughout the year. Our fundraisers are instrumental in helping Safe Space to grow and continue to provide critical programming to nearly 10,000 disadvantaged youth and families in New York City.

WILL: How does your program make decisions and structure leadership?

SAFE SPACE: We believe in a comprehensive team approach to making decisions. Whenever possible, we invite youth to community meetings to share their thoughts and ideas on various program decisions. We encourage young participants to voice their opinions about programming.

WILL: What services do you offer?

SAFE SPACE: Safe Space's Youth Services Division has developed an integrated system of progressive services, such as our Drop-In Center and our residences for runaway homeless youth between the ages of thirteen and twenty-one. Our two Youth Drop-In Centers in Jamaica and Far Rockaway are the hub of our Young Adult Services programs. In the last year, Safe Space reached 7,689 youth through our outreach services to young adults. Beyond those touched through outreach, we also had 118 clients enrolled in case management at the Jamaica Drop-In Center and fifty-five in Far Rockaway. Safe Space also operates two transitional living facilities to support at-risk, homeless, and runaway youth.

Safe Space has been operating a peer-education program specifically for those engaged in sex work since 2007. Project Gain is a non-judgmental, harm reduction program that trains youth, thirteen to twenty-one, who currently, formerly, or know other youth who have engaged in sex work to become peer leaders and outreach workers. The program aims to highlight safety in a therapeutic and self-esteem-raising atmosphere in order to reduce risks and mobilize young people to make healthier choices about HIV prevention within their community. In addition to group counseling and creative expressions, young people are also introduced to relevant community resources, services providers, and events that inspire social justice, activism, and community organizing.

WILL: Who qualifies for your services (e.g., age, gender)? Why have you focused on these groups?

SAFE SPACE: Our Drop-In Center is for all youth, ages thirteen to twenty-one. Our goal is to provide services and programs that will protect runaway, homeless, and at-risk youth.

Project Gain is for participants ages thirteen to twenty-one who currently, formerly, or know other youth who have engaged in sex work.

WILL: What do you require before a youth can participate?

SAFE SPACE: In order to become a member of the Drop-In Center, youth must complete an intake with one of the staff members. To become a peer educator in Project Gain, they must complete an application form and have an interview with the Project Gain Coordinator. When choosing our peer educators, we look for those with motivation, strong interpersonal skills, and a desire to become more knowledgeable about safe sex and HIV prevention.

WILL: Do you partner or collaborate with law enforcement in any way? If so, how? If not, why not?

SAFE SPACE: We have collaborated with law enforcement. We have visited precincts, informed officers of youth services, and discussed important youth issues (such as LGBTQ needs, for example) regarding interactions with law enforcement.

Safe Horizon Streetwork Project
Type: Harm Reduction Services
Location: New York City, NY
Demographic: homeless youth, young sex workers, young drug users, twenty-four and under

In 1984, Streetwork started as a research project on juvenile prostitution in Times Square. Since then, Streetwork has expanded and evolved. Based in Manhattan, the project consists of two daytime drop-in centers, two shelters, a peer-education program and a citywide outreach program.

Every year Streetwork reaches more than 18,500 young people. We recognize that the sex trade is a reality of homelessness, especially for young people. Some of our clients have been forced or coerced into sex work and others have found it on their own. We recognize that in street level economies, people often fill multiple roles over the course of their lives. Many of our clients exist outside of labels such as "prostitute," "pimp," "victim," and "oppressor."

WILL: How does your program make decisions and structure leadership?
STREETWORK: Streetwork is a part of a larger organization, Safe Horizon, with its own board of directors and leadership structure. Programmatic decisions at Streetwork are generally made by the staff members and, if possible, are done on a consensus basis. Our program is continually soliciting feedback from our clients.
WILL: Do you include the leadership of the young people affected by your programs and services? If so, how?
STREETWORK: The Harlem drop-in site has a formal client advisory board that meets regularly. The Lower East Side site has regular informal "town meetings" and the shelter programs hold regular house meetings. All sites involve the clients in interviewing job applicants, and Streetwork often brings former clients onto our staff team.
WILL: What services do you offer?

STREETWORK: We offer meals, food pantry, showers, clothing, laundry, computer access, counseling, case management (including advocacy and referral), medical services, psychiatry, syringe exchange, overdose prevention training, low-threshold buprenorphine assessment and treatment, assistance obtaining identification, acupuncture, street outreach, hygiene supplies, safer sex supplies, advocacy, groups, night time shelter, and a place to stay during the day.

WILL: Who qualifies for your services (e.g., age, gender)? Why have you focused on these groups?

STREETWORK: Anyone who is under twenty-four years old and homeless is eligible to become a client of Streetwork. Anyone who is under twenty-four and injects drugs is eligible to become a Streetwork client. Streetwork operates a youth-specific syringe exchange program. Our clients represent people of all gender identities and sexualities.

Historically, homeless youth services have focused on rescuing young people from "the streets" in ways that prevent them from engaging in services when they need them the most.

WILL: What do you require before a youth can participate?

STREETWORK: Clients generally receive an intake when they first access one of our programs. Clients are not required to have any documents or identification and are allowed to use an alias.

WILL: How do you find and identify the young people you provide services for? How do you determine their needs?

STREETWORK: We do street outreach every night of the week. However, the vast majority of our clients come to us through peer referrals. We determine the needs of our individual clients by listening. All of our services are 100 percent voluntary and clients are never mandated.

WILL: Do you partner or collaborate with law enforcement in any way? If so, how? If not, why not?

STREETWORK: Streetwork tries to maintain a relationship with law enforcement and we advocate for clients within law enforcement systems, but we have not collaborated because police often mistreat our clients, and collaboration is not necessary in our day-to-day work.

Young Women's Empowerment Project

Type: Community Project and Collective
Location: Chicago, IL
Demographic: young women engaged in the sex trade and street economies, twelve to twenty-three

YWEP is a community-based, youth-led project that was founded in 2001 by a radical feminist and a harm reduction-based collective of women and girls involved in the sex trade and street economy (ages twelve to twenty-three). We offer girls involved in the sex trade and street economy non-judgmental support, harm reduction information, and resources, and we have job opportunities and paid volunteer positions. This work is personal to us because it is about our lives.

YWEP's mission is to offer safe, respectful, free-of-judgment spaces for girls and young women impacted by the sex trade and street economies to recognize their goals, dreams, and desires. We are run by girls and women with life experience in the sex trade and street economies.

WILL: How does your program make decisions and structure leadership?

YWEP: YWEP is a member-based social project led by and for young women. We are a consensus-based organization, meaning, everyone

> "I did what I did for my kids. What I did was I sold my body for money. I did that when I was pregnant so I could eat and keep a roof over my head. To be honest that's not the only reason why I sold my body. It was also because I had a drug habit. So yeah, I did it to the point that I did not care anymore. My second pregnancy I did it until I got locked up. When I was pregnant with my third child I did it until I was eight months cause I was living in a hotel and I had to pay every night to stay there. I quit when I got into a shelter. I started working again when my baby was two and a half months old because she needed things like diapers and clothes."
>
> —Julia Rosas, 19 years old

in the organization must agree on a decision before moving on. Unless everyone is in agreement with the idea, we continue to talk until everyone is in agreement.

WILL: Do you include the leadership of the young people affected by your programs and services? If so, how?

YWEP: We are an organization based on social and transformative justice. We don't provide social services; we are run by and for girls (including transgendered girls) with current or former experience in the sex trade and street economies. Girls hold power at every level of our organization and are in charge of everything from fundraising to making political and project decisions.

WILL: What services do you offer?

YWEP: From member to part of the executive team, every single girl who comes to YWEP has a job. We offer the following activities as part of our activism and leadership development: Girls in Charge (GIC) is our paid, weekly leadership group open to new girls. We use political education and work on projects together. GIC makes all of the major decisions at YWEP. Girls get paid for GIC, and we offer bus fare and twenty dollars to any girl who stays and works during the meeting.

After you have come to GIC for one month, participants can join our outreach team! After they complete a paid, forty-hour training, girls can become workers with us and reach other girls in the sex trade with condoms and life-saving support. Outreach workers also receive a stipend for their outreach work. We also offer access to clean syringes.

After girls have completed the Outreach Worker training, they are able to get more involved with our social justice work. Our social justice group, YAK (Young Activist Krew) is currently working on turning the results from our research into a social justice campaign. YAK created the YWEP Bad Encounter Line, a forum for girls in the sex trade and street economy that warns other girls about bad experiences with institutions they've worked in. This will help us further narrow down the focus of our social justice campaign. YWEP travels to common hangouts for young people and leads interactive discussions. Girls respond to questions about the sex trade, and we draw on the knowledge of all participants' answers.

WILL: Who qualifies for your services (e.g., age, gender)? Why have you focused on these groups?

YWEP: YWEP is open to all girls (including transgendered girls) who are currently or were formerly involved in the sex trade and street economy. We are led by and for girls of color. We do not require ID or use intake forms.

WILL: What do you require before a youth can participate?

YWEP: A girl is not required to exit the sex trade. YWEP is harm reduction based, and we will travel to wherever the girl is located. We understand that sex trade is a complicated issue, and that exit is not always possible, so instead we work with the young woman in order to come up with positive change that she views as beneficial to her life.

WILL: Do you partner or collaborate with law enforcement in any way? If so, how? If not, why not?

YWEP: YWEP does not work with law enforcement at all. We strategize as much as possible about reducing our exposure to the criminal legal system and reducing the harm by engaging with the law.

Streetwise and Safe
LGBTQQ Youth of Color Standing Up to Police Abuse and Criminalization (SAS)
Type: Legal Services, Policy Advocacy
Location: New York City, NY
Demographic: LGBTQQ youth of color, young sex workers, 24 and under

Streetwise and Safe: LGBTQQ Youth of Color Standing Up to Police Abuse and Criminalization (SAS) is a collaborative multi-strategy initiative to develop leadership skills among LGBTQQ youth of color who have experienced gender and sexuality-specific forms of race- and class-based policing, particularly under the context of "quality of life" policing and the policing of sex work.

We work with queer and transgender youth of color up to age twenty-four who have experience trading sex for money, food, shelter, clothing, or other survival needs, as well as LGBTQQ youth who have experienced homelessness and criminalization. SAS also creates opportunities for LGBTQQ youth of color to claim a seat at policy discussion tables as full participants. We not only directly empower LGBTQQ youth of color, we also challenge sex workers' rights groups, mainstream LGBTQQ organizations and anti-police brutality initiatives to integrate the voices, experiences and perspectives of LGBTQQ youth of color around policing and punishment.

WILL: How does your program make decisions and structure leadership?

PCYP: Currently, staff members and consultants of PCYP primarily make the decisions. However, youth play a key role in setting the direction of SAS. Additionally, they can also decide how to use the tools they develop and messages they disseminate through community education efforts. As they move through the leadership program, participants have greater involvement in decision-making at PCYP.

WILL: Do you include the leadership of the young people affected by your programs and services? If so, how?

PCYP: Once they graduate from the first cycle of SAS, youth are able to join two teams connected with PCYP: the Community Educators Team and/or the Policy Advocacy Team. Community Educators regularly share information with their peers using the tools developed through SAS. They also meet once a month to discuss issues raised and policy advocacy opportunities suggested by their interactions with their peers. These experiences will facilitate their assumption of leadership roles in local LGBTQQ, sex worker rights, civil rights, human rights and police accountability organizations and movements. Through peer education efforts, they will also identify additional LGBTQQ youth of color with the capacity for and interest in achieving systemic change. Additionally, graduates of SAS will play a central role in refining and implementing future youth leadership development initiatives at PCYP.

WILL: What services do you offer?

PCYP: For over fifteen years, PCYP has addressed the legal needs of these communities through a blend of legal organizing, legislative advocacy, and direct representation. PCYP has developed considerable experience in "know your rights" workshops for LGBTQQ youth, and in advocacy on behalf of youth within the juvenile justice and criminal legal systems. Legal services include advocacy in immigration, housing, income support, and child welfare matters.

> "I have been a trans sex worker since the age of sixteen, I did it to help my mother put food on the table for my brothers, and to keep us from getting evicted. This became my life . . . this is my truth . . ."
>
> —from *This is My Truth*, a "know your rights" video created by SAS for LGBTQQ youth of color who experience "quality of life" policing and policing of sex work

WILL: Who qualifies for your services (e.g., age, gender)? Why have you focused on these groups?

PCYP: All LGBTQQ youth under the age of twenty-four in the greater New York City area are eligible to receive legal representation. PCYP has focused on providing services to this group because other providers underserve them. They also have unique needs and experiences that would benefit from a nonjudgmental approach.

WILL: What do you require before a youth can participate?

PCYP: A meeting with SAS project staff or a PCYP attorney.

WILL: Do you partner or collaborate with law enforcement in any way? If so, how? If not, why not?

PCYP: PCYP and SAS do not formally collaborate with law enforcement. We believe that it is essential to create a space without interference from the criminal legal system. If a young person asks for assistance interacting with law enforcement, we will support them in doing so.

BRENDAN MICHAEL CONNER—also known by his pseudonym, Will Rockwell—is a former escort and *$pread* editor. He currently works as a police misconduct and prisoner's rights attorney for people in the sex trade and street economy in New York City. Brendan has also worked both independently and as a research editor with Avrett Consulting for organizations such as Safe Horizon's Streetwork Project, UNDP, USAID, the HIV Young Leaders Fund, and the Open Society Institute.

ALPHABET HOOKERS: B IS FOR BOBBI

Morgan Ellis

ISSUE 2.2 (2006)

Bobbi was a woman who couldn't say no. Not in the old-fashioned, fallen woman kind of way: Bobbi was one of those infallibly polite women who didn't like to say no, for fear of insulting someone. This is a dangerous quality in an escort.

A Germanic blond in her forties, Bobbi was the last woman you'd assume was an escort. Originally, she'd been a chanteuse, singing songs in piano bars and lounges. Since this stopped being a lucrative occupation roughly around 1972, it's no wonder she needed a little something extra to top up her monthly income. Escorting seemed to be the solution, since she liked sex, men, and money, in roughly that order.

Bobbi liked to call me and update me on how her dates had gone. Her phone calls were inevitably so over-the-top incredible that they became almost legendary among our group of friends. We started referring to her as "No Bobbi," since that seemed to be the response that almost any conversation with her inspired.

"Well, Morgan, he was a very nice man, but I didn't like it when he tied me up, blindfolded me, and then took photos of me."

"No, Bobbi! Don't ever let anyone do that if you're not comfortable, and it wasn't negotiated in advance!"

"Well, Morgan, he wanted me to put a . . ."

"A what?"

"A broomstick. In my you-know-what."

"Jesus! In your pussy?"

"No . . ."

"Where?"

"In my . . . bottom."

"Oh my god! No, Bobbi! You didn't let him, did you?"

"Well, he was very nice, otherwise. Morgan, this man tonight . . ."

"This man what?"

"He had a video camera, and . . ."

"Bobbi, no! Don't let anyone videotape you! You have no idea where it might end up!"

"I had a nice date tonight, Morgan."

"For a change! That's good to know."

"Yes, but I wish he'd told me that two of his friends were going to be there, as well."

"Bobbi, for God's sake! Learn to say fucking no, OK? You're going to get killed. Jesus!"

"No Bobbi" worried me, constantly. We tried, all of us, to convince her that she had the right, and the obligation, to say no to things that she didn't want to do. She just wasn't raised that way, I suppose. In her world, women were polite to men, even when the men didn't return the favor. Nice girls, I suppose, just didn't say no, even if they were saying no to being abused for pay.

"Morgan, I was very angry at my date tonight."

Well, that was a change. Bobbi didn't get angry. Being angry wasn't in her lexicon, from what I'd always known of her.

"Why were you angry? What did he do?"

"He wanted to hit me, on my bottom. He had a paddle and some whips."

"Jesus. Bobbi, what happened then?"

"I told him no."

Bobbi is retired now, happily tending her garden and her grandchildren. When I talked to her last, she'd ditched her

Illustration by Shannon Taylor.

serially unfaithful husband and was planning a cruise to the Caribbean. She says no to all kinds of things now, on a regular basis.

Yes, Bobbi.

MORGAN ELLIS wrote "B is for Bobbi" as part of her *Alphabet Hookers* series on her blog. It was republished in *$pread,* Issue 2.2.

SHANNON TAYLOR is an artist and arts educator living in Toronto.

MEDIA AND CULTURE

INTRODUCTION

Damien Luxe

Giving a voice to the voiceless is a basic journalistic responsibility, but sit down with an issue of this already controversial title and you'll realize how effectively the mainstream media have denied sex workers a place at the table. Smart and culturally revealing, this quarterly magazine aims to educate, inform, and provoke discussion about the state of sex work.
—*Utne Reader*, after awarding *$pread* "Best New Title" in 2005

In a climate of sensationalism and stigma, the mass media treats sex workers like we can only be spoken for, and yet our community produces writing, creative strategies, art, and public education projects that stand on their own. *$pread* was media made by sex workers, as well as a documentation of how we exist in the mainstream culture as well as our own subcultures.

By speaking about, speaking for, or simply not listening to sex workers, the mainstream media negates our voices and distorts the picture. In the wake of the Eliot Spitzer scandal, Caroline Andrews explored how sex workers became caught up in the media frenzy. "The Real Media Whores" shows how sex workers learned, sometimes painfully, how to navigate the mass media's minefields of shame and stigma in their quest to speak out through daily newspapers and cable TV shows. In Radical Vixen's interview with "DC Madam" Deborah Jeane Palfrey, this idea—that sex workers are supposed to retreat in shame—is further challenged when Palfrey comments, "These people can come after me, destroy me, take every shot they possibly can at me, and I'm supposed to just sit back and be quiet? That's why I'm doing this interview with you."

The shiny silver lining of the media's fascination with sex work is that some of us have found ways to leverage it. Porn star and self-described "man with a pussy" Buck Angel has managed to do just that, and Audacia Ray's interview chronicled how a "whirlwind of history making and boundary pushing brought Buck into the spotlight and gave him a platform to speak." Likewise Craig Seymour, the subject of an interview by Will Rockwell, has segued his life as a former stripper into a successful career as a journalist and writer. "When something is published," Seymour said, "it's a validation of a certain experience . . . you cannot applaud any of my more socially acceptable accomplishments without my stripping experience." Media by sex workers, in other words, shows a full-picture narrative of the sex industry: our whole stories, in print, in public, for the record.

There is no singular sex worker point of view, and media also creates a space where we can disagree. The relationship between feminism and the sex worker movement, for example, can be particularly contentious. While exploring how novelist Tracy Quan represents her sex worker activist characters, she told interviewer Rachel Aimee that she didn't "want to see female sex workers make unhealthy alliances with feminists who may try to influence the politics of our movement." In contrast, Eliyanna Kaiser's interview with Canadian pro-choice activist Joyce Arthur reflected her belief that a feminist reproductive rights ideology is, at its heart, about self-determination and control over one's body—the same issues the sex workers' rights movement is concerned with. "You need to keep emphasizing female sexual autonomy," Arthur said. "From an activism point of view, this is a long process of public education."

This long process of resisting mainstream cultural representations in the media did not begin only when *$pread* started to capture it, nor did *$pread* have the capacity to document all of the work being produced. Sex workers are also prolific visual artists, gallery owners, performance artists, video artists, eloquent public speakers, and journalists—and we write, we write, we write.

DAMIEN LUXE is a Brooklyn-based, queer femme, liberationist artist, digital technologist, and community organizer who creates, produces, and performs political and participatory multimedia works all over the United States and Canada. Her recent works include: Exorcize, a satirical and serious healing aerobics program for all bodies; Hot Pink Mass, a church service that invokes the deity Trisha; and Femmes Fight Back, an interactive installation honoring queer herstories while resisting the State. She is cofounder of Heels on Wheels, a working-class-led, multi-racial, queer femme performance art, which produces the Glitter Roadshow and monthly Opentoe Peepshow. She is currently writing a book on the history of raised fists in political art.

SEX WORK AND THE CITY:
AN INTERVIEW WITH TRACY QUAN

Rachel Aimee

ISSUE 1.3 (2005)

Every good, sex work-positive activist recognizes that "sex work is work," but what we're not always ready to admit is that reading some of the books out there about sex work can start to feel like a chore. So, when I came across Tracy Quan's first novel, *Diary of a Manhattan Call Girl*, two years ago, I was relieved to discover that it was pure pleasure. I immediately found myself caught up in the glamorous world of Nancy, Allison, and Jasmine as they swish around Manhattan buying shoes, getting waxes, and gossiping about men, much like the characters in *Sex and the City* except that they're hookers. And except that Carrie Bradshaw and friends don't invent fictional copy editing careers for themselves, shred their mail, change their outfits in hotel restrooms, or attend NYCOT (New York Council of Trollops) meetings.

Nancy Chan, the heroine of *Diary of a Manhattan Call Girl* and now the sequel, *Diary of a Married Call Girl*, is decidedly skeptical about the sex workers' rights movement from the outset and fears that her idealistic friend Allison is putting everyone's safety in jeopardy by becoming a public spokesperson for NYCOT. She and Jasmine are far more concerned with keeping a low profile, maintaining their secret double lives, and getting away with turning tricks "[i]llegally. The way it's supposed to be done." Since I knew that the author was herself a sex work activist and member of PONY (Prostitutes of New York), I assumed that her central character would eventually come around and see the value of the movement—that the activists would save the day or something. If I'd known anything about Tracy, I wouldn't have been so naïve.

Although Tracy has been an activist for many years, she's admitted that she has a love-hate relationship with the movement, and she's always saying things that seem deliberately designed to shock or offend other activists. I realized this when, having finished her first novel perplexed as to why she hadn't given her fictional activists a better rap, I looked up every interview I could find in an attempt to figure out what Tracy Quan was really all about. I have to admit, I developed a bit of an obsession with this enigmatic former call girl who calls herself a sex worker while complaining that the label is overly politically correct, who speaks openly about her experiences in the sex industry but rails against the puritanism of the political emphasis on coming out, who is a leading figure in a social movement that seeks to destigmatize sex work but believes that social change is threatening to prostitutes.

A lot of activists dismiss Tracy's books because they're sugary, or because they don't agree with some of her libertarian politics. I personally disagree with a lot of Tracy's views, and I'm sure I'm exactly the type of twenty-something feminist with an aversion to catcalls that she'd make fun of in her novels, but I can't help being endlessly fascinated by her smart, funny, sometimes offensive, and often outrageous comments and somewhat in awe of her fierce, witty logic. As well as being totally hooked on her novels. Tracy's books are certainly addictive, and if you enjoyed reading about Nancy in her initial incarnation as the heroine of Tracy's *Salon* columns, or in the first novel, you'll love the married version just as much. Even if you don't, it's hard to deny that, with thousands of people all over the world lapping up her unapologetically realistic representation of hookers as functional, guilt-free human beings, Tracy is helping to bring about social change whether she likes it or not.

RACHEL: I love your novels because they're so much fun to read and it's really rare to find intelligent books about sex work that appeal to a wide audience. Was it a conscious decision to write about sex work and sex worker activism in a genre that appeals to people who like *Bridget Jones's Diary* and *Sex and the City* as opposed to academics and activists who are already reading about this stuff?

TRACY: Paying the rent is almost always the result of a conscious decision, as I think most of your readers in the sex trade will agree! My decisions about how to make a living as a writer have been informed by many years in sex work. Okay, it is true that, as a prostitute, I was kind of exclusive, but as an author, I want to reach the largest number of readers. And, even when I was being exclusive, I did my best to keep my options open and appeal to more than one kind of customer! So I'm following my sex-working muse here.

I often wonder if serious activists will dismiss my work because it's entertaining and because, though an activist myself for many years, I have a strong Bridget Jones component to my personality. A lot of the activists I meet are a bit severe and they don't seem to care as much as I do about "Having a Boyfriend."

RACHEL: Your central character, Nancy Chan, lives the exclusive life of a high-class escort in Manhattan, but she started out turning tricks in hotel bars as a teenage runaway. I understand there are parallels between her experiences and your own. Why did you choose to write about sex work from the perspective of Upper East Side call girls, and have you considered writing in more depth from your experiences in less "glamorous" areas of prostitution?

TRACY: Well, Upper East Side prostitution is something I know about in great detail. I spent a few years doing the other stuff, but I like to show how an indoor call girl with a small, private client base can have a secret past that her clients don't know about. It's emotionally fruitful to explore the tension between her current image and her past experience. I got into prostitution at age fourteen, and by the age of nineteen I was entering the private call girl scene.

But I don't think being an Upper East Side call girl is glamorous! It's hard work, it's a real grind at times; it's also dangerous when the cops are sniffing around. With rents like we have today, being a Manhattan call girl is not an easy, laid back lifestyle. It's very competitive, and more so today than it used to be.

RACHEL: I see your point. I guess I really meant that Nancy, Allison, and Jasmine's lifestyles in general seem glamorous or at least exciting, rather than the work itself being glamorous, although I'm curious to know if you ever get accused of glamorizing prostitution.

TRACY: I guess so, but I don't think that's a very astute accusation. My characters shop at Duane Reade, too. They worry about getting everything at a discount. They make decisions like "expensive bag, cheap wallet," because you do have to choose sometimes when you're a working girl. I think only a very unobservant reader would regard this as sheer glamour. What I'm actually doing is showing readers some of the shopkeeper logic that lies beneath the glamorous image of a call girl.

RACHEL: I've read that, like Nancy, you decided you wanted to be a prostitute at a young age, but what about writing? Did you always aspire to be a novelist, or was that something that came later? Was it a difficult transition to make?

TRACY: At thirteen, I wanted to write a novel and took note of all my conversations with my father, that sort of thing, but I didn't realize I was already living a life that was worth writing about. I had no idea that my experiences as a babysitter would, one day, have some literary value, much less my first encounter with oral sex.

The transition to writing was invigorating but it took its toll on a relationship I was having at the time. As I grew into being a full-time writer, I changed and that relationship ended. I don't regret it and neither, I think, does that particular guy, but you can't really grow in a new career without going through some discomfort.

We always hear about how sex work disrupts your romantic life, but it's a mistake to think your personal life will get simplified just because you quit hooking. Or dancing. Or spanking, for that matter. I hear too many people saying they want to quit the sex trade in order to get married or have a better personal life. It just depends on where you are at in general and who your partner is. My partner discovered that living with a writer was much more complicated than being involved with a hooker!

RACHEL: Now that she's a married call girl, your central character, Nancy, works hard at playing the perfect wife and worries about turning into the kind of frumpy woman that her clients come to her to escape. What's your view of marriage?

TRACY: My parents are divorced so I've got mixed feelings about this. Sometimes I wish they had stayed together because they were a good combination as parents—in another period of history, they would have done that, but my mother was a restless, modern woman.

People who see wives as prostitutes are very short-sighted. In some Manhattan circles, the husband is the prostitute going out to hustle every day, and the wife's like a traditional pimp—motivational, giving him a sentimental reason to make his quota, making him feel like he's got a partner in crime. For this reason, I'm a lot more cheerful about the concept of the pimp, even though I never had one. Now, if my mom had been that kind of wife, perhaps my 'rents would still be together! But she wasn't interested in that.

RACHEL: Nancy continues to hide her work from her husband, turning tricks by day and playing the conservative banker's wife by night. I've read that you believe hookers who hide their professions from their partners are often healthier, happier, and more functional than those who are open about it. What would you say to those who argue that it's politically important for sex workers to come out, whenever safe and possible, in order to challenge a society that doesn't accept sex work as legitimate work?

TRACY: Yeah, well, this seems kind of preachy to me. I'm always intrigued by the fantastic stories sex workers tell their relatives and lovers and straight friends in order to keep their work a secret. We are such creative, twisted, inventive people—let's celebrate that, too. We can fake orgasms, we can fake not having orgasms, we have orgasms that we keep a secret from our clients. We can keep a relationship or a double life going for years without being discovered. This is a major intellectual talent, a human skill that puritanical American culture condemns. It's part of our joyless Protestant heritage. It's so literal-minded, and it's unimaginative.

Stop moralizing and stop being so puritanical about the so-called truth! Maybe when a hooker tells a story about where she was that night to her husband, it's a metaphor, a kind of performance art; maybe she's just taking poetic license. If I can be a little strident for a sec, it is moronic to lecture sex workers about truth and legitimacy. We have our own truths. Our own code of ethics. I don't care if a prostitute lies to the straight world; I care if she does the right thing by her coworkers. You can lie as much as you want to your family but you should be a stand-up girl in your profession. Make your best effort to satisfy the customer; don't fight dirty when you're competing with other hookers; be honorable in your dealings as a whore. And above all, never, ever stoop to becoming an informant or any kind of rat. That's more important than coming out of the closet.

Instead, we should be giving workshops on how to be creative with the "truth". We should perhaps have PONY sessions where we coach the sex workers who are afraid to lie because they think, on some level, they'll be struck down by thunder.

While I was shopping my first book, I kept my *Salon* column a secret from my family and a lot of people I knew. That really contributed to the creative tension, helped me produce a better, funnier story and enabled me to get on with my own work. If writers are permitted to have double lives, why not prostitutes? One thing I have learned is that society cuts the artist a lot of slack but other people—prostitutes, executives—are considered workaholics or mentally disturbed or victims if they live like artists. To lie about your work is, very often, a way to put your business first: you refuse to let your personal life interfere with your output. If you tell everybody that you're a sex worker, you may spend endless free time explaining yourself and micromanaging other people's feelings. This is time you could be spending on yourself, on your business, hanging out with your friends in the business!

If you are ready to tell people about your sex work, then go for it, but nobody has the right to browbeat you into coming out of the closet. And don't confess to being a sex worker if you are doing it to get somebody's approval.

RACHEL: Despite her secret life as a call girl, Nancy has some old-fashioned ideas about women's roles; she takes pride in being a dutiful wife, dressing and behaving in a ladylike manner, and letting her husband believe he's supporting her financially, and she's put off by the "airy fairy feminist" ideas of her activist friends. What's your personal stance on feminism and its relationship to sex work?

TRACY: I would not call Nancy Chan a dutiful wife, but she likes to be feminine! She's using her wifely image as a cover for her secret life; she's actually quite a self-serving creature and if anybody is dutiful in the relationship, it's her husband.

I've been around feminism and feminist organizations since the age of ten, so I don't take it as seriously as some people do. My mother was very feminist and I've worked out a lot of my separation issues by rejecting her ideology. I feel totally entitled to my place at the feminist table so

I feel very confident about walking away from it. Or, better yet, giving it to some other sex worker who feels less secure about her relationship to feminism.

When I read Lily Burana's memoir, *Strip City*, I got the impression that she still wants to establish her feminist cred. That's because she was very attached to her mother who was a suburban housewife. My mother couldn't wait to push me out of the nest, so she could get on with her life, her career. She didn't want me to get too attached and I think an attachment to feminism is, in American life, a sign of needing approval or affection from your mother. It may even be a sign that you spent your childhood in the suburbs, which I did not.

One of my heroes, Jane Jacobs, felt that suburban life created a matriarchal bubble that was not very healthy for children. They would grow up having very little interaction with male shopkeepers and pedestrians; they would see the occasional deliveryman or repairman. And she's right. I see the symptoms of this early alienation from men and this over-attachment to mothers in a lot of adult women. I spent most of my childhood in mixed-use neighborhoods, very little time around my mother by comparison, and I think that's why I'm not very attached to feminism.

RACHEL: Your novels comment on some of the tensions and conflicts between "regular" sex workers and sex worker activists. Nancy, who sees her work as "a job, not a cause," is horrified by her idealistic friend Allison's involvement with NYCOT and can't relate to the activists who proudly label themselves whores, refuse to shave their pubic hair, and chant about sexual harassment. Do you think a lot of sex workers feel alienated by the radical politics of the sex workers' rights movement, and should the movement address these issues in order to be more inclusive?

TRACY: I think the movement is doing fine, actually. It's very inclusive and when you're inclusive you'll have some culture shock, some squabbles, some thong cleavage, and some excessive piercings. It really is true that thirty-something hookers come to PONY events and laugh about the twenty-year-olds who are complaining about sexual harassment, but it's with a certain affectionate glee because it's also great to know that the movement continues to attract these feisty newcomers. When I was seventeen, sidewalk harassment was very upsetting to me, too. Of course, I was wearing a halter-top and had no idea I was actually inviting the looks and the comments. Now I think it's funny and I have more control over the experience.

I don't worry about radical attitudes—radicalism can get people moving and talking. But I worry sometimes about alienating the guys in our industry. That, I think, is a valid concern because guys play an important role in the sex trade—as providers or consumers—and in the sex workers' movement. Some women get very turned off when we feel an anti-male vibe in the room. I don't want the movement to be dominated by feminism; I don't want to see female sex workers making unhealthy alliances with feminists who may try to influence the politics of our movement. In order for our growing political power to remain in the hands of sex workers, feminism has to be kept in perspective, not allowed to completely dominate. We have made lots of progress globally because, in the last fifteen years or so, male sex workers have begun to play a leadership role. This has helped us to become a human rights movement rather than a puppet of feminism. And I still hear of instances where males are excluded or alienated so I know this is still a problem.

Having said that, if someone feels the need to rant about "the patriarchy" at a PONY meeting, I just smile and listen. I think there's room for all of us.

RACHEL: Considering your views seem quite different from a lot of the activists I know, I'm interested to know how and why you initially became a sex worker activist and what you see as the main goals of the movement.

TRACY: I just can't imagine life without the hookers' movement. I joined up before the term sex worker was en vogue and I can't even remember why. It just felt like the natural thing to do. I knew that prostitutes had to leave their political imprint; not to be part of that was unthinkable to me. I understood that it was historically inevitable and I wanted to be part of it.

The goals change and differ depending on where you live. It's a global movement. The main goal, however, is to give prostitutes political power and a chance to participate fully in democracy. This is pretty broad, but thought control and parsimonious finger wagging don't have to be part of that process. Okay, and in some cases, the urgent goal is to keep prostitutes alive.

RACHEL: How have sex worker activists responded to the way they are represented in your novels?

TRACY: I think many activists are too busy to notice! Or perhaps I've disguised my characters effectively. Nancy's friend Jasmine is very critical of the activist scene, which she sees as a jungle filled with these outsize egos vying for dominance, and there is some truth to this. One reason I have remained a gadfly in the movement and have never been connected to any of the funding from the WHO [World Health Organization] is my desire to stay friends with everyone.

At the end of the day, a novel is a product of the imagination. I don't know if activists are represented in my novel. They are reborn! But I think the neurotic problems of activism are well represented there.

RACHEL: I hear that your first novel, *Diary of a Manhattan Call Girl*, is going to be made into a film. Do you have any more information about when that's going to happen or who might star in it?

TRACY: Darren Star's going to produce the film and Revolution Studios optioned the novel. Claudia Shear is working on the screenplay. She did a fantastic show about Mae West, called *Dirty Blonde*. She's a very funny writer who knows a lot about life. I'm pleased about her involvement.

RACHEL: So does Nancy retire as a literary heroine—if not as a call girl—or will there be a third novel? What are you working on at the moment?

TRACY: I'd like to write a nonfiction book. *Diary of a Married Call Girl* is being translated into Dutch and Italian as we speak. Those editions will come out in the spring of 2006. I'm not sure what Nancy will do next. She likes to keep her readers guessing so we'll just have to wait and see!

RACHEL AIMEE cofounded *$pread* magazine in 2004 and was an editor-in-chief for four and a half years. Now a parent and freelance copy editor, she also organizes for strippers' rights with We Are Dancers. She lives in Brooklyn with her family.

UP IN BUCK'S BUSINESS: AN INTERVIEW WITH BUCK ANGEL

Audacia Ray

ISSUE 2.2 (2006)

It seems like every press release for an adult movie makes wild claims about a first-time something-or-other or a crazy new innovation that makes this one release out of the twelve thousand adult movies produced each year worth your time. However, genre-busting female-to-male transsexual Buck Angel has truly broken with the traditions of porn merely by being who he is: a self-identified "man with a pussy." Buck has also done what many people in the adult industry are envious of—he has gotten media attention outside porn and has been written about in a variety of newspapers and magazines that are fascinated with this very masculine man who was born in a woman's body.

Much of the mainstream coverage of Buck and his career hovers around fascination with his sex change as well as his bisexual identity—nothing about Buck allows anyone to pin a specific label on him, which seems to frustrate and terrify many people. Buck's recent appearance on *The Howard Stern Show* left Stern's staff members stunned, as they grappled with pronouns and said that Buck was "disgustingly fascinating," and the "most unique guest we've ever had." These reactions to Buck are pretty standard among straight men and people who can't comprehend transsexualism. Buck uses them as "teachable moments," but he also has a sense of humor about other people's hang-ups and has forged ahead in an industry that sells sex but is often surprisingly conservative.

Buck started his career as a porn performer after he'd been working as a webmaster for other people's porn sites and became acutely aware that while there were plenty of male-to-female (MTF) porn stars, there weren't any female-to-male (FTM) ones. He took matters into his own hands and launched his paysite, Transexual-man.com, in early 2003. Buck's site doesn't intentionally cater to any specific audience, but rather is a catalog of his sexual interests and fetishes. In addition to web content, Buck self-produced DVDs until he signed a twelve-movie production deal with Robert Hill Releasing in November of 2004, becoming the first FTM to be signed to a major studio. When his deal with the company went sour, Buck returned to producing his own porn, this time with a distributor. His movies can now be purchased in fifteen different countries.

In the past year, Buck has made all kinds of porno history. He shot a scene with MTF porn star Allanah Star, and his movie, *Buck's Beaver*, was a nominee for *Adult Video News*'s "Best Transsexual Release" award in 2005. He has also gotten a lot of interest from gay men, and filmed a scene in a movie for the renowned gay porn company Titan. In March of 2006, Buck was a featured performer at the Black Party, a major annual gay circuit party, where he had sex in front of 6,000 gay men. This whirlwind of history making and boundary pushing has brought Buck into the spotlight and given him a platform to speak about issues affecting porn performers, transsexuals, and sexual misfits more generally.

A few years ago I saw Buck speak on a panel about porn, and people really wanted him to be an activist supreme, speaker of the Transman Voice—but he resisted this call-to-arms with stoicism. He stuck to his guns and was adamant that he was making porn, not creating a political movement. However, it seems that more recently Buck has been put to the test, and he has, a little reluctantly, begun to embrace his position as a cultural icon in the realm of sexual politics, though he is still careful to recognize that many transmen do not support his work and that he does not speak for all—or even most—FTMs.

Especially over the last few months, it seems like every time I check in on Buck, he's just finished doing an interview with some publication or other. Most of the interviews don't get past the obsession with his transsexualism and his very fluid bisexuality. In this interview, I attempted to move beyond the media fascination with Buck's sex change and ask him questions about his unique perspective on working in the sex industry.

AUDACIA: What drew you into the sex industry?

BUCK: Sex! I am a pretty sexual guy so I wanted to work in an industry where I would like to show up for work everyday. I also wanted to add something positive to an industry that always seemed to be getting a bad rap.

AUDACIA: What is it that's so different about the transitioning process for transmen and transwomen that leads so many transwomen into the sex industry and not transmen?

BUCK: I think that because MTFs are "men" first they have a much higher sex drive. So it just seems natural that they would get into sex work. I also think MTFs are much more comfortable with their bodies [after transition] whereas FTMs are not. I am sure I am finally changing that now but FTMs have a long way to go. They are mostly focused on the penis and feel like they cannot be men without it.

AUDACIA: You have the unique experience of having worked in the non-porn modeling industry as a woman before you made your transition. In what ways do sexism and sexual harassment play out differently in the straight and adult modeling industries?

BUCK: It's not very different. Actually, I think they are quite the same in some respects. As a man now I do not get much sexual harassment in the way I did when I was modeling as a woman. I hated it so much because these gross men would just slobber all over me and have no boundaries. If I was a woman in porn I am sure I would be getting the same kind of treatment. Now I just get stupid straight guys telling me how disgusting I am!

AUDACIA: When you are interviewed by the mainstream media, is it more about being transsexual or about being in porn?

BUCK: Both. First they want to talk about my transition and how that all came about. Then they are fascinated by how I got into doing porn. I think it is because I am the only "Man with a Pussy" in the adult business.

AUDACIA: All of your porn was self-produced and self-distributed initially. What were the advantages and disadvantages of working that way?

BUCK: The advantage was keeping ownership of all my movies. The disadvantage was not having the means or connections for getting my films to a wider audience because of the distribution you need to do that.

AUDACIA: What made you decide to make movies for someone else? What are the advantages and disadvantages of working for someone else?

BUCK: After making my own movies for a while, I had to get my foot in the door so more people could see my work, and I needed to have a company that was able to do that for me. But I have since left that company (Robert Hill Releasing) because they ended up being very slimy and not paying me. I have gone back to producing my own videos and just have distribution. I am now distributed by Avalon and I am very happy with them. They treat me with respect.

AUDACIA: When you first started making porn, what kind of market did you have in mind? Has the interest that gay men have taken in you been a surprise? What other kinds of audiences would you like to see enjoy your work?

BUCK: I thought for sure the transsexual men would be all over my work. Surprise! They hated me. They were very rude and disrespectful, sending nasty emails and saying all kinds of crap to me. That has since turned around and now they have come to their senses and find what I

Photo courtesy of Buck Angel.

am doing very hot. But they still are the more infrequent group of buyers. I had no idea the gay market was going to embrace me the way they have. It has been amazing. I would really like to see more women get into my porn. As you know, they tend not to be big porn buyers, but damn, I would like to change that.

AUDACIA: You've spoken about being a porn performer as a means to an end—what is this end? Do you feel that being a porn performer was, personally and professionally, a necessary part of that process?

BUCK: That end is basically getting behind the camera full time and just producing films with other FTM guys being the porn stars. I do not want to be in front of the camera when I am fifty. I just think I needed to get that ball rolling and get the guys interested and let them know it's okay to be a man with a pussy. It was totally necessary for me to do it this way. No one else was going to. These guys are way too hung up on the cock thing.

AUDACIA: Have you always seen your work in porn as a political thing and a way to connect with other transmen, or is that a recent development?

BUCK: Oh, no way—all I wanted to do was make hot, nasty porn. I never could have imagined that it would turn into this. To be honest, I really do not even consider myself a transman anymore. I think that I have fully evolved into a man. I am no longer in a transitional state. So connecting with other transmen tends not to happen so often.

AUDACIA: Only in very recent interviews have you revealed any information about your personal life. Do you find it difficult to explain to people that there is a difference between exposing your body and exposing your life? How do you draw this line?

BUCK: It is difficult to explain this line. Reporters have always wanted to know about my personal life, but I really am not comfortable talking about my private life. That is why it is called "private life." I have exposed some of it when I have felt comfortable, but that is very rare. I usually just let them know that is off-limits in the interview. I recently got a request to do a "reality TV show" on my life, but that is just not going to happen.

AUDACIA: Your movies are some of the very few that I've seen where condoms are used for blow jobs and on sex toys. Was this difficult to negotiate with the companies you've worked with? Why is it important to you to show safer sex in your movies?

BUCK: Totally, the folks I've worked for hated it when I used condoms on my toys. They were like, "Man, you can make way more money if you fuck without condoms." Yeah, but when I die from AIDS I won't be able to spend the money, will I? It is very, very important for me to show safer sex in my movies. I feel like it is my duty, as someone who has lost many friends to AIDS, to show that you have to be responsible when having sex now. It's not 1970. You can no longer have unsafe sex without consequences. I also wanted to show that safe sex is just as hot as not using a condom. Actually, I think it is even hotter. I really don't give a shit if people like it or not. I would be very irresponsible if I didn't do it.

AUDACIA RAY is the founder and executive director of the Red Umbrella Project (RedUP), a peer-led organization in New York that amplifies the voices of people in the sex trades through media, storytelling, and advocacy programs. At RedUP, she publishes the literary journal *Prose & Lore: Memoir Stories About Sex Work* and she has taught media strategy workshops for sex workers in New York, San Francisco, Las Vegas, and London. She is the author of *Naked on the Internet: Hookups, Downloads, and Cashing in On Internet Sexploration* (Seal Press, 2007) and has contributed to many anthologies. She joined the *$pread* staff in 2004 and was an executive editor from 2005 to 2008.

INTERCOURSES:
AN INTERVIEW WITH PRO-CHOICE
ACTIVIST JOYCE ARTHUR

Eliyanna Kaiser

ISSUE 2.4 (2007)

Joyce Arthur is a prominent pro-choice activist in Vancouver. For almost two decades she has authored a respected
Canadian pro-choice quarterly newsletter, *The Pro-Choice
Press*, and held numerous leadership positions in local and
national pro-choice organizations. As the prostitution debate
has taken center stage in Canadian feminist circles, Joyce
has emerged as a thoughtful voice on the side of decriminalization. In this interview, Joyce is speaking as an individual,
not for any particular organization.

ELIYANNA: You are one of the most openly pro-sex worker
rights feminist activists in Canada. What got you interested?

JOYCE: When I joined PAR-L [Policy Action Research List], a
feminist listserv in Canada, there was a lot of discussion
off and on about prostitution, so I started paying attention
and thinking about it. When I was younger, I was an exotic
dancer for a couple of years. In fact, it was the best job I
ever had because it was a lot of fun and I made pretty good
money for a young woman in that time. I liked dancing
and having the attention of all those men.

I took offense to some of the women saying, "All sex
work—everything—exchanging your body for cash is always
wrong, wrong, wrong." Who are they to tell me what my
experience should have been? It took me a while to sort
through the issues though. I can see both sides. It was

interesting to enter the debate without a position, more or less.

ELIYANNA: You wrote an essay on your blog called, "Why prostitution cannot be abolished . . . and should not be abolished." Was one of the things that connected the issue of abortion and prostitution for you the fact that you can't abolish either?

JOYCE: That's how I came at the issue initially and that's why I'm involved in the reproductive rights issue. We are sexual beings. To deny that or try to control that in either ourselves or others is not only futile but counterproductive and dangerous. That was the point I made in the essay: trying to eradicate prostitution is really and hopelessly naïve.

ELIYANNA: The feminist listerv you mentioned, PAR-L, has these occasional eruptions about sex work. Why do you think it's such a heated topic? The members are all feminists that mostly know each other and generally agree on things.

JOYCE: People take sex personally, and anything involving sex becomes controversial. That's the common denominator. I can understand some of it. Someone who works for a crisis center, for example, they see the women who need the most help, so they translate that to the whole sex industry.

I think we're all really trying to help women, but the abolitionists sometimes don't see that. They go into attack mode and take it personally. There's a mindset that says a woman's sexuality—and sex itself—is supposed to be sacred and special. Obviously, prostitution sex isn't special so therefore it's "wrong" and "bad for women." This is a very prurient, old-fashioned attitude and it puts [the abolitionists] in the same league as those other people who believe that any time sex is divorced from procreation or love suddenly it's wrong and bad and must be stamped out: the Christian Right, the anti-choice movement, and the anti-gay movement.

Obviously, there is a lot of exploitation and violence in sex work that really needs to be addressed. But sex work is diverse. I think where the abolitionists go astray is labeling prostitution itself as bad. It's better to argue that it's the conditions and the illegality that cause the problems. I'm not saying that sex work is a great job. Maybe it's a lousy job, like waitressing. But it's a job.

ELIYANNA: You've been very vocal on the similarities between "feminist" arguments against abortion and "feminist" arguments against prostitution. Here's an excerpt from a piece you wrote:

What is the difference between these two arguments?

1. *Prostitution is always violence against women. It's physically dangerous, it victimizes them, robs them of their sexuality, and inflicts lasting psychological harm. Women never truly choose prostitution; they are forced into it by men, poverty, desperation, etc. We must give women better options by abolishing prostitution and helping them out of it.*

2. *Abortion is always violence against women. It's physically dangerous, it victimizes them, robs them of their motherhood role, and inflicts lasting psychological harm. Women never truly choose abortion; they are forced into it by men, poverty, desperation, etc. We must give women better options by banning abortion and helping them keep their babies.*

JOYCE: It all comes down to women's sexual autonomy, and that's what people are really scared of. They see a limited role or how women are supposed to feel about and engage in sex. Women who fall outside that must be "coerced," they must be "victims," or simply not know what they're doing.

From an evolutionary perspective, women get pregnant and therefore have to be a bit more picky about who they have sex with for the survival of the species, so they can have help raising their children. Whereas men, they can just have sex with whomever they want to try to spread their seed and maximize their reproductive potential. Well, that sort of makes people very uncomfortable with women sleeping around. It makes that "Who's the father of your child?" thing an issue. Maybe I'm getting off topic here—

ELIYANNA: No. I think you're talking about control of female sexuality and patriarchy. And I think that it's right that you link the control of female sexuality with the abortion issue and the prostitution debate. There's a link between the stigma and shame that prostitutes and women who have abortions share. This paternity and legitimacy stuff means that you need a clear division between women who have abortions or prostitutes on the "bad women" end of the scale, and wives and daughters on the "good" end.

JOYCE: Exactly. If a woman has an abortion, that's kind of proof that she's been engaging in illicit sex. She's a "fallen woman" [in] the same way that a prostitute is.

ELIYANNA: There's a big difference between you and I sitting here having a philosophical conversation about how the abortion issue and prostitution are connected, and the reproductive rights movement championing the cause of decriminalizing prostitution. How do you see that happening?

JOYCE: Boy, that's a tough one. You need to keep emphasizing female sexual autonomy. From an activism point of view, this is a long process of public education. Media is especially important, like publishing, film, and news.

Successfully decriminalizing prostitution would have a major impact. I think Canada's abortion ban being struck down in 1988 led to a more liberalized attitude toward abortion. If prostitution is fully decriminalized here, I think you might see a similar thing happen in a couple decades.

ELIYANNA: The US Supreme Court decision that legalized abortion, *Roe v. Wade*, was based on the "right to privacy," not on women's right to abortion or gender equality. Sex worker rights advocates sometimes appeal to the same idea, arguing that sex work is a "private arrangement" between individuals.

Many people in the reproductive rights movement say

that it was to our detriment that *Roe* was decided based on privacy grounds. Do you think it's dangerous for sex worker rights advocates to go this similar path? Appealing to a libertarian perspective is so seductive because people accept it so easily.

JOYCE: I'm actually one of those feminists that thinks *Roe* was unfortunate in many ways. If you read the decision, it was really about protecting doctors. I think it would have been stronger under the Fourteenth Amendment [the Equal Protection Clause]. I like to think that if America ever passes the ERA [Equal Rights Amendment], it could strike down abortion restrictions on the basis that they discriminate against women. It's similar for prostitution, because most prostitutes are women. There's a group in Canada that's suing the Crown [the Canadian government] because the current prostitution laws violate various human rights protections—and this harm disproportionately falls to women.

ELIYANNA: The term "pro-choice" has a consumerist slant; it's about being able to make decisions in the marketplace. Like, I have the right to go to the grocery store and buy Granny Smith apples or Macintosh apples, just like I can "choose" to go to an abortion clinic. I'm wondering if you think the "choice" tactic has been positive or negative overall? There are identical questions about how to cast a sex workers' rights movement. Is it about the choice whether to become a prostitute, or is it about sex workers having rights?

JOYCE: I think in the beginning the choice rhetoric was a useful strategy. But over the long run it is less useful and in some ways, it's been harmful to our progress. "Choice" tends to trivialize abortion, like the choice between apples at the grocery store. Some women are coerced economically into abortion and the same thing with prostitution. Maybe they don't really want to be prostitutes or to have an abortion. We need to recognize the complexity and gravity of the situation. Casting it in terms of a "right" is much more effective because it's put on a more serious and profound level.

ELIYANNA: "Rights" also seem to make the message more inclusive. Historically, people have been critical of the pro-choice movement because, for example, while white women were marching for the right to choose, women of color were fending off forced sterilization. I don't want to suggest that the leadership of the sex workers' rights movement is the same as 1970s abortion rights activists. It's 2007 and we've had the benefit of learning from other movements. But to some extent there are more privileged sex workers out there who act like the only issue is, "What do you care if I choose to become a prostitute?" conveniently ignoring the complexity of how constrained other peoples' choices are.

JOYCE: It just shows how diverse the whole thing is. Some women actually do choose, and it might be because they are middle-class or whatever, and others are in a much more dysfunctional situation.

As soon as you start talking about women's rights, it allows you to bring in the more complex, difficult issues, like being coerced into an abortion or sex trafficking. Preventing a woman from working in the sex industry if she wants to, and preventing a woman from being forced into the sex industry if she doesn't want to, become the same issue: self-determination. You don't want to violate it one way or the other. The same is true with abortion.

Women can make mistakes and they need to be allowed to make them. Controlling women is paternalism, the idea that women need to be protected from themselves. But no, we need to allow women to screw themselves up if that's what they end up doing sometimes. Women need to take responsibility for their own lives and be treated like adult women, just like men. The anti-choice and the prostitution abolitionists want to treat women like children.

ELIYANNA: The abolitionists also focus a lot on male demand. You posted a creative answer on PAR-L about ending demand for prostitution . . .

JOYCE: Yep, we need to promote casual sex! But I don't know how far that can go because I think that women have a natural reticence to casual sex with many partners. I think abortion and contraception afford the opportunity for women to engage in casual sex for fun with no real consequences. A lot of women probably do have casual sex, but because of the shame associated with it, they don't talk about it.

ELIYANNA: Do you see a danger—and I think this is a rhetorical question—in the reproductive rights movement being associated with a pro-decriminalization agenda for prostitution?

JOYCE: There really might be. I'm even worried about that right now, just in terms of this interview. Obviously, there are people in pro-choice groups in Canada that do not think the way I do. I don't think we would ever agree to a position. The issues are going to have to stay separate until feminists have a consensus. I'm optimistic that maybe that will happen down the road because the issues are connected.

ELIYANNA: In 2000, the Pro-Choice Action Network (PCAN) in British Columbia joined a coalition opposing an anti-sex worker bill called the Secure Care Act, which would have allowed for the extra-judicial detainment of street-involved youth. Few other feminist groups joined, and many actually supported the bill. Do you think feminists principally involved with reproductive rights are more likely to be in favor of sex worker rights?

JOYCE: Pro-choice feminists have more of a tendency to be out there and have a broader perspective. Abortion itself is a controversial issue. The controversy—the root issue—in both movements is sex. People who are strongly pro-choice are probably more likely to see those issues in the prostitution debate.

ELIYANNA KAISER is a former executive editor of *$pread* magazine. She is currently raising her two children in Manhattan. In her spare time, she writes fiction.

IN HER OWN WORDS: AN INTERVIEW WITH DEBORAH JEANE PALFREY

Radical Vixen

ISSUE 3.3 (2007)

I first heard of the "DC Madam" case in March. Her client list tantalized. Which hypocritical politicians would be exposed? Which moral majority leaders would be shown to love the very "sins" they preached against? I'll admit that when the phone records became freely available I got myself a copy. Am I searching them? Yes, but I haven't found anything.

I've been disappointed with how the mainstream media portrayed Deborah Jeane Palfrey and, to an extent, the adult industry. I wanted to see coverage treating sex workers as just that—workers. I wanted to hear discussions of how politicians impose anti-sex politics on the world, yet are clients themselves. I wanted to read articles about how the government seizes people's homes and savings before even trying them in court.

So I asked Ms. Palfrey for an interview. To my utter delight, she granted my request. The full interview was one hour long, so what follows is only a portion of our whole conversation. To read the full transcript or listen to the audio file, visit www.radicalvixen.com/blog.

RADICAL: How do you feel being called the DC Madam? In a way, it's judging you before your day in court.

JEANE: I've been called worse at this point, and I'll be called worse before this is all over. I can assure you that's not too hard to imagine in my situation. "DC"—well, it's true, it was a DC-based business. "Madam"—even though I contend the business was based on legal sexual behavior, I guess the word "Madam" would be applicable here. I certainly don't think the word "pimp" is applicable. It certainly refers to a man and it also refers to a predatory individual; I am neither. In a way, I don't mind it, in another way, I can see how some people consider the moniker to be rather unkind.

RADICAL: I've been wondering about your old employees. What's your relationship to them now?

JEANE: Well, first of all, every time my attorney hears someone use the word "employee" he gets very nervous. It's all subcontractors, so I have to differentiate.

I have no relationship because none of them have contacted me and I have not contacted them. I have no idea who my accusers are. I can assume some—if not all of them—are my accusers. But at this point in time, no one has come forward to identify themselves as one of the witnesses for the government. This has been ongoing, [it] started on October 4 of last year and I have not had one gal, except for a person who worked for me back in the mid-90s, come forward and say, "I'd like to help you . . ." She's come forward and she's spoken on my behalf. But she's done so in shadow. The other ones, nobody wants to come forward, and of course, none of the clients want to either.

RADICAL: It sounds like everyone has run into the shadows.

JEANE: Boy, I'll use another metaphor. Rats jumping from a ship. Every last one of them has jumped.

RADICAL: After the [July] press conference from Senator Vitter (R-LA), I'm curious, of all the scandals that have come out of the phone records, has any one incident surprised you more than the others?

JEANE: No. I think there's a script for some of these folks. I mean they kind of go into hiding for a few days, they pull themselves together, then they come out either with their wife on their side, carrying on about how strong their marriage is, or they go off into rehab somewhere. And you don't really see or hear from them for another month or two until everything dies down.

[The reaction has] been anything from "I've sinned," as David Vitter said, to Harlan Ullman who said, "the accusation is beneath the dignity of a comment," to Randall Tobias who said, "Hey, nothing happened, I just had a couple of gals come over for a massage." So none of these reactions have surprised me.

RADICAL: Vitter supports abstinence-only education, he's against gay marriage, he's very, very anti-choice. As the bedrock of the moral conservative movement, he comes out [with] "I'm a sinner, please forgive me." Do you view it as ironic?

JEANE: He's getting such a free pass, isn't he? Because he's an unindicted coconspirator in all of this, along with all the other 9,999 estimated clients who used my service. I'm being charged with [running a] racketeering enterprise, RICO [Racketeer Influenced and Corrupt Organizations Act], and conspiracy. So in essence, the man is getting a free pass, and I'm looking at fifty-five years in prison.

RADICAL: He gets to have a press conference and say, "I'm sorry," and then he gets to wash his hands of it.

JEANE: He goes back to work.

RADICAL: Yeah. He goes back to work and maybe it comes up in his re-election campaign.

JEANE: Well, I'm sure it comes up every night at home. He's not living a life of roses at the moment. But the bottom line is he's not a coconspirator, he's not being indicted. He's not being put in a position where he's looking at incarceration. He didn't have his entire life savings, all his property, frozen and seized by the US government. He's embarrassed; of course he's embarrassed. He's professionally shamed; his life at home is probably horrendous. However, he is not in the position I'm in right now. I've been professionally embarrassed, personally humiliated. I've had all of that, but I'm still looking at fifty-five years in a federal penitentiary, which in essence is the rest of my life.

RADICAL: I've heard you say the mainstream media is more interested in who you went to prom with than the story. If you were a man, do you think the case and the media coverage would be different?

JEANE: It might be different, it might not be. The dividing line here isn't with sex and gender anymore, it's between real news (and real journalism) and entertainment. We have a culture that thrives 80, 90 percent of the time on entertainment and fluff, and really only looks at news and journalism and important issues maybe 10, 15, 20 percent of the time.

If only somebody like ABC, who has the real power and punch behind them to get a story like mine out there, would take it on. But they won't do that. They'll milk it for all it's worth with regards to sweeps week and ratings and then just stop.

Prostitution is not a federal crime, it's a state crime, by the way, it's a misdemeanor state crime in the lower courts in the states. They have literally federalized prostitution in my case in order to support [charges of] money laundering, conspiracy, and racketeering, which are the crimes, which can then [be used to] support civil asset forfeiture. They've come down on me like I was the Gambino crime family. I ran a little cottage business out of the laundry room of my home, my little Martha Stewart home in the San Francisco Bay Area for thirteen years, harmed no one, had no arrests, no problems, but yet they've come down on me. My situation is very, very disturbing on a lot of levels and in a lot of ways.

You know I was under observation as far back as March 2004. And until the trigger was pulled on me on October 2006, thirty-one months they observed me, à la J. Edgar Hoover. You and I both know being in this industry that a sting operation by the local vice squad can be put together in a few days. It doesn't take thirty-one months for a prostitution case. They were not watching me for prostitution related activities. They were watching me for some [other] reason, and the only reason I can logically conclude [is] this powder keg of information that I was holding onto for all these years.

I didn't realize the value of my phone records. Now when they came here into my house on October 4 and executed the search warrant I think they were looking for the traditional Heidi Fleiss black book and they didn't find it because I never had a traditional Heidi Fleiss black book. However, they walked by the now infamous 46 pounds of phone records numerous times. I don't think they ever connected the dots that every one of my phone calls to and from Washington were long distance, therefore they would be itemized and documented. And as a result the real black book was in the phone records.

RADICAL: With you being observed, my first thought is it costs money to pay people to observe you. All the money spent to do these things to you while our highways are falling apart, we're getting social programs cut . . .

JEANE: Not really. Let me tell you why. You see, I'm it. I'm a special person here. There's never been a case like mine before. There is no other service in the DC area [that] has had this happen to them in the last ten months, or the last ten years for that matter. It's just me and me alone.

You know as well as I do that running a business like mine for thirteen years is a bit of an anomaly. And in a place like Washington DC, in a Mayflower Madam-like setting, all of a sudden it takes on a whole different import than many of the other agencies. When I closed the business rather unexpectedly [they got] a little nervous. I made a little wire transfer to Germany, I transferred $70,000 to Germany last September 28 [and] the next day [the investigation] went into warp mode. On October 3, a couple of postal inspectors flew out from DC. They were trying to gain access to my property posing as a couple being transferred from Washington to the Bay Area. My real estate agent had to inform them that I was not in the area. If anyone wanted to see the property I wanted to be present.

It's at this point in time, from what I gather, that they went up to Sacramento and got a search warrant based on information that was three to five years old. Now for the average person, that doesn't mean a lot. But very rarely is a search warrant ever executed in this country—in any case—on information that is older than six months.

RADICAL: I find that pretty disturbing.

JEANE: That's very disturbing. [The warrant] was written in [the] third person by one of the postal inspectors about generic people, times, and places from three to five years ago (which is now four to six years ago). And somehow they got [it]. They pulled the trigger the next morning, they executed it, [and] they got into the property here. I think they came on a fishing expedition and they found absolutely nothing. I think it [was] at this point that they had to carry on like this was a "regular prostitution case." I don't think they could even explain. They'll never admit why they were really watching me all this time. It's very scary, isn't it?

RADICAL: It is, [especially] the civil assets forfeiture. It seems like a lot of people don't know about it because it doesn't affect most Americans.

JEANE: [Civil assets forfeiture] actually affects about two million Americans each year in one matter, shape, or form. It's becoming a more egregious act [by] the police as every day goes by. If you are caught in any sort of situation where you've committed a felony and it's attached to property—for example let's say you have an eighteen-year-old son who's living in the basement and is growing a little pot in a little flower bed—if the police can prove that you knew your child was growing a couple of pot plants in the basement, they can take your property from you. Most people think that the civil assets forfeiture only happens in drug-related cases [and that] it's only after the person has been convicted that they can take the property. Oh no, they take it right up front. They froze all of my assets on October 4 of last year. They stripped me bare.

RADICAL: It's such a scary thing that they took all that from you and you haven't even been found guilty or not guilty.

JEANE: No, I haven't. And I don't intend to be found guilty. I expect this case, despite the naysayers, to fall apart fairly quickly. We have tremendous legal arguments on the table.

RADICAL: You were saying earlier there hasn't been a case like yours before. After yours is all said and done, do you think this situation will set some sort of precedent?

JEANE: Oh God, I hope so. As a matter of fact, one of the motions we have before the court right now—one of the nine motions we have—is called a privacy motion. It's building on the *Lawrence vs. Texas* case of a few years back, the homosexual rights case in Texas. The argument in that case was that two consenting adults have the right to do as they see fit in the privacy of their home or domicile, that it is none of the government's business, and that government intrusion is completely off-limits. What we're doing is adding the element of money to it and saying what two people do in the privacy of a domicile is entirely their business and none of the government's concern even if there is the exchange of money. If that flies, I'm praying to God this wonderful woman, Judge Kessler, rules in my favor on this one.

RADICAL: Wow, that could have far-reaching effects.

JEANE: It would have tremendously far-reaching effects. And this case could indeed be the one, and she could be the judge to do it because she's a Clinton appointee, she's about to retire, she's a woman, she seems to be a bit of a feminist, she seems to be a protégé of Ruth Ginsburg and Sandra Day O'Conner. She is a Harvard Grad, back in the 50s, 60s, went to law school. This is a woman who came up the hard way. If there ever was a judge to do it and if there were ever a case to do it, it couldn't get much better than my situation at the moment.

RADICAL: If there was a ruling to make prostitution legal, it seems like it would have to be a by-product of a case like this, because what senator is going to try to pass a bill?

JEANE: Oh, no senator is going to try to pass a bill. Nor did any senator try to pass abortion years and years ago in the 70s.

RADICAL: Yeah, it took *Roe vs. Wade*.

JEANE: Nor has anybody come to the plate to say that homosexuality is okay from a legislative standpoint. This has all been done through the courts and through the interpretation of the Constitution and the Bill of Rights and so on and so forth. It is our right for the government not to intrude in our bedrooms. I believe I have a good chance in other areas for this case to fall apart, but for the sake of everyone else [I hope] that this one goes through.

RADICAL: Absolutely. That would be wonderful.

JEANE: I'm not playing the game the way they want me to play it. They want me to sit back and to be the dutiful little defendant and take my beating and go off to prison. And that's not the way it's going to be. I'm going to fight them in the gutter if I have to, with everything at my disposal. I will push and I will push and I will push until finally [in] this ridiculous case, there is an infusion of sanity and it's over.

RADICAL: That's the impression I got. They really expected you to plea, hang your head down, and go away.

JEANE: Some of the attorneys that I have had and that are no longer in my life or will not be soon have said things to me like, "Jeane, [why] don't you just go to prison for eight months? You'll be out in eight months. It's going to take at least eight months to fight it." I thought this person was the biggest buffoon—and he's an attorney. Only a buffoon would say [to] give up your liberty for eight months. I wouldn't give up my liberty for eight minutes. I've had people say, "Don't say anything, don't give any press conferences, don't speak up, just be quiet, don't aggravate the situation." Don't aggravate the situation? You've got to be kidding me. These people can come after me, destroy me, take every shot they possibly can at me, and I'm supposed to just sit back and be quiet and dutiful and well mannered?

That's why I'm doing this interview with you. These people who are telling me, "Just take it," these people scare me to death. I just don't understand them.

RADICAL: That kind of attitude leads to a police state I think.

JEANE: That's where we're pretty much at right now. We're not too far away. You know the wire transfer, the one that triggered all this last September/October? It was picked up on one of those terror watch lists where they're supposed to be watching terrorists and not the American people. When I wired $70,000 dollars to Germany to buy my little retirement flat over there, it was picked up on one of those terrorist-tracking programs.

RADICAL: That's what's so frustrating about the mainstream coverage of your story. The list is tantalizing and interesting: What hypocritical senator is going to be outed next? But that's just the surface of the story. The real meat of the issue is far, far beneath that.

JEANE: I absolutely whole-heartedly agree. It takes a while to answer questions and to get this story out. For people to sit back and go, "Oh my God, this has nothing to do with Senator Vitter." If anything, you may want to even argue that Senator Vitter is a bit of a victim in all of this. Because he may have been one of the people that they, whoever they are, wanted to out eventually, or maybe even wanted to protect, and in that case he wouldn't have been a victim. But by the records coming out in the manner that they did, he has become a victim in all of this.

If the government had just not pulled the trigger on October 4 and executed that search warrant or had I been home to entertain Joe and Maria, and give them a tour of the house, to explain to them why I'm selling the house, to let them feel me out and go on their little fishing expedition, I think at that point they might have just gone back to Washington, DC.

RADICAL: In a way it's a sad commentary on our society that they assume you're up to no good, that you're doing something sinister, and really all you were doing was retiring.

JEANE: Well, that's right. What might be the biggest irony in all of this when it's all over is that those forty-six pounds of phone records were considered of no value to me until the time I was criminally indicted.

When my attorney, Mr. Montgomery Sibley, said to me,

"Jeane, you need good criminal counsel. The only way I can possibly think that you can ever get the two, three, four hundred thousand dollars you need to get a good criminal attorney would be to sell those phone records." And at the time I said, "they are worth something, let's sell them." Well, we pulled off [of] that idea because we didn't know who the ultimate buyer was. We didn't know what intelligence agency around the world would be the ultimate buyer, and how many layers of attorneys we would go through, or they would go through, to get it to the ultimate buyer, so to speak. So we backed off that idea within a week or so. Then after that, we decided we still need those records to be investigated. That's when ABC came along and said, look, we won't pay you for the records but we will investigate the records for you. We thought, this is great. They'll investigate the records for leads and exculpatory evidence and that kind of thing. We all know that ABC played me for ratings and nothing more.

Nonetheless, in the process of all this, it came to our attention that we should probably put those records out for the hypocrisy angle and for the possibility and susceptibility of blackmail. Because not only were there people who violated the public trust like David Vitter, hypocrites, but there are also people we believe and we were told by very reliable sources that individuals were most likely set up through the service, and ultimately blackmailed. People who had security clearances and political connections and that kind of thing. And we thought, you know, what if we just out everybody? We're going to free those people and nobody's going to be in a position where they can be blackmailed anymore.

We figured the way people came to us and said, look it's your public duty to put those records out there on the open market, so to speak, so that [the] public can thoroughly investigate those records. And that's indeed what we did. So in the final analysis it was more for patriotic or altruistic reasons. I still don't want—and it doesn't appear as if it's happening—a lot of innocent people being slaughtered by the wayside here. It appears that only a few people are being outed, and it seems to be being done in a reasonable fashion. Because it takes a lot of time and a lot of work to go through those records and the only people who are willing to go through those records in a responsible manner are usually responsible, conscientious bloggers or journalists or what have you. So I see the outing of people to be anywhere from a few dozen ultimately to a hundred or so, many of whom will not be well-known names but there will be quite a few people outed along the way.

RADICAL: Is there anything else you would like to share?

JEANE: I think what is disturbing about this situation is that this appears to have started as an observation of Deborah Jeane Palfrey, her life, her assets, her finances, her day-to-day dealings for business, etc. This never appeared to have been an investigation into prostitution-related activities as much as it appears to have been some sort of observation of Deborah Jeane Palfrey's life. Which is very scary [and] makes you kind of wonder, what were they watching me for? Because you know what, I'm just an average, ordinary person. I think that's what I'd like to leave with your audience: that there is something very disturbing at the core of this case, that someone like me was being used for probably political purposes.

RADICAL VIXEN is a hippie, activist, and blogger. In addition to her own blog she wrote for *$pread* and Sugasm. An avid knitter, she dreams of one day raising llamas to spin their fleece into yarn. When not traveling, she and her husband live in the Southwest surfing the web off solar power. She blogs about peace, porn, and politics at RadicalVixen.com

THE REAL MEDIA WHORES: UNITING AGAINST SENSATIONALISM IN THE WAKE OF SPITZERGATE

Caroline Andrews

ISSUE 4.1 (2008)

When the news broke that New York Governor Eliot Spitzer had been arrested for his involvement with a "prostitution ring" (later identified as Manhattan's Emperors Club), I doubt I was alone in thinking at first that perhaps he had invested some money poorly, or maybe one of his advisors or campaign people had been caught in a brothel raid. These things happen. I'm not naive; I'm a veteran Manhattan escort and my old client list predictably included men of considerable power and wealth (usually both). But I was taken completely by surprise with the news of "Client No. 9."

In some of the more complete news coverage, non-New Yorkers found out why the Big Apple was so blindsided. To begin with, understand that the former governor ran on a platform of doing things differently. "Day one, everything changes," was the oft-repeated campaign mantra that assured New Yorkers that the corrupt, scandal-ridden government we are so used to here was a thing of the past. Also, as a candidate, Attorney General Spitzer was internationally renowned for being the tough-talking prosecutor who cleaned up Wall Street. He even busted up some "prostitution rings."

Once elected governor, and throughout much of 2007, the New York State Legislature negotiated what eventually became landmark human trafficking legislation. Over many months, service providers for prostitutes and trafficking victims faced off with the anti-prostitution lobby in closed-door meetings, with one side fighting for funding for trafficking victims while the other side pushed to use the trafficking bill to further punish clients of regular prostitutes. Eventually, Governor Spitzer intervened in his usual heavy-handed manner, introducing a governor's program bill, which essentially put a stop to any further debate on the question. The governor's bill included some major concessions to the anti-prostitution lobby. A May 16, 2007, press release from the governor's office announced that a deal had been reached on the trafficking bill and pronounced that it would include an amendment to the penal code, "[s]uppressing the demand for prostitution by elevating the lowest-level patronizing a prostitute crime from a B to an A misdemeanor." In New York, a class A misdemeanor is punishable by up to one year in jail and/or a $1,000 fine.

The trafficking bill was signed on June 6, 2007, with fanfare. The lead-up to the vote in Albany was marked by public hearings, press conferences, carefully planted op-ed pieces in major print dailies like the *New York Times*, radio and television appearances, and statements released from the governor's office. He was so proud of his new law that he bragged about it in his 2008 State of the State speech—just two months before his arrest.

The anti-prostitution lobby had discovered, to their delight, that they had no better friend than New York's governor, Eliot Spitzer. The day the agreement was announced, Equality Now's Executive Director, Taina Bien-Aimé, released a statement in which she praised "the extraordinary leadership of Governor Eliot Spitzer and his deeply dedicated staff."

What About "Kristen"?

For most of America, the Spitzer scandal bled old but familiar wounds. It seemed like mere minutes before newscasts were digging through their libraries for old reels of Bill Clinton's famous "I did not have sexual relations with that woman, Miss Lewinsky" speech. And how could we forget the country's first "Gay American," former New Jersey Governor Jim McGreevey? Closely themed, Senator David Vitter's prostitution liaisons and Randall Tobias' high-profile White

House resignation were back on the tube. We even got to revisit the hilarity of US Senator Larry Craig's airport bathroom footsie with an undercover cop.

Everyone, particularly late-night comedians and tabloid headline writers, seemed to be having a good time with the gossipy, middle-school style fun of reading about the juicy details, walks of shame, and requisite stand-by-my-man press conference. But for sex worker and prostitute advocates, the whole saga was one of apprehension.

Media moments like these inevitably push prostitution into the limelight. In a world where, "How does someone hire a prostitute?" is a question that many people actually don't know the answer to, it makes sense for the media to ask those kinds of questions. But the depth of ignorance can be difficult to overcome: Who are prostitutes? Are they all abused? How do prostitution businesses work? Why do men see prostitutes? The list goes on.

The media seems to have established a formula for reporting on prostitution every time the topic cycles back into the public conversation: First, find some random prostitution opponents (Google works for this), name them experts, and ask their opinion on important, timely issues of substance. Name their credentials, no matter how scant. Next, find some prostitutes. Lull them into thinking you care about their perspectives and use them for some stock narrative copy about girls gone way too wild or reluctant whores, whichever works. For credentials, get photos or detailed descriptions of what they look like; be sure to ask how much they charge. Last, but most importantly, find out as much as possible about the prostitute of the moment; build her up, tear her down, and don't come back to the newsroom until you get pictures of her (a) naked, and (b) age twelve or younger, looking very, very innocent.

The day after the Spitzer story broke, Sex Workers Action New York (SWANK), Prostitutes of New York (PONY), Sex Workers Outreach Project (SWOP-NYC), and Desiree Alliance released a statement titled, "What About Kristen? New York Sex Worker Organizations Respond to Spitzer Scandal." They began by noting, "As sex worker advocates, we are concerned about the representation and fate of 'Kristen' and sex workers who are being thrust into the spotlight because of the investigation into the Governor." SWANK's (and *$pread's*) Shakti Ziller pleaded for journalists to think about the impact of the bust on sex workers as people and not just as salacious news bits: "Nobody is talking about the impact of this story on 'Kristen' and other women, men, and transpeople who are currently working in the sex industry," she said. "Prostitutes disproportionately face punitive action after arrest as compared to clients. Whether or not she will face prison time, 'Kristen' has been dragged into the spotlight and will be subjected to public humiliation. Shouldn't the police emphasis be on catching perpetrators of violent crime and protecting sex workers—not exposing adults who are consenting to a transaction? All she did was try to make a living."

Eventually, the inevitable transpired and the *New York Times* tracked Kristen down and exposed the woman behind the pseudonym: twenty-two-year-old Ashley Dupré. The press even called her mother who made a brief statement supporting her daughter (As Stacey Swimme rightly pointed out on sex worker blog *Bound Not Gagged* [boundnotgagged.com], no one called Eliot Spitzer's parents to find out how he grew up to be a john). In a heart-wrenching statement to the *New York Times*, Ms. Dupré's fear of what was to come was apparent. "I just don't want to be thought of as a monster," she said.

The topless photos of Ms. Dupré that soon appeared on the cover of the *New York Post* were taken by photographer Wesley Mann who sold them to the tabloid for a tidy profit. *The Associated Press* took photos from her MySpace page and began publishing them without her permission (including a number of photos of her friends and family, some of whom are very young children). In a statement, the *AP* said, "[We] discussed the photos obtained from the MySpace page in great detail and found that they were newsworthy. We distributed the photos that were relevant to the story. Those photos did not show nudity, nor were they explicit."

Dupré's attorney, Don Buchwald, responded: "While the circumstances surrounding Governor Spitzer's resignation are newsworthy, some publications, in violation of journalistic norms, have used the occasion of Gov. Spitzer's political misfortunes as an excuse to exploit Ms. Dupré's persona for commercial purposes."

After the sex worker advocates released their statement, the media requests began pouring in. While some TV segments, radio appearances, and newspaper interviews provided constructive opportunities to raise sex workers' issues, it became overwhelmingly apparent that the media by and large wasn't interested in telling the kinds of stories that sex workers wanted to speak about.

"Have You Been a Whore?"

That was the question posed to blogger, renowned author, *Village Voice* columnist, award-winning filmmaker, Columbia Master's degree graduate, former Executive Editor of *$pread* and—yes—former sex worker, Audacia Ray by a scout for MSNBC vetting for a segment on *Live with Dan Abrams*. Needless to say, Ms. Ray declined to appear on the show. MSNBC executives later denied that their staff member ever used "that word."

On her blog, *Waking Vixen* (wakingvixen.com), Audacia Ray details her dealings with the media in the wake of the Spitzer scandal (see her March 11 post titled, "Why sex workers aren't represented in the media"). In a suitably angry moment, she funnels her ire directly at the journalists who have contacted her: "You want to talk about exploitation of women, media? Look at your own goddamn questions, the exposure you ask us to engage in, the personal questions you want us to answer. Look at the sexy container you put us in, all sultry bad girl secret story, no room for brains with the boobs. We don't want to tell you our naughty secrets. What's in it for us? You won't give us the space and air time to talk about issues that matter to us, we won't give you the dirt."

I, too, fielded a number of media requests in the weeks following the scandal. In one particularly memorable exchange, a writer for a free daily, *AM New York*, called looking to talk to a "high-priced" call girl. I let the high-priced part go (is the alternative to say, "no, sorry, I was just a cheap whore"?) and didn't mention that I had quit escorting some time ago. He wanted to know what I thought was meant by the released transcript in which Emperors Club manager Tameka Rachelle Lewis told Ms. Dupré that from what she had heard, "he would ask you to do things that, like, you might not think were safe . . . basic things." I told him I thought the meaning was pretty obvious: they were talking about condom use.

The reporter seemed genuinely disappointed. "You don't think it could be anything else?" he prompted. I asked him what he had in mind. "Maybe anal or getting tied up?" I spent a minute explaining how common it is for clients to request sex without condoms before trying to bring the conversation back to my preferred message. Isn't it interesting how the governor was so famous for being a bully and always getting his way, but twenty-two-year-old "Kristen" is quoted in that transcript as saying that she got him to behave? Sex workers are very skilled at dealing with these sorts of situations, even if the law and society doesn't back them up or provide them support. The reporter cut me off. "How much did you charge? Can you describe what you look like and would you be willing to have us take a picture of you if we hid your face?" I quickly got off the phone.

On March 16, the *New York Times* published an article titled "The Double Lives of High-Priced Call Girls," in which two of my friends were interviewed under pseudonyms. They spent hours with the reporter in a Brooklyn coffee shop having carefully rehearsed what they would say to stay on message: they were there to talk about politics and the rights of sex workers, not to be used for a story they didn't care about. The reporter seemed friendly enough and promised to emphasize the issues they cared about. The resulting article at first glance wasn't horrible—it presented sex workers as people—but there was no mention of the political issues that my friends were promised they would be quoted on. Basically, it was a fluff piece profiling three women. What's more, personal identifying details made it easy for two of the women to be recognized by their friends, family, coworkers, and clients, despite the fact that they had been promised anonymity. The two women fought back and a corrected version of the original print version is now in the *Times* website's archive, accompanied by an unusually long retraction.

The Silver Lining

Former New Jersey Governor McGreevey's threesomes and new Governor Paterson's past marriage problems have shifted the spotlight for the moment, but it's always just a matter of time before the next scandal pops up and another sex worker is exploited by the media while the rest of us are used as props. Have we learned anything?

For maybe the first time ever, the media has been called to task (a little bit) for its dealings with sex workers. Not only did the *New York Times* editors go through the embarrassing process of heavily correcting a lengthy article because sex workers fought back, but enough of the paper's general readers wrote critical notes to its editorial board that they were prompted to post an answer in their FAQ section to the question "Why did the Times track down and identify 'Kristen,' the prostitute in the case?"

Sex workers are improving their media skills. All over the country, there is a growing recognition that we need to be making our own media and becoming experts in engaging with the mainstream media. Undoubtedly, this will be a topic of much discussion at this summer's upcoming sex worker activist conference organized by the Desiree Alliance in Chicago. The newly founded New York-based nonprofit Sex Work Awareness (sexworkawareness.org) has established a website, Sex Work 101 (sexwork101.com), which provides a central location for basic information about sex work from a worker's perspective, so that outsiders can use it for education while sex workers can use it as a template to answer many common questions from the media.

Sex workers are not falling for divide and conquer tactics anymore. Maybe it's advances in technology and what it makes possible, but it was a wonder to watch a dozen or so representatives of sex worker organizations from all over the country edit the same Google document simultaneously to polish their joint press releases. Through email, phone calls, blogs, texting, Google Docs, and instant messages, press requests were centralized and analyzed by the group, and respondents were selected. At times it even felt like we were gaining control of the situation. Though we couldn't always guarantee that our stories would be told the way we wanted to tell them, this coordinated effort maximized our ability to do so and made it harder for any one of us to be fed to the wolves.

Sex workers are getting better at making demands. Even though the *Times* didn't play nice, I remember smiling when the pro-domme in the "Double Lives" story told me how she insisted to the reporter that she was there to talk about politics. She had never spoken to the press before, but she had the chutzpah to demand a say in how she was presented and what her story was. Then she had the sheer audacity to bare her teeth when he didn't do as he promised. I am equally awed by Audacia Ray's dealings with MSNBC. No, you giant multi-billion dollar corporation, you can't call her a whore. Because as fast as she can type it, she's going to tell her five thousand friends and then none of them will go on your stupid show.

Eventually, friends, this kind of stuff spells power.

CAROLINE ANDREWS is the pseudonym of a former street worker and escort who lives in New York City. She took her first and last names from Mayor Rudy Giuliani's two children, because Giuliani treated us all like children.

DIRTY WORDS: AN INTERVIEW WITH CRAIG SEYMOUR

Brendan Michael Conner, writing as Will Rockwell

ISSUE 4.3 (2008)

$pread's Will Rockwell took a stroll with Craig Seymour in New York's Lower East Side to get the dish on the debut of Seymour's recently released memoir, *All I Could Bare: My Life in the Strip Clubs of Gay Washington, DC*. Seymour set out to document the gay stripper scene of America's capital in the 90s and recount his life as a stripper boy, "if not for sale, then at least for controlled-access rental." This interview traces Seymour's life and workaday skills from nudie bars like Secrets, Wet, and La Cage to reporting for *The Washington Post* and tackling an editorship at *VIBE Magazine*. In the midst of this 90s nostalgia, Seymour finds the time to comment on the mounting "Pink Scare" in the States and DC's $400 million development of the district's southeast quarter, which stamped out Seymour's former workplaces.

WILL: Did you research other stripper memoirs in preparation for *All I Could Bare*? If so, was there much male-identified content you could choose from?

SEYMOUR: I avoided reading too much to keep it original, but I had read some stripper memoirs like Lily Burana's *Strip City* and Elizabeth Eaves's *Bare*. I don't know of any other male stripper memoirs. It was really important for me to get a major publishing company to put out a book by a guy stripper. It's so easy to dismiss experiences of strippers or sex workers in general, and people made a lot of jokes while I've been promoting the book. But when something is published it's a validation of a certain experience, so the historical record of the DC scene is now valid in a way it wasn't before I sat down at Starbucks and wrote this thing up.

WILL: Besides pulling off a blend of memoir and entertainment column, *All I Could Bare* often reads like a coming-of-age novel. Was the sex trade your rite of passage as a gay-identified man?

SEYMOUR: DC clubs were the first places [where] I felt comfortable expressing my desire for other guys. I think that's why I find sex establishments welcoming to this day. I was also in a long-term relationship at the time I started working and had only had sex with one person, so when I started stripping I was finally able to relate sexually to all these other people, just by getting jacked off by customers on the bar. I came to terms with myself as a sexual person. Stripping gave me the courage to be who I was.

WILL: What kind of questions have reviewers asked about the book?

SEYMOUR: People are just interested in the personal story, why I did it, and generally the racier aspects, but some of the reviews—*Publisher's Weekly* and *The Bay Area Reporter*—have actually misrepresented what my experience was because, you know, they called me an ex-prostitute, and I don't want to claim something that I wasn't.

The *Dallas Voice* said the book was both "bawdy and sweetly nostalgic at the same time," and I appreciate that because it was hard to make a mainstream readership feel nostalgic about a bunch of strip clubs in DC. One guy wrote and said "you've given me my life back." And still some people read it as a morality tale in which I emerge from this deep, dark world of stripping.

WILL: While *All I Could Bare* is presented simply as the story of your working life, would you say it has an agenda?

SEYMOUR: In writing the book, I wanted to make it very clear that I feel prostitution should be decriminalized. But some people might have breezed by those aspects that others took the time to notice. In *All I Could Bare*, I hope I relate in a conversational way how stripping is a lot like other types of work. I write about how I was attracted to stripping because I didn't feel comfortable with my body, for instance, but there could be plenty of not-so-good reasons why I chose to go into journalism, too. Maybe someone had a trauma in their childhood and it led them to become a nurse, or a lawyer, but because people stigmatize sex work, they try to find a traumatic moment in your past and say, "There!"

WILL: The one possible "root" you do mention involves you in the backseat of a car as a child off DC's Fourteenth Street, watching a bunch of queens walking on the strip.

SEYMOUR: I've always been fascinated with prostitution. I looked it up in the dictionary as a child, and I remember hearing that Jesus would hang out with prostitutes. I would always focus on the prostitutes. [Laughs]

WILL: In discussing the sometimes-intimacy you experienced with clients, you write, "Money was simply how each story began."

SEYMOUR: Even for the most hardcore, stone-faced, "I'm just here for the money" dancers, relationships happened, and I think it happens in any kind of sex work, because it's always an exchange between two people. I mean, I guess it could be more than two people depending on your scene! [Laughs] But it's still an exchange between people. It's almost impossible to reduce the relationships purely to money. In *All I Could Bare*, I meant to show some of that complexity in describing my interactions with customers. It's so easy to dismiss customers as losers, and I think a lot of sex workers do that too, and I do understand psychologically why people do that, but I really wanted to humanize the whole experience.

Going back to your question, it's almost like we don't have a language to discuss the intimacy that occurs in sex work. When I found out some of my customers had died there was a real sense of loss, but how do I describe who they were to me?

Photo by Steve Becker.

WILL: In some passages, you highlight the racism you experienced among your client base once they were made aware that you were African American. Was there a noticeable difference in tips? How were differences in skin color visibly dealt with, or not dealt with, by your coworkers and management?

SEYMOUR: It was hard to tell if people didn't tip because of my race, of course, but there was one time a customer told me he liked me better when he thought I was Latino. I had friends who danced and had maybe a darker shade of skin than me—one friend was performing and this white drag queen pulled her purse closer to her when he walked by on the bar. I never felt it from management, but, I don't know, maybe managers did hire less dancers of color. The thing is that racism is systemic, so of course it sometimes manifested itself within the clubs. But I have certainly experienced racism outside of the clubs as well. But within the context of the clubs, and perhaps the sex business as a whole, the issue of race becomes very complicated because you can't force someone to pay for something—or someone—that they don't want, whether their desire—or lack thereof—is motivated by racism or not.

WILL: But you can affect racist hiring practices?

SEYMOUR: Yes, but it's not just management, racism manifests in a lot of different ways. Sometimes there's internalized racism. I've heard some African American dancers say they don't like dancing for African American audiences because they don't tip as well as the white guys. But at the same time I know a lot of dancers who like to only strip for older guys because they tip better than younger ones. So, rarely are these situations just about race. In this case, it's a combination of race and economics.

WILL: How was the sex sector perceived by your coworkers in general? What did they think of their own jobs?

SEYMOUR: In my experience, most guys didn't like to talk about it. I think a lot of sex workers learn to compartmentalize that part of life. And in this case, it was also complicated by the fact that a great percentage of the guys led straight lives outside of the club. It was something that they did, not something they wanted to talk about.

WILL: Not something they identified with or as?

SEYMOUR: Exactly. Most dancers didn't own being a "stripper," certainly not a "sex worker," as an identity. Dancing was seen as temporary even if they'd been five years in a club. [Laughs] For me, I was always a "sex worker." I always felt there was a continuum between what I was doing and other types of sex work, like prostitution.

WILL: The DC loophole that allowed for nude dancing closed pretty quickly when the Alcoholic Beverage Control (ABC) Board started issuing citations, and management instituted a new policy at Wet: "Not to be touched, fondled, fingered, or stroked." How did this affect the dancers?

SEYMOUR: My dick got very lonely. [Laughs] I thought to myself: "What are we supposed to do—dance?" I mean, really, though, I think it's crazy the way we police sexual activity among consenting adults whether money is exchanged or not—I see a continuum between sex work establishments and sex work. I just re-read a piece by E.M. Forster, where he was writing about anti-gay laws in nineteenth-century Britain, and he said that it wasn't that people felt that strongly against homosexuality but that they didn't want to think about it. And I'd say sex work today is very similar. I don't think people sit around and worry whether or not you're going to work a guy in a bar. But to change laws on sex work, people have to think about it. And that's when all the moralism and everything else start to kick in.

Since the clubs were demolished and the laws have been changed, DC gay male stripping has changed too. I hate seeing guys dancing in G-strings. People might think it was raunchier when people were allowed to touch, but to me there was something more intimate and personal about dancing nude and being touched. I liked the touching.

WILL: Have you heard of the recent "Pink Scare" raids, busts and closings in New York City? If so, what do you make of the anti-sex "scare" some sex workers have declared here in New York? Is the situation similar to the DC closings?

SEYMOUR: It's clearly what's happening. All across the country there's been this real movement to close public sex venues, strip clubs, escort agencies, and, in fact, the harshest effects come less through police persecution than real estate. If you talk about the loss of New York sexual establishments, it was all done through zoning regulations. Even if you turn to DC's gay clubs, it was a question of wanting the space for the Nationals stadium, and zoning regulations made it nearly impossible to find places for the clubs to reopen.

I read an article recently in *The Village Voice* about how younger people aren't as interested in sex establishments because of Internet sex culture, like Craigslist. I think if there were more interest in public venues, the raids wouldn't have the same effect. The unfortunate part about it is [that] it's all happening in real time and these are our lives. It's taking a human toll now.

WILL: In your memoir, you connect skills you learned at the Follies and your later literary career at *VIBE Magazine* and *The Washington Post*, as well as your professorship. Could you speak more to this?

SEYMOUR: Part of being a journalist is relating to people, and my skills got sharper after years of stripping. It would have been easy for me to wipe the stripping from my history but the truth is that stripping in DC is central to the person I have become. I felt that it was an obligation to say that. I wrote the book because I thought I had something to say about sex work, and I wanted to use the platform I have as a professor and a journalist. The fact is that you cannot applaud any of the more socially acceptable accomplishments and put down my stripping experience. You can't take my accomplishments à la carte. Stripping is as much a part of who I am as my PhD or an article I wrote for *The Washington Post*. In fact, it's probably more of a part.

BRENDAN MICHAEL CONNER—also known by his pseudonym, Will Rockwell—is a former escort and *$pread* editor. He currently works as a police misconduct and prisoner's rights attorney for people in the sex trade and street economy in New York City. Brendan has also worked both independently and as a research editor with Avrett Consulting for organizations such as Safe Horizon's Streetwork Project, UNDP, USAID, the HIV Young Leaders Fund, and the Open Society Institute.

THE HISTORY OF *$PREAD*
A TIMELINE

March, 2004—Rebecca and Rachel meet organizing a benefit for the Prostitutes of New York (PONY) and hatch the idea for a sex worker magazine.

May, 2004—Rachel and Raven meet at a barbecue in Brooklyn and Raven jumps on board.

June, 2004—We coin our infamous name and come up with our illuminating tagline.

July, 2004—Call for submissions goes out.

September, 2004—First *$pread* benefit at a random sports bar where the bartenders refuse to turn the baseball game off.

December, 2004—Second *$pread* benefit at Rififi; one *$pread*-ster gets drunk and almost loses all the money.

January 3, 2005—The New York Press gives *$pread* its first media mention.

January-March, 2005—Production Deathmatch: *$pread* Publishing Novices vs. Design Software, Printers, and Customs Canada.

March, 2005—Launch party for Issue 1.1 at the Slipper Room. *New York Post* gossip columnist creeps us out with his plastic leprechaun. We begin to understand the reality of publishing when we lug sixty pounds of magazines to the post office in a suitcase. *Time Out New York* quotes Raven saying, "It's not intended to arouse, but people are aroused by all kinds of things, so maybe someone will be turned on by sex workers fighting for social justice."

May, 2005—*$pread* takes a road trip to Stella's Forum XXX conference in Montreal and mingles with sex worker rights activists from around the world.

May, 2005—First one hundred subscribers!

July, 2005—Mailing Deathmatch! After two days of organizing mailings by zip code, we end up sorting envelopes of Issue 1.2 in the bulk mail center parking lot in the hot July sun.

November 7, 2005—*$pread* hosts a sex worker fashion show at Galapagos Art Space in Brooklyn.

January 6-8, 2006—*$pread* staffers go on our first annual retreat to a cabin called the Otter House in upstate New York, beyond the reaches of cell phone reception.

January, 2006—*$pread* hosts the Sex Worker Olympics at the Slipper Room to launch Issue 1.4, the one with Rich Merritt, our first cover dude.

January, 2006—*$pread* goes to the Independent Press Association's Annual Conference and Utne Independent Press Awards in San Francisco where we receive the "Best New Title of 2005" award. We drink with publishing idols from *Bitch*, *Venus*, and *Lip*.

February-April, 2006—Taxes Deathmatch: *$pread*'s grant from Citizens for NYC has staffers and interns running around the city to help sex workers do their taxes. In an ironic twist of fate, *$pread* fails to do its own taxes on time.

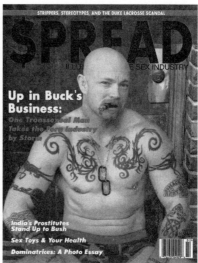

March, 2006—Sex TV produces a ten-minute featurette on *$pread*.

March 29, 2006—*$pread*'s first birthday! We launch Issue 2.1 (the one with a mystery *$pread* girl's hot body on the cover) at our *Sex Worker Visions* art exhibition at the LGBT Community Center. We all wear tiaras and eat birthday cake.

March 30, 2006—*$pread* cosponsors the Sex Work Matters conference with CUNY and The New School.

May, 2006—We conduct our first readers' survey and are surprised to discover that johns read *$pread* too!

June 3-4, 2006—Second *$pread* retreat at the Otter House. On the agenda: "Strategies for avoiding burnout and hatred."

July 1, 2006—*$pread* gets its first office in a creepy building owned by a religious cult. We paint a pink city skyline on the wall and spray-paint a gold dollar sign on the door.

July, 2006—Printer Deathmatch: Issue 2.2 is late because our printer decides to go gambling at Mohegan Sun instead of printing our magazine. When we finally get the issue, we find two articles missing all the "i"s and resolve to switch printers yet again.

July 9-12, 2006—*$pread* launches Issue 2.2, the one with Buck Angel on the cover, in Las Vegas at the first Desiree Alliance conference.

September, 2006—*Bitch* prints a feature length interview with *$pread*, and subscriptions go through the roof.

October 21, 2006—We launch our first themed issue, "The Relationships Issue," at a strip club/veterans hall in Philadelphia. The bartenders teach us some mean pole tricks.

October, 2006—The *Village Voice* crowns us "Best Sex Worker Support System of 2006."

December 3, 2006—*$pread* throws a benefit party at the Delancey. Confused stockbrokers mingle upstairs while

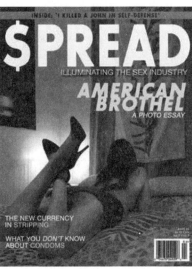

our friend Rose Wood fucks herself in the ass with a bottle of whiskey in the basement.

December, 2006—*Clamor* magazine (who runs our online store) goes bankrupt and almost takes us down with them. Thanks to our generous fans, and a grant from the Louis Rabinowitz Foundation, we get back on our feet.

February, 2007—Printer Deathmatch: Our printer adds its own page twenty-nine to Issue 2.4. Eventually we get a whole new print run.

April 8, 2007—*$pread* cohosts Easter at Avalon with Transmission, an experimental Easter service focusing on Mary Magdalene.

March and April, 2007—Sex workers in Toronto, Chicago, Minneapolis, and New York decorate dildos and send them in for "One Nation Under Dildo," the opening night exhibition for our art show *Sex Worker Visions II*.

May 1, 2007—We launch Issue 3.1, the Money Issue, at the opening gala for Sex Worker Visions II at Arena Studios, where everyone scrambles to bid on the decorated dildos.

October 20-21, 2007—*$pread* drives to Baltimore for the Mid-Atlantic Radical Bookfair and presents on how activists can support sex workers.

November, 2007—*$pread*'s first international launch party in Toronto to launch issue 3.3, the one with the DC Madam on the cover.

January 19-21, 2008—Another *$pread* retreat, this time in snowy Albany. We give up on our dream of commercial viability (aka ever paying staff) and decide to focus, instead, on stepping up our outreach program and increasing community distribution.

February, 2008—Mailing Deathmatch: After finally being approved for periodical mailing privileges, we spend three days transporting copies of Issue 3.4 back and forth

between the office and the bulk mail center in an attempt to comply with insane post-office rules, breaking boxes, spilling magazines on the sidewalk, and pleading with angry cab drivers.

February 24, 2008—We break our record for outreach mailing, successfully packing up and sending over 500 magazines to sex worker programs across the country.

April 1, 2008—We say goodbye to the creepy cult members who populate our office building and move downtown. We get a table stuck in the elevator.

July-August, 2008—Our friends at Different Avenues help us kick off our voter registration drive, Grind the Vote 2008, with a party at Be Bar in DC. For the New York edition of Grind the Vote, at which we also launch Issue 4.2, we host a burlesque show at the Slipper Room.

October, 2008—Moving Deathmatch: When the photography studio we're renting from goes out of business, we head back uptown to the creepy cult building.

November, 2008—*$pread*'s first Boston launch is a dance party to celebrate Issue 4.3, the one with Craig Seymour on the cover.

April, 2009—With the original editors and art directors gone, *$pread* struggles with staffing shortages, and Issue 5.1, the Alt Porn issue, makes it to press three months late.

May, 2009—*In Our Own Image*, a documentary about the making of *$pread*, premieres at Bluestockings Bookstore in New York.

August, 2009—*$pread* finally succeeds in leaving the creepy cult building and resettles in a converted warehouse in Brooklyn. There are still no windows, but we paint it "Gem Turquoise" and make it home.

November, 2009-January, 2010—We come up short on printing costs, and launch a Twitter donation drive that doubles *$pread*'s donor income for the year. This brings tears to our eyes and Issue 5.2, "The Family Issue," to newsstands (finally).

January, 2010—A guest editorial collective is formed to collaborate on an issue about race and racism in the sex trades, and work begins in what will be the longest production cycle in *$pread*'s history.

January 15-18, 2010—*$pread*'s next retreat takes us to New Jersey where we hang out with a half a dozen cats and ponder if there is a future for the magazine.

January, 2010—*$pread* wins the Naked Truth People's Choice Adult Entertainment Award for "Favorite Sex Industry Magazine."

May, 2010—Launch Party Deathmatch: We celebrate the launch of Issue 5.3 without Issue 5.3.

August 21, 2010—At $pread's fifth anniversary reunion we decide to call it quits, but only after we publish the two issues currently in production. Sadly we later abandon one of them.

June, 2011—Members of the final issue's guest editorial collective talk about its production on a panel at the Allied Media Conference.

July, 2011—$pread closes down its physical office.

August, 2011—Issue 5.4, the Race Issue, is finally printed.

November, 2011—The Race Issue is launched in San Francisco.

January, 2012—We say goodbye to $pread with a reading hosted by Red Umbrella Diaries at Happy Ending.

ACKNOWLEDGMENTS

Special thanks to Bhavana Karani, whose tireless work on this anthology made it not only possible, but much, much better.

The hard work of the volunteer staff of *$pread* is what made the magazine possible. Thank you to: Sarah Louise Allen, Kristie Alshaibi, Theresa Anasti, Heidi Baez, Aubree Bernier-Clarke, Sarah Jenny Bleviss, Shanna Bowie, Amanda Brooks, Rachel Burt, Mary Christmas, Christina Ciccelli, Dylan Cox, Stephen Crowe, Denise Cumor, Moira Cutler, Lisa Davis, Alice Dietz, Melissa Ditmore, Andile Dube, Kevicha Echols, Olivia Edith, Jose Estevez, Severine Feist, Fly, Paul Gagner, Chloe Genius, Frank Griggs, Rachel Grinstein, Malcolm Hamilton, Darby Hickey, Sara Howard, Chelsey Johnson, Brian M. Johnson, Hawk Kinkaid, Pony Knowles, Meena Kumari, Eryn Alana Leavens, Viveka LoraX, Lulu, Sadie Lune, Damien Luxe, Rebecca Lynn, Manny, Jasmine McKay, Letha Muth-Kimball, Sarah Elspeth Patterson, Stephanie Pekarsky, Catherine Plato, Ali Poison, Eric Reidmiller, Andrea J. Ritchie, Susan Rohwer, Alysha Rooks, Maura Roosevelt, Kenan Rubenstein, Jenni Russell, Jenny S., Dorothy Schwartz, Monica Shores, Erin Siegal, Christina Simpson, A. Bowie Snodgrass, Lauren Spencer, Ellen Stockburger, Raven Strega, kaitlyn tikkun, Tania Torres, Courtney Trouble, Jeanne Vaccaro, Jose Vega, Radical Vixen, Jennifer Waller,

Anna Weaver, Rose White, Bianca White, Noreen Wolfe, and Shakti Ziller.

We would especially like to thank Brendan Michael Conner, J. Kirby, Aisha Sattar, and Xandra Ibarra for reading this book's introduction and providing helpful edits.

We would like to thank Amy Scholder, Jennifer Baumgardner, Elizabeth Koke, Julia Berner-Tobin, Jeanann Pannasch, Drew Stevens, and Jisu Kim at Feminist Press for believing in *$pread* and turning our "real" magazine into a *real* book.

In addition to our volunteer staff, *$pread* was made possible by the many writers and artists who contributed to its pages, the subscribers, donors, and advertisers who gave their financial support, performers and other artists who brought crowds of delighted partygoers to our fundraisers, and the long-suffering families and loved ones of our over-committed volunteer staff. We are forever grateful to you all.